Media Mindfulness

ALSO BY WILLIAM INDICK
AND FROM McFARLAND

*Media Environments and Mental Disorder:
The Psychology of Information Immersion* (2021)

*The Digital God: How Technology Will
Reshape Spirituality* (2015)

*Ancient Symbology in Fantasy Literature:
A Psychological Study* (2012)

*The Psychology of the Western: How the American
Psyche Plays Out on Screen* (2008)

*Psycho Thrillers: Cinematic Explorations
of the Mysteries of the Mind* (2006)

*Movies and the Mind: Theories of the Great
Psychoanalysts Applied to Film* (2004)

Media Mindfulness
Building a Balanced Diet for the Brain

WILLIAM INDICK

McFarland & Company, Inc., Publishers
Jefferson, North Carolina

ISBN (print) 978-1-4766-8781-0
ISBN (ebook) 978-1-4766-5084-5

LIBRARY OF CONGRESS AND BRITISH LIBRARY
CATALOGUING DATA ARE AVAILABLE

Library of Congress Control Number 2023048916

© 2024 William Indick. All rights reserved

No part of this book may be reproduced or transmitted in any form or by any means, electronic or mechanical, including photocopying or recording, or by any information storage and retrieval system, without permission in writing from the publisher.

Front cover images: © metamorworks/ Vasya Kobelev/Shutterstock

Printed in the United States of America

*McFarland & Company, Inc., Publishers
Box 611, Jefferson, North Carolina 28640
www.mcfarlandpub.com*

For Sophie and Casey

Table of Contents

Preface	1
Introduction: Media Mindfulness, Media Balancing	7
Chapter One. Two Ways of Attending, Eight Ways of Knowing	13
Chapter Two. The Principles of Media Engagement	19
Chapter Three. Linguistic Media: Anxious Depression and the Primary Environment	47
Chapter Four. Logical-Mathematical Media: The Twin Demons of Time and Money	66
Chapter Five. Nature: The "Ground of Being"	89
Chapter Six. Music Therapy for Your Self	100
Chapter Seven. The Body: Medium of the Self	126
Chapter Eight. Visual-Spatial Media: Addiction and Counterbalance	156
Chapter Nine. Interpersonal Media: The Paradoxes, Illusions, and Delusions of Social Media	176
Chapter Ten. Intrapersonal Media: The Spiritual Dream in the Temple of Sleep	203
Conclusion: The Message/Medium Mind Flip	229
Epilogue: Stop Fighting Your Self	231
Chapter Notes	233
Bibliography	239
Index	243

Preface

Media:
    1. Plural of MEDIUM.
    2. The main means of mass communication.

Medium:
    1. The middle quality between extremes.
    2. ***The means by which something is communicated.***
    3. An intervening substance through which impressions are conveyed to the senses.
    4. The material form used by an artist, composer, etc.

Mindfulness:
    1. Taking heed or care.
    2. Being conscious.

The terms "media" and "mindfulness" have been co-opted by academics and clinicians to such an extent that I feel it necessary to state my definitions first, pointing out that they're the simplest definitions available, taken directly from the *Oxford English Dictionary* (OED). My use of these terms may seem novel to readers accustomed to the more complicated, culture-laden interpretations. By "media," I'm simply referring to the plural form of the word "medium," which is anything that acts as an in-between. This book is a medium for me to get my thoughts into your head. It's a relatively ancient medium, but it still works quite well—ironically better, in many ways, than much more modern media. ***Most often, the simplest medium is the best one.*** Let's call that lesson number one.

OED's second definition of "media" focuses specifically on mass communication. Media psychologists are generally interested in the effects of media content on people's minds and behaviors. Does watching violent television make you violent? Does watching pornography turn you into a social deviant? Does buying this book make you a sucker? This approach, though fruitful, is generally unedifying for the average person, who is unlikely to engage in violence despite watching *Game of Thrones* and who is equally unlikely to become a sex offender despite watching internet porn. For the average person, the much more significant psychological effect of media engagement doesn't come from the content of the medium, whether it be *Game of Thrones* or *Sesame Street*. The significant effect comes from our prolonged and repeated engagement within the medium itself. The media that capture our attention, hold our minds, mold our thoughts, and shape our expressions are the invisible environments that surround us, and they're constantly influencing our feelings, our behaviors, and our experience of consciousness. Hence, the focus in this book is on managing the psychological effects of all media—not just the means of mass communication—though those influences will be covered as well.

The so-called information age has forced humanity as a species to engage in daily prolonged immersion within specific media of thought that, over time, become **toxic media environments**. To be clear, I'm not arguing that certain media (e.g., video games or TV) are toxic. I'm also definitely not arguing that certain kinds of media content (e.g., violent shows or porn) are toxic. ***Toxicity doesn't come from any specific medium or media content; it comes from prolonged immersion in one single medium, resulting in a state of mental imbalance.*** Take alcohol as an analogy. One drink isn't toxic because unless you're an extreme lightweight (like me), one drink doesn't intoxicate you. That is, the toxic effects of alcohol aren't harmful until the level of alcohol in your system reaches a certain level of toxicity, resulting in symptoms of intoxication. Similarly, immersion in any one information medium is not toxic … until it is.

Our minds naturally thrive when our thoughts are allowed to be expressed and received in multiple modalities. In contrast, when we're forced to overspecialize our intellect and overfocus our attention within one specific medium of thought for too long and with too much strain, our minds respond with the symptoms of being stuck in a toxic environment. Those symptoms feel like anxiety, restlessness, difficulty concentrating, distractibility, boredom, indifference, lethargy, depression, nausea, and fatigue. In short, your brain is trying to tell you that your media environment is toxic and it wants out. The current state of opinion in the twin industries of clinical psychology and psychiatry, however, maintains that the symptoms I just mentioned are primarily caused by "chemical imbalances" of neurotransmitters in our brains, which are best treated, apparently, with drugs manufactured by pharmaceutical companies that people can only get by paying clinicians for prescriptions so they can pay pharmacists for drugs. This system is close-minded at best, criminally negligent if less than best. In the worst case, it's a legitimized system of convincing people that they have physical deficits in their brain, when they absolutely do not, to get them hooked on drugs that don't work and they don't need. I'm sorry if I'm making it sound like a big scam, but a spade is a spade, regardless of the credentials of the people telling you it's not. My argument in this book is that symptoms of anxiety and depression, for most people, are not generated spontaneously from inside of our brains. The symptoms, in fact, are symptoms of **media intoxication**. The symptoms are our brains' response to the toxic media environments within which we imprison them.

If we immerse our brains in toxic media environments for hours and hours on end, day after day after day, should we be surprised when the brain responds with unhappy feelings, thoughts, and behaviors? Although the simplest solution may simply be to take a pill that makes you seem less unhappy in your toxic media environment, the simplest solution is not necessarily a good option because the pill isn't addressing the problem; it's just addressing the symptoms of the problem and it generally does a poor job at that. Changing the environment that's generating the problem is a more complicated approach because it requires an actual understanding of how the media environments affect each of our minds, and every mind is different. This book is an attempt to bring sanity into a world of applied psychology that seems to have gone completely pill crazy—*addicted to its own supply*—and negligent of the real harm it's perpetrating. By pointing the finger of culpability squarely at the information environments we immerse ourselves in (rather than at our brains and the brains of our children), I hope to hasten the day when the thought of putting powerful psychoactive substances into the brains of toddlers is considered as repulsive and reckless as it truly is.

OED's first definition of a medium is "the middle quality between extremes." So, too, a healthy media environment is one in which extremes—such as prolonged immersion within any single medium of thought—are avoided in favor of balancing multiple modes of engagement. **A healthy media environment is a "happy medium,"** an environment in which engagement is balanced across the mind's modalities in such a way that thought is expressed and received as freely as possible.

OED's third definition of a medium is an "intervening substance through which impressions are conveyed to the senses." In the digital age, all information is deconstructed into digits and morphed into virtual images and virtual sounds. With increasing frequency, the "intervening substance" we use to convey our impressions is no substance at all. As living physical beings, this disconnection from the physical dimension, this preference for the virtual and remote over the physical and present, has a deteriorating effect on our sense of time and place in the real world. The virtualization of much of human life is also an important element in the toxifying effect of our modern media environments. Balancing our media environments requires a very deliberate and mindful rapprochement with the natural physical world, matched with a very critical and mindful consideration of the toxic effects of the steadily encroaching domain of the immaterial virtual world, the invisible environment that's swiftly enveloping us.

OED's fourth definition of a medium is a "material form used by an artist, composer, etc." We must not forget that the sweet sound of a child singing is a medium as well, as is the canvas she paints on, and the words she uses to tell her little stories. The human palette of communication is naturally broad, encompassing all of the arts and sciences, all physical and symbolic forms of expression, every possible way in which I can pass my thought or feeling on to you, and every possible way I can express my thoughts or feelings to myself. A child, without encouragement, will naturally sing and play, dance and draw, tell stories, play make-believe, and express herself freely. When given a healthy media environment, she will engage in multiple modes of media engagement, either simultaneously or sequentially. Her "material form" will be the sound of music, the sculptor's clay, the dance floor, or mommy's old dress-up clothes. Only later on, in the unhealthy and unbalanced toxic media environment of the classroom, will the child, quite unwillingly, be forced to narrow her palette of expression quite rigidly for prolonged periods of strained attention within the media of symbolic letters and numbers. With her "material forms" unnaturally restricted within her toxic media environment, she's more likely to cry than to sing, as her wings of creative expression have been clipped. If she cries too much or sings rather than reads, she's at risk of being labeled with "attention deficit" or a "behavioral disorder." No worries, though. We have pills for that.

OED's definitions of "mindfulness" are perfect in simplicity, bereft of all the mumbo jumbo and psycho-jargon that's been applied to the construct in the past few decades. To be "mindful" is to "take heed" and "care" in what you're doing, not for the sake of Zen enlightenment or some guru's version of nirvana but simply to be aware that the media we engage in—all of the screens, devices, symbols, languages, games, thoughts, and dreams—are experienced within a media environment composed of its own particular ecology. It behooves us to be mindful of that, especially if our aim is to modify our media environments to improve our mental and physical health. Mindfulness is simply "being conscious," not only of what we're doing but also how we're doing it. *"What medium am I using to express or receive this thought, what's the effect of the medium on this thought, and how could manipulating the media environment enhance my experience of this thought?"* Mindfulness, ultimately, is simply being conscious of being conscious. In turn, **media mindfulness is being conscious of the media we use to experience being conscious**. It's as simple as that, but please read on if you'd like more details.

When the coronavirus pandemic hit in early 2020, I was working on a broad theory of media engagement. Suffering from massive underenrollment, my university furloughed much of its full-time faculty, me included. Suddenly, I found myself in the perfect situation for an extended research experiment. It was a pandemic, so I was sequestered at home for what turned out to be nearly two years. Work, mortgage payments, bill payments, plans for the future—everything was put on hold. Where once there was no time, there was now a surfeit. I had a theory, some time to test it, a more-than-willing subject in myself, and nothing to lose. Beyond that, I was also feeling anxious and depressed—not just because I was worrying about how to support my family, but because I was unhappy with myself—physically, emotionally, psychologically, and existentially. Like a broken-down old car, I needed to take myself apart, put myself back together, start her up, and see if I could get all eight cylinders firing in sequence. Erik Erikson spoke of the "midlife crisis" and the choices we make toward either "generativity" or "stagnation." This was my midlife crisis, sure enough, and I was ready to get generating! This book summarizes the process I went through between 2020 and 2022 as I applied my own theories of media psychology to my Self.[1]

Introduction

Media Mindfulness, Media Balancing

> *One thing about which fish know exactly nothing is water, since they have no anti-environment which would enable them to perceive the element they live in.*
> —Marshall McLuhan

You wake up one morning to find yourself adrift on a life raft in the middle of a vast ocean. Your brain immediately gets to work, adapting itself to this strange and treacherous new environment. How on earth did you get here? Where are you going and where have you been? How will you survive? Every neuron in your brain is focused intently on figuring out the new rubrics and boundaries of your novel environment so you can understand it, adapt to it, and eventually master or escape it. We, the human race in the 21st century, find ourselves in this exact position, at this exact moment in time, if not literally, then figuratively. The human brain has evolved over millions of years to do exactly one thing—to adapt to its environment. "Intelligence" is a construct that's been delineated in many different ways by psychologists, but the broadest and therefore the most inclusive and most correct definition of "intelligence" is **the level of adaptation one has within one's environment**. A well-adapted mind is an intelligent mind for that person in that environment. The intelligent person's mind will adapt to survive on the life raft until the person is rescued. The unintelligent person who cannot adapt will die.

The brain's ability to adapt is its core asset and prime function. However, the brain cannot directly interact with its environment. Similarly, in a computer, the microchip cannot directly engage with the internet because the computer needs an "operating system" for the commands to be transliterated into codes that can be communicated to the internet. In the same way, the brain needs an operating system for the user (the *mind*) to engage the system (the brain) in mental activity (thought) and to connect this activity with the thoughts of others (communication). "Media" is the blanket term I use to refer to the interacting operating systems in our brain and in our environment that enable us to be aware of our own thought processes and to communicate thought with others and to ourselves. I refer to these interacting systems both within the brain and in the brain's surroundings as "media environments."

What Is a Media Environment?

Since the brain is safely tucked away in the hard shells of our crania, the brain has no physical interface with its environment. The brain therefore can only adapt to the information it receives about its environment. Each thought, each expression of thought, each reception of thought from others is merely an aspect of the brain's continual process of real-time adaptation to its information environment. We're all surrounded at every moment with information. Unlike the body, which evolves and adapts physically to its physical environment, the brain evolves and adapts metaphysically, responding only to the information it receives, by creating, strengthening, cutting, or weakening neural connections generated by the information it receives and expresses. It may take centuries, millennia, or even millions of years for a physical adaptation such as an opposable thumb to evolve. For the brain, however, adaptive evolution is a real-time process that occurs instantaneously in response to environmental pressures. As you read these words, your brain is creating or strengthening neural connections in response to the information you're receiving. If you pause for a moment to be mindful of the information process, you could actually feel your brain working as it continually adapts to its media environment by rearranging its neural connections.

What Is Media Mindfulness?

Most media environments evolved gradually, giving our brains time to collectively adjust and adapt to them. Oral language was a new medium for our species in the Paleolithic Age that evolved out of more primitive communication systems (grunts, growls, gestures) over hundreds of thousands of years. Literacy was a new medium introduced in the Iron Age that evolved out of the combination of oral language and ancient modes of written communication (pictograms, hieroglyphs, logograms) over thousands of years. As a species, we're still trying to adapt to the literacy environment, and we're still trying to figure out the effects of this environment on our minds and our brains. A very large minority of people have brains that are still not well adapted for literacy. (Those people are labeled "dyslexics" merely because the media environment they're forced to engage in at school is unamenable to their particular kind of brains.) Unlike oral language or literacy, digital media, in all of their manifold environments, are brand-new media, only a few decades old. Nevertheless, we find ourselves completely immersed, irrevocably engaged, and unwittingly entrapped in this new overwhelming environment, an environment that we don't understand and cannot control. Without knowing how we got here, what we're doing here, where we're going, and how it's affecting us and our children, we awaken in the middle of this vast ocean of information, our brains frantically flailing in the ether, desperately trying to adapt to this strange and treacherous new environment, even as it changes at every moment. The desperation is real. The need to adapt is immediate and dire. If we don't adapt to this invisible environment that we've somehow floated into, we'll soon find ourselves and our children hopelessly drowned. Like the deep ocean, the digital media environment has a strong tide. Anyone floating on its shore will drift into its ebb, get sucked in, and immersed. Before even realizing it, we're pulled into the deep sea. Sight of land is lost. We begin to sink. The more we tread water, the more it seems that the ocean itself is pulling us into itself, with its long invisible arms. If we don't start adapting real quick, we're going to sink to the bottom.

"Media mindfulness" is a construct that I developed while considering all of the mental health issues that may be caused or exacerbated by media usage and overusage, issues that I covered in depth in my previous book, *Media Environments and Mental Disorder: The Psychology of Information Immersion* (2021). In this current book, I present the process of "media mindfulness" as a coping mechanism for people living in "unbalanced media environments"—environments that foster overusage and dependency on one particular medium of thought—to the exclusion of others. If much of the anxiety and depression related to modern living is a direct result of existing in unbalanced media environments, then the mindful process of understanding the different modes of media engagement in our environments and then balancing those modes of engagement in a more adaptive manner will naturally relieve those symptoms of mental unbalance. This process has worked for me and I know it can work for you as well because the basic ideas are actually very simple and the process itself is primarily intuitive once the principle theories and methods laid out in this book are understood.

Media mindfulness is not about exorcising various forms of media from our lives to avoid their potential side effects. Although it may seem nice to dream about a world in which the internet, social media, texts and emails, and all of the other means of telecommunication no longer exist, that scenario is simply unviable for the vast majority of us. Technological progress invariably moves forward, not backward, even though we're blind to what lies ahead. Opting out of digital communication completely for a modern person would be tantamount to becoming a hackneyed version of the Luddite hermit, living alone in a log cabin on top of a mountain in the woods, cut off completely from the world and everyone in it. Even though cutting the digital cord would solve the problems related to media dependency and overusage, disconnection in and of itself would for most of us inevitably raise more problems than solutions. How would we work in a world that is now an integrated digital media environment? Our only options are to adapt to the environment, to drown in it, or to become an obsolete reject. (If that sounds like only one option to you, you're right.) **Media mindfulness is not about disengaging from media environments but about understanding them and then balancing them so that they serve us, rather than the other way around.**

Modern humans face the predicament foretold in nearly every science fiction scenario—the predicament of "technocracy," the point in evolution when the technology we create becomes smarter and more powerful than us. In a technocracy, humans think they're in control, but they're actually just "servo-mechanisms"[1] to their own digital devices. Go to any public place and you'll see what I mean. The average human has become a stooped and shadowy figure, constantly gazing down toward a screen, continuously and instinctively responding to every bleep and bloop emanating from their device, avoiding the sun because it glares the screen, avoiding the outdoors because there's nowhere to charge their phones, avoiding real people and real life in favor of virtual interactions. We may think that we're in control, but in actuality, we're rapidly becoming a race of mindless automatons, enslaved by our own technology, pawns in a game set by technocrats, servo-mechanisms locked away behind the invisible bars of the media environments that imprison us.

What Is Media Balancing?

Media balancing is a natural response to the process of being mindful about our mental and physical engagement. To a large degree, media mindfulness and media balancing are essentially the same thing, as the latter follows unvaryingly from the former. A child who touches a flame will naturally respond by retreating from the fire. The next time the child sees the flame, she'll be more mindful of its effects and avoid getting too close. In time, she'll figure out how to use the fire in a balanced way so that the light and heat serve her purposes while not burning her in the process. Media mindfulness and balancing follow the same process, but because our media environments are largely invisible and rather complex, it's not as easy to figure out if and how the fire is burning us and how we could avoid it. The purpose of this book is to illuminate our media environments so we can be mindful of their effects and balance our engagement within them. The end result will be a host of custom-made nontoxic media environments created specifically for you by you. These new self-created media environments will help you adapt to this scary, maddening, and confounding world of digital everything.

In his seminal book *Frames of Mind: The Theory of Multiple Intelligences* (1983), Howard Gardner proposed a now well-known and eloquently arranged model in which he proposed seven different modes of "intelligence," or seven different ways that we process thought. Each different intelligence reflects a different mode of mental engagement—a different medium of attention and thought. Gardner argued that humans have seven mutually exclusive and relatively independent modes of intelligence: linguistic, musical, logical-mathematical, visual-spatial, bodily-kinesthetic, interpersonal, and intrapersonal intelligences. After publishing his original theory in 1983, Gardner suggested the addition of an eighth intelligence—naturalistic—which most textbooks include in his model and which I will also include in my model of "media mindfulness" and "media balancing."

The model provided in this book works by routinely, deliberately, and mindfully balancing our minds' engagement in multiple media of intelligence (e.g., music, art, etc.), rather than overusing and getting stuck in just one or two media of intelligence (i.e., linguistic and logical-mathematical). Deliberately balancing our media engagement is the simplest way to balance the contribution of both hemispheres of the brain in our thought processes. When we change our media environment, our behaviors must change to adapt to the new environment. When our behaviors change, our thoughts in turn must change to adapt to our new behaviors. The same idea, expressed more simply, is the mantra for this book: ***Change your behaviors and your thoughts will follow.***

CHAPTER ONE

Two Ways of Attending, Eight Ways of Knowing

When you follow your bliss ... doors will open where there were no doors before.
—Joseph Campbell

Just as the Covid-19 pandemic hit, I published a book called *Media Environments and Mental Disorder: The Psychology of Information Immersion*. My theory was that a lot of the conditions that we refer to as "mental disorders" or "mental illnesses" are actually symptoms of maladaptation to our media environments. It's a complicated model because each mental disorder is different, but the river of ideas running through my book was inspired by Iain McGilchrist's seminal tome *The Master and His Emissary: The Divided Brain and the Making of the Western World* (2009). The basic premise is that every human being has two brains because each hemisphere of the brain is more or less capable of functioning without the other. We know this because there have been cases in which individuals have had major portions of one hemisphere of their brain removed—due to lesions, injuries, tumors, and so forth—and after surgery, most of these people went on to function quite normally. We have two brains, and the twin hemispheres work in tandem like dual processing units in a computer bank. This is not redundancy. Each hemisphere has its own distinctive way of understanding and engaging with its environment. In a later book, McGilchrist called them two different "ways of attending to the world."[1]

The left hemisphere is adept at focusing deeply into matters: analyzing, deconstructing, examining discrepancies, discovering problems, finding solutions, and figuring out exactly what's what. The right hemisphere takes a holistic approach to the world, looking at the big picture, recognizing overall patterns, sensing relationships between subjects, and getting a general sense of things. The two ways of attending are complementary and, when balanced, provide us with the ability to get an intuitive "big picture" grasp of anything, while also having the option of thinking about something very specifically, logically, and systematically. Young children are very intuitive, approaching new stimuli with spontaneous curiosity. Later on, once they've started attending school, they adopt a more deliberate, contemplative, self-conscious approach to something new—studying it *before* they explore it. This shift from an intuitive style to a thought-out logical approach recapitulates the shift in hemispheric dominance that gradually occurs as we grow from a child into an adult. Babies' and children's brains are right hemispheric dominant; adults' are left hemispheric dominant. In his book, McGilchrist argues that this left hemispheric-dominant type of Homo sapiens is relatively new to this world, a product of the intellectualization of Western society over the past few centuries. Before then, it was likely that most adult humans had a more balanced style of cognitive engagement within their environments in which each hemisphere's particular way of attending could be achieved together in harmony. McGilchrist's final thesis is that the modern world—the information age—has become an unfriendly environment for the brain because it disrupts the primordial balance between the hemispheres.

The right hemisphere's way of attending, which grounds us in the real world through intuition, has been dethroned and silenced by the left hemisphere, the way of attending that focuses on letters and numbers and other symbolic representations of things, rather than actual physical objects, people, and relationships. In my previous book, I related this imbalance in hemispheric dominance to the mental "imbalances" that result in psychiatric disorders. Symptoms of autism, for instance, could be understood as the expression of a mind whose brain is dominated so much by the left hemisphere that necessary right hemispheric input is shut off to the point of dysfunction. The "hemispheric imbalance" model worked well for my book on mental disorders, but disorders are examples of abnormal psychological subjects. When I tried applying a "balancing" model to a theoretically "normal" person (i.e., myself), I found it either too simple or too complex: too simple because most of the things I do involve combinations of both left and right hemispheric functions, too complex because the brain is so intertwined and interactive that it's extremely hard to nail down what exactly is going on in any one part of the brain at any one moment. I needed an additional model to work with.

"Eight Ways of Knowing"

Howard Gardner referred to his model of multiple intelligences as eight "*different ways of knowing the world.*"[2] Each "way" is a discrete and mutually independent medium of mental engagement. When taken as a whole, Gardner's eight ways are equally distributed between the hemispheres. Linguistic and logical-mathematical intelligences are very clearly dominated by the left hemisphere, while musical and visual-spatial intelligences are usually dominated by the right hemisphere. On a broader level, we could perceive interpersonal intelligence, with its affinity for sensing relation, as right hemispheric, while intrapersonal intelligence, if conceived as a deliberate process of theological, philosophical, psychological, and existential contemplation, would seem quite left hemispheric. Bodily kinesthetic intelligence must, by master design, be bi-hemispheric, as each hemisphere controls the contralateral side of the body. Naturalistic intelligence is not so much bi-hemispheric but either-or. My personal approach to nature's flora and fauna is intuitive and holistic. I enjoy the flowers and trees without needing to know their scientific names, and I relate to them as one natural being to another without finding the need to study or examine them. Another person's approach could be completely deliberate and studious, the person who knows or wants to know the scientific name of each tree, flower, plant, or bug. As a whole, I was comfortable moving beyond the primary model provided by McGilchrist (the two ways of attending) to the secondary operational model based on Gardner's theory (the eight ways of knowing). My self-experiment would proceed along the lines of the scientific method:

1. Observation: I am anxious, depressed, chubby, and generally unhappy with myself.
2. Hypothesis: My imbalanced media environments—a steady diet of books, articles, student papers, emails, text messages, memos, bills, budgets, grades, and reports—are having a negative effect on my mental, physical, emotional, and spiritual health.
3. Proposition: Balancing my media environments may improve my condition.
4. Test: By mindfully balancing my media engagement across Gardner's eight ways of knowing while gauging my physical, mental, emotional, and spiritual health as well as my productivity and performance in all other domains, I can assess the effects of the balancing process on myself.
5. Report: As a final step, I will publish my results, probably in book format. How do you like it so far?

Spoiler Alert: The Experiment Was a Success!

Things won are done; joy's soul lies in the doing.
—Shakespeare, *Troilus and Cressida*

You wouldn't think I'd write a book about a failed experiment, would you? The experiment was, of course, a success. When I first resolved myself to run this experiment, I wrote down the following equation with a sharpie and pinned the paper to my bedroom door: $B = f(P,E)$.

The relatively well-known equation, attributed to the great psychological theorist Kurt Lewin, expressed the idea that behavior is a function of a person in their environment. The equation was a focal point for me, a symbol composed of symbols, reminding me that the inner struggle I was experiencing could only be resolved if it was externalized and acted out through my behaviors in my environment. My toxic media environment had turned me into a passive media consumer. I needed to amend the way I interacted with my environment to deliberately become active rather than primarily passive, creative rather than primarily reflective, and generally more well rounded rather than going along with the "stuffy old professor with his nose in a book" stereotype that I had become.

The first thing I discovered was that simply changing my perception of the location of the struggle was tremendously helpful. When I perceived an inner struggle, I felt trapped in my brain and body, a victim of bad genes, poor choices, and happenstance. I didn't know what was wrong with me, and I didn't know how to fix it. When I changed my perception and looked outward at my media environment, then, like the fish who can finally see the invisible water it's immersed in, my eyes were opened to the true nature of my reality. I had immersed myself in a toxic environment of information overload, and then I wondered naively why I always felt so cognitively fatigued, and why my body and mind felt like the slaves of a cruel and indifferent master. Simply externalizing the focus of my gaze was liberating. I—my delicate and vulnerable sense of self—was no longer under the scrutiny of the left hemispheric microscope, that laser light beam of conscious attention that excels at finding faults and discrepancies. Now that third-degree light was turned outwardly, toward my environment. As it turns out, there was nothing really wrong with me; the problem was in my media environment, and that's what needed to be fixed!

I envisioned each day of the experiment as an opportunity to create the optimal environment for my own development, not as a psychologist or as a writer or as a theorist but my development as a *whole person*. My first real challenge was giving myself permission to not be productive. I had to convince myself that it was OK to limit myself to one or two hours of laptop screen time per day, even though as an academic, my work on the laptop was and is my livelihood. I had to trust in the experiment and also con myself into it a bit by convincing myself of the inherent value of the experiment, on both the personal and professional levels. Once I committed to the experiment, I discovered the second immediate benefit. When

I stopped forcing myself to do things for hours and hours on end, things that I clearly didn't want to do, I released a tremendous amount of psychological energy, energy that could then be devoted to other tasks. It seems absurdly simple, but the absurdly simple is precisely what's elusive to the person whose thinking is dominated by the unintuitive left hemisphere. Here's the same absurdly simple idea drawn out logically and linearly for your left hemisphere's pleasure:

1. F (force) requires E (energy)
2. W (work) requires E
3. $F \times W = E^2$ (Forcing yourself to work requires exponentially more energy than doing work that you want to do.)

The switch to working at home full time during the pandemic quarantine provided the perfect setting for an extended behavioral thought experiment on myself. Each morning, I allowed myself to turn off my laptop after about an hour or two of work, which was just about enough time to do my academic work, email correspondence, pay my bills, and take care of anything that needed to be done by computer. After turning off my laptop, I immediately found that I had a wellspring of energy that fueled me through the rest of the day. That energy burst stood in direct contrast to my usual state of lethargy and fatigue that consumed me all day as I sat chained to my device. All the energy I was using to force myself to work was now free and at my discretion to apply toward media of engagement that were less linguistic and logical-mathematical. It was spring in the Northeast of America when my experiment began, a beautiful time of year, so I hopped on my bike and took a long ride—at 10:00 a.m. on a Monday, no less! I wound up riding for hours and hours, driven not only by the energy freed from not forcing myself to work but also from the extra energy that's generated naturally when we're doing something that we love. "Autocatalytic behaviors" are the things we do on our own initiative, for the joy of our own soul, with no external pressure or motivation. My experiment would involve the deliberate rebalancing of my mental and physical engagement so that the majority of my behaviors were autocatalytic rather than forced labor. I never had to force myself to ride my bike, to play my piano or guitar, to garden or spend time playing with my kids and my dog. Those processes were inherently rewarding, and the joy I experienced doing them only increased my energy to do other things because they are energy-generating activities. The surprise that's probably not so surprising was that *not* focusing predominantly on productivity made me more productive in many ways.

To sum up for now, diversifying my mental and physical engagement by balancing my media environments made me mentally and physically healthier, more well rounded, more productive, and a much happier person. In the process, I reacquainted myself with my inner musician, made new friends, and enjoyed new experiences that I never would have if not for the experiment. I got more in touch with nature, especially in my sense of rootedness to the nature that surrounds and fills my home. I became more athletic and physically fitter, and I explored new artistic and intellectual pursuits. I also nurtured my relationships with family and friends and found new intimacy in my "primary relationship"—my relationship with my Self.

As I write this page, however, I clearly see that the process encouraged me to blossom as a writer as well. Prior to the experiment, my identity as a writer was tied up in the notion of being a person who wrote scholarly books for my academic work. "Publish or perish" is the name of the game in academia. The effect of the pandemic on my job—getting furloughed under the threat of a permanent layoff—released me from that game, as I had published a lot and seemed to be perishing anyway. The experiment allowed me to reconsider my writing identity. With little pressure to write for work, I stopped forcing myself to write. I soon found that when I didn't pressure myself to write, my ideas flowed more freely and of their own accord. It wasn't about forcing the words out; it was about allowing them to pour forth. By not deliberately focusing on writing for an extended time, I turned into a better writer because it opened my mind to new forms of expression, which were liberating and eye opening. It also helped that my experiment gave me lots of ideas that I wanted to write about, and that was the point—I began writing because I *wanted* to write, not because I *had* to write. I also eased the focus on what I was doing, releasing myself of the burden of always having a product to create. I allowed my ideas to be written as pure ideas first, without premolding them into chapters and sections for a book in progress. By separating my Self from my work, I was able to perceive my Self as the medium for my own thoughts. The books and articles I write are the content of my medium, the figures that I and my readers focus on, but the ground of my medium is my own identity, my own ability to process thought as written word. It's wonderful to be able to write as a means of creative expression, without judging or prequalifying the merit of the expression, even before it's written. It's quite liberating, and I've found the whole process very personally rewarding, but I suppose it's up to you, the reader, to decide if this particular bit of media content has value to you. I hope it does, but if not, I won't take it personally. I am *not* my work, and neither are you!

CHAPTER TWO

The Principles of Media Engagement

In the humanity of which we are a part, intuition is, in fact, almost completely sacrificed to the intellect.... It throws a light feeble and vacillating, but which none the less pierces the darkness of the night in which the intellect leaves us.
—Henri Bergson[1]

Media mindfulness is a deliberate process of adaptation to our environment. It's designed to be complementary to the unconscious instinctual adaptation process that's perpetually occurring behind the scenes. One of the most important things to remember when being mindful of your media engagement is that the conscious mind tends to be left hemispheric dominant in its cognition. That is, our conscious thoughts tend to be reflective, analytical, and deconstructive. In its need to take the situation apart, find the problems, and fix them, the conscious mind is likely to overfocus on specific issues, while remaining blind to the bigger picture of what's going on. Consciously deliberate thought processes are very impatient. Since we're focusing on results, we expect to see them posthaste, and we'll rush toward fixes and solutions that are shortsighted. Intuitive processes, on the other hand, tend to work at a global and glacial pace. The brain itself is never in a hurry; only the conscious mind feels the sense of time ticking away in the background.

Oftentimes, what's needed is a process of being consciously mindful of the unconscious processes at play and a mindful resignation to not interfere with these processes, to be aware of them but not necessarily change or control them. The left hemisphere always thinks it knows best, so it will inhibit the intuitive right hemisphere's processes and completely take over. The left hemisphere has the power to do this—to inhibit right hemispheric input or at least ignore it—because the left hemisphere controls the means of argument, the medium of internal discourse, also known as internal verbal thought or the voice of consciousness. Many mindfulness practices, especially those of the "Zen" variety, focus on silencing the inner voice of consciousness. With practice, that technique can be mastered, but the effect is simply that of shutting down the process of consciousness to the point where you're not aware of it.[2] Shutting down consciousness is a good technique to know, but it's not particularly adaptive because rather than consciously controlling our media engagement, we're basically just shutting it down. If you want your child to watch less TV, the most direct way is to simply shut off the TV and pull the plug. Your child will certainly stop watching TV after you pull the plug, but later on, when you're not around, he'll just plug it in again. Consciousness is just like that little kid: you can control it by shutting down the flow of content, but the minute you stop the shutting-down process, the stream of consciousness gets plugged back in again. There is no "cure" for consciousness. It's a curse, and we're all stuck with it. You can spend all your time and energy trying to shut it down, in which case, you're primarily engaged in fighting yourself, and we all know how efficient that is. The only way to efficiently employ both your conscious and unconscious mind to achieve a state of balance within your media environment is to know exactly what principles of media engagement are at play, how they're affecting your mental engagement, and how that mental engagement is affecting your mental and physical health.

Media Appetites and the Saturation Principle

The saturation principle is the most basic principle of media psychology to be aware of and the hardest principle to mindfully employ. Any physical material that absorbs another substance is prone to saturation. A sponge can absorb only so much water until it becomes saturated, at which point, it cannot hold any more. Similarly, the human stomach can only absorb so much food. Once it reaches its saturation point, you feel completely full and you can't eat anymore. Although information is metaphysical, it does have certain physical properties that can lead to saturation, just like water or food. "Time" as measured by "duration" is a physical property measured on a clock. "Quantity," in terms of the amount of information being processed, is also measurable, such as the number of pages read in a book. "Attention" can also be quantified in terms of both duration (how long I pay attention to a certain stimulus) and quantity (how much information can I absorb and process from a certain stimulus within a certain duration).

To apply a simple but apt metaphor, we all have "media appetites" for different forms of media content, such as TV shows, movies, books, magazines, music, video games, social media, and so on. These media appetites are not unsimilar to other appetites, such as our appetite for food or sex or for anything we desire. When we indulge our food appetite and eat a large quantity in a short duration, we feel full, or saturated, so we stop eating. However, sometimes we eat so much so fast (i.e., a "binge") that we oversaturate ourselves, which is unhealthy and leads to obesity. Oversaturation is obviously not our goal, so why do we do it? We do it because we're indulging our appetite for food in such an unmindful way that—though it feels good in the moment—it's ultimately maladaptive and extremely self-destructive. Oftentimes, we're feeling emotionally or interpersonally "empty" inside, so we use food to fill us up, even though food, as a physical object, can never satiate emotional or interpersonal needs. Media appetites and media saturation work in much the same way, but since media content is informational rather than physical, we either fail to recognize the symptoms of saturation, or we fail to act on them. Also, we tend to use media content to "fill up" our empty lives, even though we know that the "parasocial relationships"[3] we form with our media content are not real and that they can never make us feel emotionally "full" or not alone.

Recognizing the feeling of saturation is an extremely important part of the method of media mindfulness. In fact, it's the most important part because the internal cue to abandon one mode of media engagement in favor of another is usually prompted by a feeling of saturation with the medium being engaged in. When eating, for example, it's better to eat as slowly as possible because it takes a while for the digestive system to communicate the feeling of fullness to the brain. Bingeing, therefore, is more about time and impulsivity than it is about food. When we eat too quickly, we're setting ourselves up for a binge because we're not allowing for the feeling of saturation to be experienced. Media binges work the same way. When we binge-watch a show, we're absorbing so much content so quickly and efficiently that we're not consciously aware of the feeling of saturation growing inside of us. Furthermore, since media content is not a physical substance like food, it's not as simple to recognize the feeling of media saturation. Nevertheless, being aware of the "**saturation principle**" by identifying the feelings of media saturation is really the first crucial step in the process of media mindfulness. Like the other principles of media engagement, the saturation principle will be a perpetually recurring theme in this book.

The Displacement Principle

Everyone knows that when you get in a bathtub, the water level rises and may even flow over the sides of the tub because the water is displaced by the mass of your body. This physical principle applies to media engagement as well because of the physical properties of media engagement discussed above. Time and attention devoted to one medium of engagement will displace time and attention that could be devoted to another. More time spent watching TV means less time reading. More time spent staring at your laptop means less time experiencing the outdoors. The principle is quite simple. If a toxic environment is one that's dominated by just one or two media of engagement, then we could say that overuse of those two media displaces the time and energy that could be devoted to the other six media of engagement. Balancing therefore requires awareness of overengagement in a certain medium (saturation) and a concomitant awareness of the need to reduce engagement in that one medium to increase engagement in other media (displacement).

In my case, I found that I was spending the majority of my time and attention focusing on linguistic and logical-mathematical media. To balance my media environment engagement, I decreased this displacement by deliberately decreasing the time and attention I devoted to linguistic and logical-mathematical media and deliberately increasing the time and attention I devoted to musical, visual-spatial, interpersonal, naturalistic, intrapersonal, and bodily kinesthetic media of engagement. The process may sound complicated, but it's actually entirely intuitive. Once you get adept at feeling the sensation of media saturation, the shift from one medium to another will happen by itself if you just follow what your brain (in the role of your intuitive feelings) is telling you. Remember, your brain knows what it needs more than your conscious mind does. You have to learn to trust it. Your brain will tell you when it's experiencing saturation; you just need to recognize the cues. Your unconscious mind will also intuitively crave the mode of media engagement that will relieve imbalance; you just need to stop forcing yourself to perseverate in an unbalanced toxic media environment. Once you're aware of the feeling of saturation, moving on to a mode of engagement will feel as natural as going to sleep when you're tired, eating when you're hungry, or laughing when you're amused. The process is not so much about doing things but allowing yourself to stop doing the things that are causing imbalance. Once you recognize saturation and displacement in your media environment, you'll see the invisible bars of your mental prison cell. After that, it's a rather simple matter of just allowing yourself to get up and walk out between the bars.

Saturation Nausea

> *I exist, that is all, and I find it nauseating.*
> —Jean-Paul Sartre, *La nausée* (1938)

Chapter Two. The Principles of Media Engagement

Immersion in any one medium over time leads to a saturation point. The first response to media saturation is typically a feeling of mental "nausea." For instance, I've always loved TV. When I was a kid, I was a "TV addict" and would spend countless hours watching. Then, at one point, I found that I was no longer watching TV because I liked it; I was watching TV because I was bored and lonely and couldn't come up with a better idea for what to do. I kept watching, even as my self-awareness grew, creating a sense of "cognitive dissonance"[4]—*"Why am I watching this stupid box that is no longer entertaining?"* Then, one day, I woke up, and the first thing I did, as usual, was to turn on the TV. Rather than feeling engaged and entertained, I felt disengaged, bored, even more lonely, and overall, rather disgusted with myself and the medium I was staring at. Although I couldn't have expressed it then, what I was feeling was the nausea of saturation. It's similar to the nausea one feels when one eats too much—the feeling of being bloated, stuffed, overfull, along with the concurrent feeling of shame for bingeing in such a lazy and self-indulgent manner. Saturation nausea is a bad, gross, uncomfortable feeling rooted in shame and self-loathing.

In his existential novel *La nausée* (1938), Sartre reflected on the notion that the mind is constantly searching for meaning outside of itself, meaning to be found in books, movies, and other media. On occasion, the mind pauses in its feverish search, perhaps because it sees that the media it's engaged in does not and will never purvey any actual meaning. It is at that moment—when our media fails us—that we realize that meaning will never be found in our media because our media, rather than providing a window to the world, is actually just a mirror reflecting ourselves. This recognition, this "real-I-zation" that the thing that gives meaning to life, the search for meaning itself is ultimately just a pointless and futile mind game pursued by a brain stuck in search mode; this is what makes us feel sick with ourselves. Like a dog chasing its own tail, we finally must admit not only defeat but that the entire process is self-defeating. The endless conscious deliberation on the problem of the Self will never result in a final solution but only in a state of saturation with the problem itself—the problem of the Self. When we become completely saturated with the eternal search for meaning and self-understanding, we're left with nothing else to feel but disgust with the oversaturated subject, which is of course self-disgust. In Sartre's words, *"I exist, that is all, and I find it nauseating."*

Media is the thing we use to fill up the unbearable emptiness of our own being. When our media fails us, we're forced to observe ourselves and our existence as we truly are, and that is truly nauseating! Saturation, the moment of media failure, gives us that rare moment of clarity that can unlock the cell that has caged our minds. That feeling of nausea with your media and yourself (the *"sweetish sickness"* as Sartre dubbed it) is your cue to immediately bail on whatever media you're engaging in in favor of another medium that makes you feel less sick with yourself. Recognizing and identifying that nauseous feeling inside your head (rather than your stomach) is actually incredibly important because it's the cue that alerts you to the toxicity in your media environment. It may be hard to recognize that feeling at first because it relies on a mental trait that's perpetually being drowned out by the hyperintellectual, meta-abstract, left hemispheric way of attending. Recognizing one's own saturation nausea relies primarily on intuition, that right hemispheric way of attending that grounds us in the real world and reflects our natural instinct to engage in the world, rather than to observe the world distantly from our vantage point deep within the kingdom of our minds via the telescope of media. Living in the digital age of virtual everything has disconnected us from everything that is actually real and natural. To even feel our feelings again, we need to get back in touch with our intuition and we have to trust it. When we're truly aware of our feelings, when we're truly engaged in a medium of thought that feels real and integrated with our environment and ourselves, when we're truly living rather than thinking about living—then we are truly a human "being" rather than a human "doing"—and only then can we reflect on ourselves without the sickly sweet nausea of self-disgust.

Medium Switching

So what did I do as a child when I felt the nausea that I could not relate to "saturation" and when I felt the self-disgust that I could not relate to existential crisis? I turned off the TV and did something else. That was my intuitive response, and I listened to my intuition, which was the right thing to do. (We adults could learn a lot from children, who have not yet cut off their intuitive selves in favor of the highly logical, rational, detached, and cut-off selves adopted by adults.) I didn't stop watching TV altogether; I just changed my habits (or I should say that my habits changed as a function of listening to my intuition). I got into the habit of not watching TV all day long (the behavior that generated saturation nausea in the first place). Eventually, I associated the feeling of saturation nausea with the experience of watching TV during the day, so I stopped doing that. I got into a pattern of watching TV only at night, and even then, only watching the shows or movies that I really wanted to watch and then turning the TV off. Much more important, I got into the habit of recognizing and identifying the feeling of saturation nausea in myself and responding to it intuitively and immediately. I practice the same TV habits to this day, and I must admit, I'm happy with the balance I've struck with that particular medium primarily because I have complete control over it. I'm no longer an addict simply because I recognize the effect of the medium on my mind and I immediately respond to that recognition with "the power of off." Consciousness does not have an "off" button, but electronic media does. Utilize the simple but awesome power of off, and you will become the master of your media, rather than the other way around.

If I'm watching a show or a movie and I start to feel nauseous, I immediately get up and turn off the TV and then I immediately let my intuition lead me to a different mode of engagement, and the nausea immediately dissipates. Significantly, I don't wait for the TV show or movie to end before disengaging; I immediately disengage. Some people have observed my behavior and found it odd, especially if the media I'm engaging in carries an expectation of completion, such as a show or video game. The idea of "not finishing what you started" or "quitting" is so anathema to the hyperfocused left hemisphere that it cannot condone any half-assed job, even if the job is just watching a stupid show. *That's nonsense!* Should I wallow in my nausea merely because my obsessive-compulsive mind demands task completion? No, thank you. I will follow my intuition and detach from my nauseating media without giving a second thought to the construct of "task completion" because my aim in life is not to complete tasks but to live freely and to engage in media for my own pleasure, rather than at the pleasure of my media.

Mode Flipping

Medium switching, ditching one medium for another (whether prompted by media nausea or not), is about as simple an application of the ideas espoused in this book as you can get. It reminds me of the old joke, *"Hey, Doc, it hurts when I go like this."* Responds the doctor, *"Don't go like this."* The punchline in the doctor joke is that the solution is a bit too simple, but no such construct as "too simple" exists in psychology. As a rule, simple solutions in psychology are invariably the best (the "rule of parsimony"). In the joke, the doctor, in his simple solution, seems to be overlooking a deeper underlying problem. We're tempted to think the same about ourselves. The root of unhappiness must be some complicated neurotransmitter imbalance that only neuroscientists can understand, or perhaps some multilayered neurotic "complex" that only a psychoanalyst can figure out, or maybe it's a faulty thought pattern that only a cognitive behavioral therapist can correct. Untrue! You are anxious and depressed because you've immersed yourself in a media environment that manufactures anxiety and depression. Simple as that. ***Change your media environment by changing your behaviors, and your thoughts will follow.***

Medium switching is the simplest way to counter saturation but not the only way. Every form of media engagement has both a receptive and expressive mode of attending. This is true because all media, in essence, are forms of communication, and communication involves either the reception of information, the expression of information, or both. Hence, any medium that you engage in will have both a receptive and expressive mode, just as any telephone must have both a receiver/speaker for you to hear things, as well as a transmitter/microphone for you to speak things. The inclination for us humans is to fall into the receptive mode of media engagement, which is generally passive, and to remain stuck in that position because it's so easy and requires little to no physical effort. We're so comfortable in the role of passive observer because it mimics the passive observer role of the conscious mind itself (the inner critic), who passively observes and criticizes everything but accomplishes nothing. The TV junkie watches a million hours of TV, but does he film his own videos or shows to post on his own internet platform or channel? The news junkie consumes a million news stories as he doomscrolls his life away, but does he ever write his own stories, articles, or essays? The avid music fan listens to a million hours of music, but does he ever make his own?

Medium switching and mode flipping are the primary devices used in this book to balance our media environments. Although both are important, mode flipping requires much more of a drastic paradigm shift in your approach to the world. Don't be afraid! Isn't that why you're reading this book—to effect a drastic paradigm shift that will change your life for the better in a lasting and significant way? Think about your modes of media engagement, the media you use to receive or transmit information—books, TV, emails, games, social media, and so forth. Now figure out how much of your media engagement is receptive, and how much is expressive. Go ahead and get a pen and paper. I'll wait.

OK, have you got your list? Good. Let's get started.

One of the first things you may have noticed when composing your list is that the receptive-expressive dichotomy is not always applicable. A good conversation is completely interactive, a reciprocal exchange of active expressions and passive receptions. Social media is likewise interactive, involving receptive tasks such as reading posts, looking at pictures, and listening to recordings, while it also involves writing posts, taking pictures, and posting images. Digital media in general tend to be more interactive, making them less applicable to the mode-flipping dynamic. That's fine. So what do you do when you're on social media and you get the first little tingling of saturation nausea? You can't flip social media from passive to expressive modes because social media is interactive, so just switch media. ***If you can't flip it, switch it*** and vice versa. So simple, yet I promise you, so effective. I used to do social media, just like everyone else. It became a black hole of time and energy, rewarding me only with anxious and depressive fears of missing out, the green demons of envy and self-doubt. When I practiced this little bit of media mindfulness—awareness of even the slightest bit of nausea and immediately responding to it—I found that my reaction to doing social media changed immediately. I became so sensitive to saturation nausea that it kicked in within one or two minutes of logging into any social media account, prompting me to bail out almost immediately. I now spend almost no time on social media. I do what's required of me in terms of familial, social, and professional obligations, and then I get the hell out of there before I throw up, and I'm so much happier for it! Simply paying attention to your intuition and responding to it as you proceed through your day is a form of mindfulness that's 1,000 times more efficient than any unintuitive path.

Another issue with the receptive-expressive dichotomy is that the active-passive dichotomy doesn't always apply. For instance, Marshall McLuhan referred to print (like this book) as a "hot medium" because it requires deep focused engagement. TV, on the other hand, is a "cool medium" because the viewer doesn't need to focus much; she could be relatively disengaged and coolly detached while still watching the show. Reading, the receptive mode of literary engagement, is not passive; it's active because it requires deep focus.[5] Reading could be hard work, which is why most people avoid it nowadays. Does this mean that when you feel that "sweetly sick" feeling when you're reading (receptive mode) that you should flip modes into writing (expressive mode)? That process actually works well for me, and I usually follow that pattern myself, but it doesn't mean it will work for you because reading can be just as active a task as writing and sometimes even more so. Again, feel what you're feeling, respond to it, and follow your intuition. If a flip doesn't feel right, try a switch to a completely different medium, such as music or visual art. The point is, try something! Change. Don't wallow in your saturation nausea. Don't allow yourself to get drawn into the vortex of a hypnotic state of perpetual passive receptivity (I'm looking at you, Netflix binge-watchers). Don't resign yourself to being a servo-mechanism of your own media devices. Instead, just feel it, then flip it or switch it. Also, don't be afraid to invoke the divine power of off.

Saturation Fatigue

> *Our fatigue is often caused not by work, but by worry, frustration and resentment.*
> —Dale Carnegie

If your workday is somewhat like mine, you work in the morning and afternoon—primarily engrossed in information embedded in screens—until you reach a point of physical and mental exhaustion, usually in the mid- to late afternoon. You hit a wall, and the wall seems insurmountable. Where did that wall come from? It wasn't there a minute ago. It just popped up out of nowhere, but the feeling of total exhaustion, though sudden, is so overwhelming. You can't even keep your eyes open, and the notion of swallowing even one more byte of information seems impossible. You force yourself, but it literally feels like torture. Why is this happening? You couldn't be physically exhausted because you hardly moved from your desk all day. It could be mental exhaustion, but why did it come on so sudden and with such severity?

What you're experiencing feels like physical and mental exhaustion, but it's actually just a variant of media saturation. Rather than feeling nauseous, you feel exhausted, even though there's no real cause for exhaustion. This is what I call **saturation fatigue**,[6] a feeling of exhaustion that arises out of a state of mental conflict with your media environment. It's not that you're exhausted; it's just that your brain has become so saturated with the specific medium it's engaged in that it literally *cannot* take it anymore. The more you force yourself to do it, the harder it becomes. The fatigue doesn't arise from the work itself but from the massive effort you're expending to force yourself to continue working in a medium in which you're oversaturated. (Remember the formula from Chapter One: $F + W = E^2$.) In short, you're fighting yourself. Guess who loses when you fight yourself?

How can you tell when you're experiencing saturation fatigue as opposed to real fatigue? Immediately turn off your laptop and phone, take a breath, walk outside into the fresh air, and engage your body and mind in some small physical task like a walk. If the fatigue goes away in a minute or two, it was saturation fatigue. Want to be sure? Go back to your screen. If the feeling of fatigue immediately returns, you know why. The same phenomenon can be seen in others. Your kid doesn't want to go to school. She lies on the floor, complaining that she's so tired she can't get up. Tell her you're going to get ice cream instead, and she's flying out the door. She wasn't lying about being tired; she really felt it, but it was saturation fatigue emanating from her conflicted motivations and her saturation with the media environment of school.

Saturation fatigue presents us with some interesting paradoxes. We feel fatigued while working but energized the moment work is abandoned. When we're doing something fun, we feel energized so that doing more of the same gives us more energy to do even more and fatigue doesn't set in even though we've expended a ton of energy. In contrast, when doing something we don't want to do anymore because of saturation, every second of work is agonizing and effortful because we're battling the counterforce of "**inhibition energy**"—the side of your brain that's arguing against the forces of saturation and actually inhibiting you from continuing engagement in that task. The energy you must expend to overcome your own inhibition is wasted energy. Stop "forcing yourself," stop "fighting yourself," stop ignoring the signals emanating from your own brain telling you to "stop." What should you do instead? In general, we should all create a daily media environment (schedule) that energizes and also maximizes mental resources at strategic times of the day and night. Be mindful of when your brain works best in relation to specific media and modes of engagement, and follow the path that optimizes the functioning of your brain, as opposed to the path set by a clock or a rigid externally imposed schedule. You'll find that if you get in touch with your intuitive sense of saturation, you will immediately recognize the symptoms of saturation nausea and/or saturation fatigue when they arise, and then instead of wasting energy fighting yourself, you'll switch media or flip modes into a form of engagement that will not only relieve your saturation symptoms but will also energize you so that you'll be more active and engaged than you could have possibly believed just moments before as you wallowed in your pit of self-imposed drudgery and boredom. That's lateral thinking at work: To avoid fatigue, expend more energy!

The Enhancement-Obsolescence Dichotomy

Marshall McLuhan, the premier media philosopher of the 20th century, proposed four principles of media effects on the individual and society. He referred to them as the "tetrad." In essence, the tetrad itself is composed of two dichotomies. The first dichotomy is enhancement/obsolescence. Every new medium that's successful provides an enhanced experience for the user. If not, the new medium would not have become successful. The cell phone, for example, is an enhancement over the landline phone because of its portability. In turn, a successful new medium will necessarily obsolesce the medium that preceded it. Cell phones make landlines rather useless and redundant, so they're becoming obsolete. Awareness of both the process of enhancement/obsolescence and the inevitability of it is key to media mindfulness. Whenever one is engaged in media, especially in the use of a "new technology," mindfulness of exactly how this technology is both enhancing our experience in one medium while simultaneously obsolescing our experience of the preceding medium is crucial. Our tendency is to be hyperaware of the enhancement because that's the draw, the attraction that the product advertisers want us to see, the thing about the product that Apple and Samsung want you to focus on, the figure of our attention that obscures the ground of the media environment behind it.

My cell phone, for example, has so enhanced my ability to correspond by text message with family and friends that I have more time to devote to other things. OK, that's great, but what does the cell phone obsolesce at the same time that it's enhancing? Upon reflection, my cell phone obsolesces my old use of phone technology. I rarely talk on the phone with anyone anymore. In fact, I avoid it because I can. I also spend less physical time with family and friends because I don't need to—I can just correspond when I need to via text message. What's more, with FaceTime, Zoom, and other teleconferencing apps, I don't even need to physically attend birthdays and celebrations—I can just phone myself in. Yes, my cell phone certainly has enhanced the efficiency with which I connect to people, but what has it obsolesced? I rarely speak to people in real time anymore, robbing our conversations of the spontaneity and reciprocity of a real-time interaction. I spend less time in the physical company of family and friends, robbing my interpersonal engagement of the real physical interactions that can never truly be simulated with digital technology. I also engage in less physical travel and less physical participation in real events in favor of virtual engagement in virtual events. It turns out that upon inspection, the experiences that my cell phone obsolesces are actually much more personally valuable to me than the enhancements that it provides. Furthermore, all the time and energy that my cell phone saves me in its efficiency are just directed right back to my cell phone in the name of net surfing, doomscrolling, social media trolling, and all the other addictive modes of engagement that wind up costing much more time and attention than any other medium in life. In short, the cell phone's enhancements are somewhat illusory because the modes of engagement they obsolesce are important and good for us, while the modes of engagement they enhance tend to be superficial and also tend to monopolize our time and attention to the point where any benefits in terms of efficiency are completely nullified by overengagement.

Wait! Don't throw out your cell phones just yet because that's not the answer. The key to media mindfulness is to find a way to live in balance with the new technology because the new technology isn't going anywhere. We're going to have to live with it, like it or not. Mindfulness is about being aware of both the obvious benefit of a medium (enhancement) while also taking into account the hidden costs (obsolescence). Once I'm aware of both of these concurrent processes, I can make better decisions regarding when and how much I will rely on my cell phone for interpersonal connection and when I will put it away in favor of a far older but far more fulfilling mode of interpersonal engagement—spending real time with real people in a real place. We all have a choice in our media engagement, but we all don't necessarily know the options and the underlying costs and benefits. It is the purpose of this book to make us aware of the invisible forces at work in the media we use so we can make better choices.

The Retrieval-Reversal Dichotomy

The second dichotomy in McLuhan's tetrad involves the ways that media engage the senses. New media technology is being developed all the time. There's no limit to the new media that society will be exposed to. Our senses, in contrast, are limited. New media tend to enhance our experience of media engagement by rearranging the sensory experiences involved. Since we have only six senses,[7] all new media will necessarily "retrieve" sensory modes of engagement that may have been previously obsolesced. For example, in ancient times, to connect with someone far away, you had to physically travel to that person and speak with them. When the technology of literacy came to the fore, an enhanced medium for distance communication—the letter—was born. The written letter obsolesced the need to physically travel to someone to connect. Many centuries later, the electric telegraph was created, enhancing exponentially the speed at which written words can be sent across vast distances. In many cases, the telegraph obsolesced the written letter, especially when correspondence was urgent. However, the speed of the telegraph also "retrieved" some of the sensory experiences of the mode of engagement that preceded written communication. Telegraphic communication was immediate, allowing for a real-time exchange of thoughts, just like an actual in-person conversation, the mode of engagement that preceded letter writing.

Not too long after the invention of the telegraph, the telephone was created. The phone enhanced the ease of communication by making it verbal rather than written, obsolescing the telegraph. Concurrently, the telephone retrieved the older means of communication—speaking—thus "reversing" the trend toward written communication that began with the letter. Recently, the cell phone has obsolesced the landline, as it offers enhancements such as mobility and the ability to create written messages as well as oral messages. Since text messaging is in many ways easier, more convenient, and more efficient than a phone call, texting is quickly obsolescing the phone call. And what is a text message if not a digital telegraph? The phone (from the Greek root "phon" for sound) was invented to transmit verbal communication. Nowadays, most of us use our phones to text and email more than we use them for actual verbal phone calls. Hence, the digital cell phone has retrieved the telegraph as a mode of communication, constituting a "reversal" in the way the phone engages our senses. We now look at our phones more than we listen to them, and we type into them rather than speaking into them. Media mindfulness requires an awareness of how our media engages our senses and how the balance of the senses in any state of media engagement affects the mind and body as a whole. Is your cell phone enhancing your connection with others, or is it changing it in a way that seems easier but is ultimately less engaging and less gratifying? We must ask the same question of all our devices and then, if necessary, make adjustments to the way we use those devices. Sometimes (or even most of the time) the simplest adjustment is the best adjustment. Just turn it off!

The Principle of Least Action

In physics, the principle of least action dictates that the natural movement of a physical object will follow the course in which the least amount of action or energy is required. This is also known as the law of least effort or the path of least resistance. In short, humans adapt to their environment by intuitively figuring out how to get the most benefits out of the least amount of effort. We're naturally lazy because laziness conserves energy, and the conservation of energy is a natural adaptive response to our environment. In terms of media engagement, we tend to overindulge in modes of engagement that require less energy (i.e., passive receptive engagement), and we tend to avoid modes that require more energy (i.e., active expressive engagement). Once again, it behooves us to be aware of our natural tendency to lazily overindulge in receptive media engagement such as binge-watching TV, binge-reading comic books, or binge-listening to albums. Sometimes we're bingeing because we're anxious or depressed and we can't think of something better to do, so we just keep bingeing even though the awareness of our unhealthy bingeing behavior makes us feel anxious about our physical and mental health and it also makes us depressed about our own state of self-pitying sloth and self-indulgence. It becomes a vicious circle: bingeing to soothe anxiety and depression actually causes more anxiety and depression—feelings that we soothe by engaging in even more bingeing. To add to the problem, feelings of anxiety and depression drain our minds of mental energy, giving us the physical sense of being fatigued and lethargic even though we've expended no physical energy while bingeing. It is this exact cycle that mode flipping can break. When we deliberately flip from a receptive to an expressive mode of engagement, the energy being subdued in the receptive state of static inertia is released through bursts of creative expression.

The irony of mental energy works both ways. When we're lethargic and bored, we overindulge in receptive media engagement, making us feel even more lethargic and bored because our creative energy is trapped inside and it actually requires energy to keep it trapped in, making us feel even more drained. We feel weak and powerless because we're fighting ourselves, and we don't even know it. Only when we flip from a receptive to an expressive mode of engagement does the energy get released, thus stimulating the release of more energy, and then all of a sudden, you have all the energy in the world. Mode flipping is very simple, it works extremely well, and it will be discussed throughout this book as a primary method of media balancing. Once you discover this simple little trick to controlling your media engagement and once you start intuitively employing it every day, I guarantee that you will become more creative, more energetic, and generally feel more positive about yourself and the way you spend each day of your life.

The Productivity Paradox

How can you find time to spread your engagement across eight different media when you're so busy with the one or two media related to your work? I get it. I'm busy too. The primary lesson of media mindfulness is that when we bury our noses in work for extended periods, we truly believe we're being super productive when we're actually being incredibly unproductive. The dark side of the productivity paradox—the fact that we're ironically at our least productive when we're forcing ourselves with all our might to be productive beyond our saturation point—arises from the sensible delusion that consciously working hard and long on a task is the quickest and most efficient way to complete that task. That point of view makes perfect sense when the task is physical, such as digging a ditch. It may be hard work, but if you roll up your sleeves and stick to the task at hand, it will eventually get done. However, the same metaphor doesn't necessarily apply to nonphysical informational labor. If I have 50 emails to answer and I push myself to answer all 50, by the time I'm done, I'm likely to have 10 new emails to answer that arrived while I was answering the first

50. Ditches don't begin refilling themselves as you're digging them, but informational work is never ending—it just keeps rolling in. The tremendous effort I put into answering all 50 emails in my inbox was relatively futile because I will always have emails in my inbox, as it's constantly refilling itself. Similarly, I'll always have another chapter to write, another paper to grade, another journal article to review—the information never ends. Putting heroic efforts into task completion by pushing through saturation nausea and fatigue is ultimately self-defeating in informational work. A much more productive and efficient process is to approach the information from a mental standpoint of maximum productivity and efficiency—*get as much done while you're in your most productive and efficient mindset*—and then quit the work when that mindset can no longer be sustained because you've reached saturation. At a later time, or maybe the next day, you can return to your work when you're not saturated, and you will be exponentially more efficient and productive in completing your work.

When we adopt the simple "get it done" mindset that's effective for ditch digging and other physical labor and apply it to informational labor, we're applying a metaphor that is not apt because of the inherent difference between physical and informational labor. When we get tired of ditch digging, that's physical exhaustion, which you can push through if you're close to task completion. When we get tired of responding to emails, that's saturation fatigue, which you can push through if you're close to task completion—only the task will never be complete because the inbox is constantly refilling itself—so there's no point in pushing through because you'll just be fighting yourself, and the process itself will be inefficient and less productive. The energy spent fighting yourself to "push through" is wasted energy. You're much better off ditching the emails and doing something else that requires a completely different form of engagement (like digging a ditch). When you get physically exhausted with digging the ditch, go back and hit those emails again, and you'll find that your ability to focus and engage are much stronger than before when you were saturated and forcing yourself to go on.

Commitment Resistance

When our mind is posed with an unwanted task, our initial reaction is that of reluctance. We don't want to do what we don't want to do (go figure!). But what if you must do that task for work? The reluctance must be overcome. You can force yourself to do something you don't want to do, but you can't force yourself to like it. So what happens to that natural feeling of reluctance once you start doing what you don't want to do? It degrades into a dull stiffness of mental acuity, a present yet subliminal and stubborn **commitment resistance**, like driving a car with the emergency brake engaged. The car is moving, but you can feel that something's holding it back, inhibiting its forward momentum, so you need to use more gas, which depletes the fuel for the task much more rapidly than it would otherwise. In other words, you're fighting yourself, but it's very subtle, so you don't notice it. *What's going on?* The mind is being forced to engage in a medium it's already saturated with. Since it has no choice, it must do what it's forced to do, but it will not "commit" to the task because it's fundamentally set against it at that moment, and it's that lack of commitment to the task that creates the feeling of subliminal unconscious resistance. It's like you have an inner mule that you use for work and that inner mule is being stubborn, not refusing to budge altogether, but you really need to force it into taking each step.

Your best friend sets you up on a blind date with one of her friends, for example. The blind date shows up and he's kind of a loser. *What do you do?* You don't want to offend your best friend by preemptively ditching the loser, so you suck it up and go out on the date, just to be polite. You will physically go out on the date, but how will you feel? Obviously, you've already determined that this fellow is a loser and that you want nothing to do with him after the date, so your feeling will be that of **noncommittal resistance**. You'll go along with it to a certain extent but grudgingly so. You'll go on the date, but you'll put no effort into it, making the date itself, ironically, much harder to get through. You'll mentally focus on the end of the date rather than the process of the date itself, and this future-oriented mindset will actually increase your anxiety and make the date feel much much longer. In short, you'll do the task while not psychologically committing to the task, and this predetermined resistance will actually make the task feel much longer, much more difficult, and completely joyless.

Inefficiency and nonproductivity result from the same problem—the inability of your mind to truly focus on a task completely—due to cognitive resistance. We're fighting ourselves, thinking in ways that we don't want to think in, and that's why relatively simple jobs often take so long to get done. Most of us have been overengaging in our specific work media[8] for so long that saturation kicks in almost immediately, only we don't realize it because we're used to it. We've become so accustomed to loathing our work that we don't even feel the hate anymore; it just feels like a dull aching pain, a sort of existential headache.

The only cure for commitment resistance is mindful awareness leading to balancing. Being aware of your resistance to a process and knowing exactly how that resistance is destroying the efficiency in which you complete that task does not in and of itself make the task easier or increase your efficiency. Awareness merely tells you that you need to switch or flip media in part because there's no way you can efficiently work when you're fighting the uphill battle of your own resistance and in part because you now know that if you ditch the task for now and return to it at another time, you'll be in a much better position to complete the task efficiently, getting it done better and quicker than you would if you were still fighting yourself. Media mindfulness cannot solve the problem of completing an unwanted task, but it can help you maximize your own mental efficiency so you can complete the task quicker and with much greater efficiency. When we stop forcing ourselves to be "productive" by perseverating on work media beyond the point of saturation, our minds will naturally process thought in ways that require much less energy because we're not fighting ourselves. The final result, ironically, is increased productivity and efficiency. When we switch or flip our media to allow our minds to channel thought without forcing it through the specific work medium that we overuse to the point of saturation, we tend to have our greatest ideas and most beneficial breakthroughs. When we return to the work medium after recovering from saturation, our work is fueled with the power of those new ideas, making the work itself seem new and interesting once again. Mindfulness of the productivity paradox is just one example of how media mindfulness can help you become more productive, more efficient, and more creative in your work.

Switching Costs and the Hidden Price of Procrastination

Media mindfulness works best when we apply it *before* we engage in work that we know will saturate us. If I have an inbox full of emails that I know I have to get through and if I know that I'll be hitting my saturation point in less than an hour, I'll be completely motivated toward the goal of answering as many emails as I can as efficiently as I can within the limited time I have before saturation kicks in and I'm obliged by my own philosophy to quit rather than fight myself. That knowledge in and of itself helps me overcome my commitment resistance because I'm acknowledging it and working with it rather than denying, suppressing, or repressing the real feeling that is begging to be addressed. It's like I'm reasoning with my own mind, telling him that I know he doesn't want to commit to the task, and I know he's reluctant and resistant, but if we both suck it up and really focus on working together as a team, getting as much done as possible as efficiently as possible, we'll do great, and also I promise to quit, at least for a while, when I feel saturated. Now that my mind and I are on the same page and commitment resistance is minimized, at least temporarily, we can get to work, all the while being mindful of the other mind games at play.

When the mind is resistant to committing to a task, it will constantly opt for procrastination over task completion. Your blind date is walking toward your front door, for example. You can tell he's a loser just by the stupid way he wears his loser hat. He rings the doorbell. *What do you do?* Well, having resigned yourself to the unwanted date, the most efficient way to get the unwanted task done is to get it started right away. "*Well begun is half done*,"[9] right? So what do you do? Invariably, you stall. You have him wait at the door, then you let him in and have him wait in the foyer while you get ready—while you *procrastinate*—because your mind is laying down a path of obstacles that reflects its own commitment resistance. **Procrastination is the most inefficient and unproductive thing we do while working, and it is the most obvious sign of commitment resistance.** The irony, of course, is that procrastination arises because we don't want to do the job, but the effect of procrastination invariably is to prolong the job. It makes no sense! *Why?* Because you're fighting yourself!

How can you stop procrastinating? You guessed it: Being mindful of your own procrastination—what it is, where it comes from, and how to dispel it—will naturally lead to your avoidance of procrastination. Specifically, there are three things that you can do to counteract your own tendency to procrastinate when faced with an unwanted task: **commitment**, **decision**, and **concentration**.

First of all, *commit to the task*, even if—*especially if*—it's an unwanted task. As all yoga teachers are required to say at regular intervals, "*Set your intention, and then follow it through*." As covered above, consciously committing to the task while simultaneously acknowledging your own unconscious resistance to committing to the task is a way of temporarily overcoming your own commitment resistance. It's like you're making a bargain with yourself to get the job done, and that bargain in and of itself lowers the threshold of the initial resistance you're feeling. Simply understanding the neurotic conflict you're experiencing, acknowledging it, and working *with* it rather than *through* it will allow you to leap over that first initial obstacle to task completion. At least you won't be fighting yourself every step of the way, and that will actually make a huge difference. We're typically unaware of how much we're constantly fighting ourselves, and we generally have no idea what a powerful and formidable adversary we are. Getting yourself to work with yourself rather than against yourself is not just the first step; it's the last step and it's also every step in between.

Once committed to the task, you must commit yourself to being decisive. ***Procrastination expresses itself primarily through indecision.*** The blind date, stupid hat and all, is getting out of his car. You have less than one minute to cancel the date before it's too late, and you risk offending your best friend by insulting her friend (the loser). **You must decide!** But do you decide? No. You hem and haw and pace the floor and deliberate with yourself. You're conflicted due to the commitment resistance you're experiencing, which is at odds with your fear of hurting your friend's feelings (and possibly out of concern for the loser as well. Losers have feelings too, you know). So, do you decide? No. By the time the loser rings the doorbell, the window of decision has closed, and now you're locked into the date, like it or not. If only you were decisive at the exact moment of decision, you could have decided to cancel the date, maybe coming off as a bit rude, but at least you would be free from the agony of the loser date. *Why didn't you decide? Why did you procrastinate?* You were indecisive because you had not committed yourself to either the task of the date or the task of canceling the date. Your lack of commitment was expressed through indecisiveness, and your indecisiveness was revealed in your procrastination, and your procrastination has resulted in the worst date of your life.

Now let's apply the same logic to a work problem. You get an email from your boss requesting some thought that you don't want to think about. *What do you do?* Do you respond to the email immediately, or do you procrastinate by moving on to the next email without responding? Our tendency is to procrastinate because we don't want to deal with it. It's easy to procrastinate because we can just move on to the next email, providing us with the illusion that we're doing work when we're actually avoiding it. This is something we do all the time. We trick ourselves into believing that by skipping an unwanted task to move on to a less unwanted task, we're getting work done, but getting work done is *not* accomplished by moving on to a new task; **work is accomplished by completing the task at hand.** That last point is so incredibly obvious that it's invisible. We're completely blind to our total inefficiency at work, yet we wonder why it's so hard to get all of our work done. Procrastination due to indecision is the most villainous of all the "time thieves" in our lives, and the worst part is, the thief is our self.

Let's break it down. The task of responding to an email consists of three separate parts: (1) reading the email, (2) understanding the email and figuring out how to respond, and (3) writing the response. Where does procrastination kick in? Obviously, it can't kick in before part 1 because there has to be an unwanted stimulus that you're avoiding for procrastination as a behavior to exist. Generally, procrastination kicks in after you read the email, digested it, understand what the sender wants from you, and in most cases, have a pretty good idea of what your response should be. Procrastination kicks in once you need to flip modes from the receptive tasks of reading and understanding the email to the expressive task of writing the response email. The volition required to actually start writing is stalled by your own commitment resistance, resulting in temporary indecision—*should I reply now or should I reply later?*—and then our reluctant behavior simply follows the path of least resistance, which is to move on to the next email without responding. You procrastinated rather than commit to the task at hand, even though you already completed two-thirds of the task (reading, understanding, and knowing your response). If you would just do that last third of the task right, then rather than procrastinate, you would be done, but instead, you procrastinated, wasting all the time and energy you already spent on the uncompleted task. The waste is due to **"switching costs"**—probably the most expensive hidden cost among all of our inefficient work practices.

Every time we switch our attention from one stimulus to another, we pay a cost in terms of time and cognitive energy. It takes time to remember where I left off with the stimulus I'm returning to, and that remembering incurs a cognitive cost in terms of mental energy expended. When I read an email, understand it, and compose an initial response in my head, I'm spending time and energy on that process. If I procrastinate by not responding to that email right away and moving on to the next email, I'll forget the gist of what I just learned. When I return to the email hours later, or the next day, or days later, I'll be obliged to reread the email to rekindle my understanding of it and remember my initial response to it. In other words, I'm spending all that time and effort again, paying twice for the same product. What's worse, if I choose to procrastinate a second time, then I'm forcing myself to pay the switching cost yet again, which means I'll be spending thrice for the same product. Each time I procrastinate, I have to pay for another round of switching costs. For people who procrastinate often, their horrible work inefficiency can be chalked up to the incredibly high switching costs they're paying to complete tasks that, for the most part, they're doing over and over again, rather than just simply completing each task once right away. The irony, of course, is that we procrastinate when we don't want to do a specific task, and that procrastination dooms us to the fate of having to do most of that specific task numerous times, rather than just getting it done the first time around in one go.

The Myth of Multitasking

Perhaps the biggest myth of the digital age is the myth of "multitasking." This is the false belief that a human being can focus on multiple tasks at once, thus doubling, tripling, or even quadrupling their efficiency. The ludicrous construct of multitasking is the biggest load of nonsense ever dumped on our species, but the digital generation is nevertheless addicted to it. My average student believes that she can write her term paper while also studying for an exam in a different class while also responding to both her text messages and emails. She believes that she's being incredibly efficient by doing four things at once, but she's actually deluding herself while being incredibly inefficient at everything.

There are some forms of attention that don't require full mental engagement, especially when the media of engagement are in different modes of perception, such as listening to music while engaging in a visual task such as playing a game on your phone. However, when the attention required for multiple tasks are in the same media of engagement and require the same mode of perception, it's literally impossible to multitask. In the case of my student, she's trying to spread her linguistic attention across four tasks, but that form of attention requires exclusive focus—you can read only one word at a time—no matter how quickly you read and no matter how good your attention is. Therefore, my student is deluding herself when she thinks she's multitasking because she is actually "serial tasking"—focusing on one task at a time—but switching frequently from one task to the other. She thinks she's being superefficient, but she's actually being super inefficient—taking much much longer to complete a task and doing a much poorer job at it—because every time she switches her attention from term paper to exam, or from email to text, she's paying a premium in terms of switching costs. The more she switches her attention, the higher the cumulative costs. Empirical research has shown that multitaskers take much longer to do anything, even when you compound their multitasked work together because the completion time for any one of their tasks is exponentially longer than the completion time for study participants who do the same tasks one at a time. Multitaskers are also much more likely to do very poor jobs because they're spreading their attention too thin, and they're also much more likely to not complete any task at all because it takes them so long to complete anything that they experience pseudo-exhaustion or real exhaustion well before they can complete even one of the multiple tasks they're trying to do concurrently.[10] Perhaps the most troubling research finding is that multitaskers tend to believe that they're truly being much more efficient in their work, even when presented with the objective evidence of their own inefficiency.

In addition, some tasks (such as writing a term paper) require a level of "deep focus" that cannot be attained when your attention is dashing around from one task to another every quarter second like a coked-up squirrel. The author Nicholas Carr referred to the above process as "skimming the shallows" in his famous book *The Shallows: What the Internet Is Doing to Our Brains* (2011). His premise is that internet-enabled multitasking makes it difficult if not impossible for users to engage in the deep-focus thinking that's generally required for college-level informational work, resulting in a generation of users who are quite adept at "skimming the shallows" of our information environment but unable to immerse themselves deeply in the kind of deep-focused unilateral attention required to understand or create extremely complex or difficult-to-understand ideas. Hence, the third thing we must be mindful of when working is **the level of concentration** *required of a task and the level of concentration we're comfortable committing to a task*. If you know that a certain email is going to require a high level of concentration and if you know you don't have the attentional resources at that moment to fund that level of concentration, then you should immediately ditch the task. The alternative—reading, understanding, and processing the email—only to procrastinate and not respond is doing two-thirds of the job before quitting. That's like working at a job Monday through Wednesday and then quitting on Thursday afternoon even though Friday is payday. If you just finish the week, you'll get paid, but if you quit and walk away, you get nothing, and all that time and energy are wasted. Similarly, by not committing to completing the task at hand prior to beginning the task, you make it likely that you will procrastinate, thus expending the bulk of your time and energy on switching costs rather than on task completion.

The paradox of productivity is revealed in the fact that we're generally the least productive when we're forcing ourselves to be productive, whereas we become more productive in general when we regularly release ourselves from the burden of productivity. The reason why forcing yourself to be productive is incredibly unproductive is because the force we're expending is being used to fight ourselves, battling our own natural counterforces of "inhibition energy" and "commitment resistance" to the task at hand. If we force ourselves to do a task we're not mentally committed to, we're much more likely to procrastinate or engage in other anti-productive behavior such as multitasking, which is essentially just another form of procrastination. Procrastination, in turn, becomes our most wasteful and inefficient work practice because the bulk of our time and energy is wastefully expended on switching costs rather than on task completion. In the end, it's clear that the main reason work is so hard and takes so long is because we're wasting so much time and energy fighting our own inhibition energy, battling our own commitment resistance, and wallowing in the mire of our own switching costs.

The mindful approach to efficient productivity is to understand the processes above so we can approach our work with the correct mindset.

First, ***commit yourself to completing the task at hand without procrastination*** even if that means you respond to only three or four emails before you reach saturation and need to switch or flip media. Actually responding to three or four emails and being done with them is exponentially more productive than reading 50 emails but responding to none of them because when switching costs are calculated, reading those 50 emails without responding was just wasted time and energy (procrastination in the false guise of productivity). Second, while working, ***always be decisive*** in your approach, as you already know that indecisiveness is usually just an unconscious expression of your own cognitive resistance to committing to the task at hand and that indecisiveness usually leads to procrastination. Indecisiveness traps us within the inner conflict of our own mind, our concurrent desire to both complete the task at hand and to avoid the task at hand. Conscious and deliberate decisiveness in either direction—*complete the task or ditch the task*—frees us from that mind trap. ***Freedom is achieved through decision.*** Whether we go on to complete the task or we ditch it and return to it at a better time, at least we're not wasting our time and energy fighting ourselves or getting bogged down in unproductive procrastination. Third, ***be mindful of the level of concentration required of the task at hand***, and either commit fully to devoting that level of concentration to the task at hand or accept the fact that you don't have the attentional resources at that moment, and immediately ditch the task. It's far more efficient to return to the task at another time rather than forcing yourself into a process that you know will be a wasteful and inefficient uphill battle against yourself. Being preemptively mindful of your own ability to commit to a task, to remain decisive and committed to that task while completing it, and to concentrate fully on that task until its completion is the best way to maximize your work efficiency and productivity, while also being mindful of your brain's natural need to balance its media engagement.

The "Medium" Path

I have a fondness for double entendre. I admire their efficiency. The "medium" path is an extremely efficient double entendre. Also known as the "path of moderation" or the "middle road," the medium path is the one in which excess in any direction is avoided. Media balancing evokes this meaning of the medium path, as the focus is on the Self—the center of one's consciousness—and the method is to avoid straying too far away from one's center. The medium path may seem contradictory to the paths of success sold to us in schools, where the goal is to "specialize" as much as possible in a single field to reap the highest possible profits from your labor. There's no doubt that most of us have had to "specialize" our attention for many years to attain a career or profession to support ourselves and our families. This specialization is a form of "self-commoditization" that could be perceived as a necessary evil of the modern world. If, like me, you're older and have already gone through the specialization/self-commoditization grinder, then you may have found, like me, that the downside to the productivity of turning yourself into a machine is that you feel like you have the soul of a machine. Media balancing brought me out of that machinelike mode of functioning and brought me closer to my center. If, unlike me, you're a young person just starting out in the world, you may be concerned that the method in this book will take you away from the specialized path you need to find to become the doctor, lawyer, entrepreneur, designer, or whatever specialization it is you wish to gain. The "medium" path sounds a lot like the path of the dilettante, the generalist, the professional dabbler, the jack-of-all-trades but master of none. If specialization is where the money is, then dilettantism is where the money isn't, and that's no lie.

However, I've found that the effects of media balancing are almost always counterintuitive. For example, as a result of deliberately cutting back on linguistic and logical-mathematical tasks for my work in favor of engaging in other media that I'd rather be engaging in, I've found that the time I do spend on those tasks is much more efficient and that I'm equally if not even more productive even though I spend less time and energy on those tasks. Furthermore, the energy I release when I stop forcing myself beyond saturation to perseverate in those tasks drives my engagement in other creative and fun tasks, which actually generate even more energy and stimulate my creative juices. The end result is that I have a lot more energy, I do a lot more stuff that I consider fun and personally beneficial, and I'm even more productive with work even though I spend less time working. Now, that's counterintuitive! Nevertheless, it makes perfect sense.

The medium path promotes **lateral growth** in eight directions, while the path of extremes promotes growth in only one or two directions. If a tree has eight boughs and the growth of six are not promoted while the growth of just two are overpromoted, the tree will grow unproportionately. The two boughs will extend very far, but the tree itself will not thrive and it will never reach its full potential. When a tree grows in a balanced way, it grows upward and outward, with the boughs on all sides in proportion to each other. The tree whose boughs are allowed to grow in all directions will thrive, eventually reaching its full potential. The tree that has grown to its full potential will eventually be taller than its twin who has grown in only one or two directions even though it may take more time to get there. For any organism to reach its full potential, it needs to grow in every way that it can grow. Lateral growth in multiple directions is ultimately much healthier and results in more development for the organism as a whole than vertical growth in just one or two directions. For the young eager person who wants to find the quickest and most direct road to success, I suggest you put this book down and find another. The path prescribed in this book is the medium path, a slow and deliberate path, and the riches to be gained, while great, are more likely to be personal rather than financial.

The second meaning of the "medium" path is a reference to McLuhan's infamous adage, *"The medium is the message."* Within that simple phrase is an entire philosophy. Whenever considering something, our attention is initially drawn to the figure standing out before us, the focal point of our attention. This is our left hemisphere doing what it does—taking over, dominating the conversation, hogging all the attention to focus *"single-mindedly"* on what it wants to focus on. If the thing we're considering is a book, for instance, our focus is on the content of that media, the meaning of the words, the "message." McLuhan's adage is a reminder to flip our attention from time to time to perceive the effect of the ground of the medium we're engaged in. Stop thinking for a moment about the meaning of the words in this sentence, and ponder for a moment the meaning of words in general. Think about the enormous psychological effect that book reading has on your cognitive tendency to think in words, your tendency to format your thoughts in the form of verbal propositions. Clearly, the effect of the medium of literacy itself is far more impactful on your mind and behavior than anything I could ever write. Hence, the "medium" path is an ongoing thought experiment, a challenge to yourself to flip your perception every once in a while to perceive the effect of the "medium" on your thought process, as opposed to focusing on only the content or message being delivered by the medium. That mind flip is the essence of media mindfulness.

I have bad thoughts: anxious thoughts about the future, depressing thoughts about myself. In the past, I would have analyzed these thoughts to the point of frustration, in vain pursuit of some deeper meaning that I could untangle and construe, as if my own consciousness was a puzzle that only my own consciousness could solve. I'd discuss these troubling thoughts with therapists and friends, family and well-wishers, but nothing was ever cured or resolved. And then one day, I flipped my perception of myself. I realized that the "medium was the message." The reason why I have anxious and depressed thoughts is because I'm an anxious and depressed person. I—the medium of my own consciousness—am the generator of anxious depressive thoughts. Once perceived that way, I realized that the content of my actual thoughts were entirely inconsequential. My thoughts are anxious depressive because the medium—me—is anxious depressive, and it's as simple as that. Trying to cure the anxious depressed medium by analyzing the content of that medium is an exercise in futility.

I had a similar revelation many years ago, but I forgot it, or at least never applied it to myself. In my twenties, I worked as a creative arts therapist and counselor at a mental hospital in New York City, where most of my patients were schizophrenic. Therapy with schizophrenics is a challenge because they often have very elaborate delusions that monopolize their thoughts and fantasies. I was trying to figure out the meaning or root behind my patients' delusions as an attempt to help them, and I consulted with the floor psychiatrist for guidance. The psychiatrist said, in so many words, that delusions were nonsense, the figments of unhinged minds, and that I was wasting my time trying to figure them out. My job when counseling patients was to make sure that they were compliant with their medication regimes and that their other psychosocial needs were being met so that they can remain stable and not become a danger to themselves or others. At the time, I was a bit disenchanted with the psychiatrist's unromantic view of my psychotic patients' delusions, but after a good deal of time listening to them, I have to admit that she was right. A schizophrenic brain is a medium for delusions, so a schizophrenic has delusions because he is schizophrenic, and that's that. *The medium is the message.* Analyzing the message (studying the delusions) may be interesting, but it will have absolutely no effect on the actual medium—the schizophrenic's brain.

On an even more basic level, let's say your dog barks. Could you get your dog to stop barking by closely analyzing its barks and trying to figure out what they mean? Obviously not. It doesn't matter what the barks mean. They may mean nothing at all. Your dog barks because it's a dog, and a dog is a medium for barking, so if you don't want to hear barking, you better get yourself a different pet medium—like a cat or something—because that dog ain't gonna stop barking no matter how much you analyze the sound of its bark. You can, of course, *train* your dog not to bark by focusing on your dog's environment and behavior and manipulating them to the desired effect. And therein lies the key. Applying the "medium" path to myself, I realized that if I didn't want to be stifled by my own anxious depressive thoughts, I needed to adjust the medium (myself) by changing my environment rather than wasting time focusing on the content of the medium (my thoughts). If I change my environment, my behaviors automatically change to adapt to the environment, and in turn, my thoughts change to reflect my new behavior. In short, **change your behavior, and your thoughts will follow.**

Impure Forms and the Sin of Reification

> *Nature brooks no sharp discontinuities.*
> —Howard Gardner

Howard Gardner found it necessary to qualify his model of multiple intelligences with an extremely important warning:

> These intelligences are fictions—at most, useful fictions—for discussing processes and abilities that (like all of life) are continuous with one another; Nature brooks no sharp discontinuities of the sort proposed here. Our intelligences are being separately defined and described strictly in order to illuminate scientific issues and to tackle pressing problems. It is permissible to lapse into the sin of reifying *so long as we remain aware that this is what we are doing*.[11]

Gardner insists that there are no "pure forms" of intelligence. All thought, when expressed or experienced through a medium, becomes metaphor, and the metaphors we use are all mixed. If I have a thought about you, that thought is likely to be "linguistic" because it's formatted in words, but because I'm thinking specifically of you, the thought is "interpersonal" as well. At the same time, I may be imagining your face ("visual-spatial") or hearing the lilting sound of your voice as if it were a melody ("musical"), and so on. Clear demarcations between media of engagement are fictional and only make sense on paper. Although I must make these fictional demarcations for the purpose of elucidation, in practice, the aim is not to single out any one mode of engagement and focus on that but to balance all of the modes of engagement in ways that are complementary. In that sense, the intention is to seek harmony—integration—rather than "balance" per se, which could be seen as divisive, a process of segregation rather than integration. My suggestions in this book rely on combinations and pairings of modes of engagement, not the isolation, discrimination, or inhibition of any of them. The "sin of reification" is most heinous when applied religiously. Misunderstanding metaphor for the "real" thing it denotes is probably the biggest mistake humans make, and we do it all the time. So, to be clear, your "mind" is a metaphor. The eight multiple "intelligences" or "media of engagement" are metaphors. The distinction between the "expressive" and "receptive modes" of media engagement is a metaphor. Every concept in this book is a construct, a metaphor. The "Self" is a metaphor, as are "consciousness" and "existence." These metaphors are useful only in so far as they help us to understand ourselves. My hope is that the metaphors I supply in this book are apt metaphors for your personal existence.

Chapter Three

Linguistic Media

*Anxious Depression and
the Primary Environment*

> *My thought is me: that's why I can't stop. I exist because I
> think ... and I can't prevent myself from thinking.*
> —Jean-Paul Sartre[1]

Before I became mindful of my media engagement, I dwelled in an incredibly unbalanced media environment. As a writer/professor, it would seem to make sense for my media to be heavy on the linguistic side (reading, writing, lecturing, corresponding via email, etc.), but the sheer level of unbalance, in retrospect, was overwhelming. Each morning, I would read for an hour or two as my mind awoke. Once awakened, I would focus my mind on writing. The late morning would find me reading and responding to emails from students and colleagues, while the early afternoon was usually consumed with reading and grading papers, delivering a lecture, or advising students. The late afternoon and early evening featured more reading and writing of both professional and personal emails as well as text correspondences and more book writing. The evenings were generally not so literacy focused until it was time for bed, at which time I'd curl up with—you guessed it—a good book. I remember, for all those years, feeling proud of myself for living the "life of the mind" that I had always aspired to.

> *My mind to me a kingdom is; such present joys therein I find;
> As far exceeds all earthly bliss, which* **God** *and* **Nature hath assigned**.[2]

Yet, if I was so content in my kingdom, why did the head that wore the crown rest so uneasy? In retrospect, I was drowning in anxious depression, excessively overweight, living an entirely insular, isolated, indoor, interior, inactive existence. My kingdom was a cage and my Self both the prisoner and the guard. I had to find the key to unlock my mind—and I did—and now I'm sharing that key with you.

Mind Your Own Mindfulness

Why is everybody talking about "mindfulness" these days? Is it just the hip thing to talk about, another passing cultural phase, or is there more to it? In essence, the mindfulness craze is addressing a problem that we're all quite aware of yet somehow helpless to overcome. We live our busy and hectic lives rushing to and fro, our minds dutifully following our slapdash behaviors. Our focus flits from here to there like a hummingbird, representing a brain that's relentlessly adapting to a media environment that's constantly changing content with no cohesion. Other books will advise you to counter your mindless unpresentness by adopting a practice of mindfulness, which may include meditation and/or other centering techniques. Those practices are great—I engage in them myself—but they will not cure the problem. The reason is simple: The mindless unpresentness of modern existence is a product of our media environments. Our media, saturated with content aimed at elevating our fears and anxieties, bombards us every second of the day. The cerebral retreat of a yoga practice or a bit of meditation is just that, a temporary retreat. Once you emerge from the yoga studio or the meditation space, blissfully centered and balanced after a mindful practice, you reenter your toxic media environment, and once again, you're almost immediately right back where you started. Have you ever noticed that? The temporary retreat of these part-time practices are useful, helpful, and healthy, and I encourage them, but they're temporary and not nearly enough.

A blind man, let's say, finds a miracle doctor specialist who says he has a procedure that can cure blindness. The blind man visits the doctor and takes the cure. Directly after the procedure, the blind man is amazed to discover that he can see clearly. He walks home without a cane, but after about an hour, his sight dims and goes away again. The blind man returns to the doctor to complain, and the doctor explains that the cure works only temporarily, providing sight for about an hour after each implementation of the procedure. If he wants to see again, he'll have to go through the procedure each time, and even then, the gift of sight will be experienced for only an hour each day. The blind man is glad to have had the gift of sight, even temporarily, and he will surely take advantage of it again, but for how long? How long until the burden of the procedure itself, and the shortness of the benefit itself, becomes too much of a hassle to deal with on a daily basis, and he either gives up the "cure" completely, or it becomes more of a once-in-a-while thing rather than an everyday thing? Sound familiar?

The part-time practices that we employ to experience the "anti-environment" to our media-saturated existences are of limited use because they confer only part-time benefits. Once meditation or yoga ends, so does mindfulness. The mindfulness gurus will argue that if you seriously study and practice mindfulness as if it were your full-time job and if you focus on staying mindful throughout the day, then the benefits of that practice will also be full time. This is true but at the mental cost of being deliberately mindful about your mindfulness all day long. So much for getting anything else done. I'm here to tell you that any mindfulness regime that requires constant vigilance and focus on the practice of mindfulness is leading you astray. Even though "constant vigilance" may be the cost of world peace, it should not and cannot be the cost of your inner peace. Unless you're a monk or a yogi, nobody has the time and patience for that level of perpetual mindfulness. You will burn out or abandon the practice—just one more approach to self-help that you tried, experienced, and abandoned. If you're considering a mindfulness regime that depends on you being deliberately mindful all day long, you will be disappointed with the outcome. The purpose of mindfulness is not to be mindful about being mindful all day long. You can clearly see the pointless circularity of that process. The purpose of mindfulness is to liberate you from the anxieties and troubles that imprison your mind in unsettling thoughts, not to burden you with an overly restrictive and regimented way of thinking, living, and being. Mindfulness will only be useful to you if it helps you live your life *without* the chore of having to be mindful of your mindfulness every damned second of the day!

In general, mindfulness practices are of limited utility because they either provide part-time relief for a full-time problem—or they provide full-time relief—but at the high cost of full-time commitment. Why are these practices so horribly inefficient? The solution is simple: The practices localize the root of your problem in your mind. Your mind, they say, is not mindful enough. To make it more mindful, you must practice mindfulness. See the circularity of the hypothesis? When the problem is identified as merely being the lack of a cure and the cure is identified simply as that thing which the identified problem is lacking, there's really not much being provided beyond the basic premise that mindfulness is good for you. Don't feel upset by this. Nearly all of applied psychology functions according to the same specious circularity.

If your child, for instance, is not doing well in school, the teacher may tell you that she's having attentional problems. You confer with the school psychologist, who reiterates the teacher's observation that your child seems to have deficits in sustaining her attention in the classroom. What can we do about it? Well, if a diagnosis of ADHD is made, then possibly some treatment, mostly in the form of stimulant medication, could be applied. What does ADHD mean? ADHD means only one thing—that the patient is displaying deficits in sustaining attention. Complete and total circularity. The "diagnosis" of ADHD is simply a confirmed observation of attention deficit in the patient. That's all it means and nothing more. The "diagnosis" explains nothing, elucidates nothing, provides no insight into the attentional issue, and has no real practical application because it's just a circular reference. Is it really helpful to say that your child has attention deficit issues because she has a condition called attention deficit disorder? That's about as helpful as telling me that I have bad breath because I suffer from "bad breath disorder." Don't spit on me and tell me it's raining. Don't let so-called experts fool you into thinking that your mind or brain is disordered in any way (or that your child's mind or brain is disordered) just because it profits them to make you believe that you or your child has a "mental disorder" because they just happen to possess the "cure" in the form of psychiatric medication or treatment.

On the same basis, don't let mindfulness experts convince you that there's something wrong with your mind—that is, you are chronically mindless or unmindful—just because they happen to have a cure to sell. **There's nothing wrong with your mind!** The problem, my friends, is in your environment. (Your media environment in particular.) Any mindfulness practice that points to your mind and not your mind's environment as the root of the problem is not only leading you astray, but it's making you think you have a real mental problem when you absolutely do not. It's the same as if you went to a psychiatrist complaining of a general lack of satisfaction in life, and the doctor diagnoses you with CDD (chronic dissatisfaction disorder). That disorder doesn't really exist—I just made it up—but the fact that it *could* exist points to the general circularity and absurdity of how we deal as a culture with mental health issues. The first thing we do is blame the "patient," pointing the finger of culpability squarely at her brain or mind. The next thing we do is to try to adjust the brain or mind (two things that we really know very little about) either by prescribing drugs to alter brain chemistry or some practice of psychotherapy or self-therapy to address the cognitive issues of the mind. Mindfulness practices would fall under the latter category. Again, both of those "corrections" will lead you astray because they mistakenly identify your mind and/or your brain as the root of the problem rather than the environment surrounding your mind/brain. They mistakenly try to address the problem by altering your brain chemistry or moderating your mind's cognition rather than changing the thing that's actually causing the problem—your toxic media environment.

Anxious Depression

> *If fear or despair continue for a long time, such a thing is melancholia.*
>
> —Hippocrates[3]

Chapter Three. Linguistic Media

In my previous book, *Media Environments and Mental Disorder*, I created the construct of "anxious depression," a term that differs from the current diagnostic terms constructed by the psychiatrists and psychologists who wrote the DSM-V (*Diagnostic and Statistical Manual of Mental Disorders*, 5th ed.). My purpose in doing so was to avoid the circularities embodied in the DSM diagnoses and also to avoid confusion. **This is not a clinical psychology book.** Clinical psychology invariably focuses on altering the brain and/or mind of patients with psychological issues. This book focuses on adjusting the media environments that surround our brains and minds. You might say that this is a "clinical media psychology book," if that helps in any way.

It's well known in the field of psychiatry that symptoms of anxiety and depression overlap to a very large degree and that pretty much everyone who is diagnosed with an anxiety disorder would also fit the diagnosis of a depressive disorder and vice versa. In practice, the vast majority of psychiatric patients suffer from both anxiety and depression, and the same patients are comorbidly diagnosed with both anxiety and depressive disorders. If, as a rule, anxiety and depression coexist rather than exist separately, then why are they considered separate disorders by psychiatrists? The long answer can be found in my previous book.[4] The even longer but far more complete answer can be found in the book *How Everyone Became Depressed: The Rise and Fall of the Nervous Breakdown* (2013) by psychiatrist and psychiatric historian Dr. Edward Shorter. In his book, Shorter explains that for nearly the entire history of medicine and psychiatry, anxiety and depression were not considered discrete disorders in and of themselves, but rather, they were considered common symptoms of one broader underlying condition and referred to conjointly as "depressive neurosis," "mixed anxiety-depression," "melancholia," or with other similar titles. The nonsensical divorce that severed anxiety/depression into two separate disorders had no clinical rationale. The separation arose out of an unholy marriage between the psychiatric industry and the pharmaceutical industry in the interest of doubling the number of psychiatric diagnoses applied to the average psychiatric patient, thus doubling the number of psychopharmaceutical prescriptions and, ultimately, doubling profits for everyone (except the patient). I will use the term "anxious depression" because it's simple, it's correct, it's a true description of what you and I are feeling, and it currently has no psychiatric or pharmaceutical connotation associated with it.

Why is it that most people feel either a little bit anxious or a little bit depressed a lot of the time with occasional bouts of severe anxious depression, mixed with times of no anxious depression at all? The reason (you guessed it) is your media environment. The reason anxious depression comes and goes is because your media environment is always changing. The vast majority of people diagnosed with anxiety and/or depression are taking psychiatric medication under the false belief that there's something wrong with their brains and that the medication is countering this unbalance. The blunt truth of the matter is the "neurochemical imbalance" theory used as a rationale behind most psychiatric medication has never been clinically proven despite many years of research and thousands of studies. Yes, that's right. The theory that everyone thinks is true has no actual basis in truth, and the millions of patients taking the medication based on this false rationale have essentially been lied to by their doctors. In the case of "clinical" anxiety and depression, the theory rationalizing the use of medication is that symptoms of anxiety and depression are caused by a deficit of the neurotransmitter serotonin in the brain. Multiple double-blind studies in which the artificial depletion of serotonin in patients did not cause depressive or anxious symptoms clearly demonstrate that the serotonin-deficiency theory in particular, and the neurotransmitter imbalance theory in general, is simply untrue. In his book *The Emperor's New Drugs: Exploding the Antidepressant Myth* (2011), Dr. Irving Kirsch, associate director of the Program in Placebo Studies at the Harvard Medical School, provides incontrovertible evidence via multiple meta-analyses of hundreds of clinical studies that antidepressants, for the vast majority of people prescribed the medication, have no significant clinical effect beyond the placebo effect. Dr. Kirsch, possibly this nation's foremost expert on psychopharmaceutical drug testing and the placebo effect, concludes, *"It now seems beyond question that the traditional account of depression as a chemical imbalance in the brain is simply wrong."*

So why do we keep blaming the brain for our anxious depression when the brain is clearly not to blame? First of all, the brain is the most obvious suspect because it's right there in our heads for all to see. Our media environments, on the one hand, are primarily invisible and also, as a construct, not physically real like the brain and also not as well known. (Have you ever heard of "media environments" before reading this book? I didn't think so.) Another reason is that although antidepressants and anxiolytics such as Prozac do not have a significant clinical effect in patients, they do have a very powerful placebo effect. Patients who believe in their doctors, and who believe in the neurochemical imbalance theory, and who believe in their pharmacists have all the reason in the world to believe that the medication will help, so it does. Mind over matter. It's as simple as that. The problem is, the very powerful placebo effect wears off over time so that patients have to take increasingly larger doses of the drug to get the same placebo effect even as issues with chemical toxicity, side effects, and interaction effects due to drug use increase with time and larger dosages. Eventually, the drugs have no real effect at all, but by that time, the patients have been taking such a large dose and for such a long time that their bodies and brains have adjusted to them so that quitting is no longer an option, as it would result in serious withdrawal symptoms. This brings us to the current situation in which millions of people religiously take their prescribed psychiatric medication every day (a sacramental ritual based on faith) even though it has no real effect. The most anxious depressive people I know are all on psychiatric medication. Does that sound off to you? Shouldn't the medication be *reducing* their anxious depression? The funny thing is, when I raise doubt about the benefits of their treatment, they stay faithful and true to the neurotransmitter imbalance theory despite all the evidence debunking it. Why so?

Life is chaotic, random, meaningless, tragic, and filled with suffering. Nothing is certain, and that's terrifying. Anxiety, the feeling of being afraid even in the absence of any real physical threat, is triggered by the terror of uncertainty. I define anxiety as **the embodied need for certainty in an uncertain world**. Psychologists also use the term "intolerance of uncertainty" as a way to measure and assess anxiety in their patients. When patients see a psychiatrist to treat their anxious depression, they're completely uncertain about themselves and their condition. They're asking for "help," but what they really crave is certainty. They want a doctor to be certain about their condition, so the doctor can make a certain diagnosis and prescribe a certain course of treatment, treatment that they are certain will cure them. All of this certainty is expensive in many ways, but they get what they pay for. After the psychiatric diagnosis and prescription, they're certain that they have an anxiety and/or depressive disorder, they're certain that the root of their problem is an innate imbalance of neurotransmitters in their brain, and they're certain they're being treated for it, and that's enough—even if they still feel anxious and/or depressed most of the time and even if they never actually get better. A little bit of certainty goes a long way, and most people in this anxiety-ridden world will suffer through anything just to get a little slice of it.

Don't let doctors fool you with phony diagnoses and impotent drugs to feel a bit of relief from your anxious depression. The root of your anxious depression is not in your brain, nor is it in your mind. See as many psychiatrists as you like, but they won't fix your brain because your brain doesn't need fixing. See as many psychotherapists as you like, but they won't fix your mind because your mind doesn't need fixing. The roots of your anxious depression are deeply ingrained in your primarily linguistic media environment. This media environment—let's call it the **primary environment**—is difficult to notice because it's entirely invisible. It consists of the words that flow through your eyes and ears and float back and forth incessantly between the hemispheres of your brain. If you listen closely, you can hear them now. **The words**. You can hear them in your head as you read these sentences, and you can hear them, too, when you think to yourself—the process of verbal conscious thought, or the "voice of consciousness." Media environments do not just surround us; they envelope and infest us. The words we read, write, hear, and speak comprise a small part of our linguistic media environment. By far, the vast majority of our linguistic media environment is experienced inwardly as the ongoing internal conversation we have with ourselves about ourselves. The voice of consciousness is always there because at the most basic ontological level, your consciousness is the thing that you most relate to as being "*you*" and wherever you go. There you are! But what if the voice of consciousness in the "primary environment" is obsessed with anxious worries or depressive self-deprecatory reflections that make you feel sad or upset? Once again, the temptation is to blame your brain or your mind because after all, the "bad thoughts" are emanating from your brain and/or mind, are they not?

Not!

The "bad thoughts" are coming from your primary environment, the linguistic media environment that monopolizes your mind. However, the medium itself is not your mind. **Your bad thoughts are not your mind. Your voice of consciousness is not your mind. The medium of linguistic verbal thought is not your mind.** The word-generating media that feed your voice of consciousness are aspects of your primary environment, which you can understand, control, and tailor to your own needs and desires. This process is the true content of this book. Before we get to the process, I do need to cover the first step: understanding what the primary environment is, how it came about, and why it tends to mire us in anxious depression.

The Primary Media Environment

The processes of verbal speech and verbal thought are dominated almost completely by the side of our brain that attends to the world as if it were a task that needs to be completed or a problem that needs to be solved. This utilitarian approach to the world and others has engendered us as a species with the cognitive power to become the absolute undisputed masters of our environment, but at what cost? The left hemisphere's way of attending is to frame each stimulus as a problem or puzzle that needs solving so it can do what it does best: analyze, deconstruct, focus deeply on differences or discrepancies that might lead to a logical solution, and then work through those solutions via the process of hypothetical deductive reasoning. Again, this approach is extremely efficient and productive, but there's a very big problem: what if there is no problem? The left hemisphere presupposes a problem because it functions as a problem solver. As such, the left hemisphere is perfectly adapted for a world approach that can engage in deep-focused problem-solving. This approach is great if we're continually stepping back from the problem to allow for a more general view of the situation as a whole. This is the right hemisphere's way of attending, an approach that doesn't necessarily see a "problem" at all but rather a whole situation, with lots of interacting parts. The right hemisphere grounds us in the world we live in, while the left hemisphere extracts us by abstraction into a state of focus that, by its own design, does not see the big picture and is, in fact, blind to it. When working in tandem, in a balanced and reciprocal way, the twin hemispheres are the perfect dance partners, the epitome of collaborative give-and-take. When unbalanced—when dominated by the left hemisphere's myopic deep focus—we run the risk of becoming dangerously ungrounded in our existence, blind to the big picture and to the world as a whole, constricted to only being able to see ourselves and everyone else as problems that need to be solved. And because the left hemisphere's process of deduction is hypothetical, the process never ends because another hypothetical problem can always be conjured, requiring even more hypothetical deductive problem-solving ad infinitum. The left hemispheric way of attending dominates our conscious thought processes because it controls the primary medium for self-communication—verbal thought—and because it locks us into a perpetual feedback loop of self-communicative deliberation. I refer to verbal consciousness as the "**primary media environment**" because we're involuntarily stuck in it most of the time, with no simple means of escape.

Let's say, for instance, you meet a psychoanalyst at a cocktail party. For a laugh, you say, *"Go ahead and psychoanalyze me!"* The analyst will then proceed to ask you questions that may reveal your underlying neuroses. In other words, she will see your mind as a problem, and she will start descrying conflicts and ego defenses in your problematic mind to reveal that problem. If you momentarily object by saying, *"Why do you assume I have issues with my parents?"* or *"Why do you presume that I have unconscious defenses?"* then you're totally missing the point. The psychoanalyst works by presuming you have problems and then proceeds by analyzing those problems in a very deliberate, sequential, and deconstructive way to identify a solution to those problems. If you don't want to be envisioned as a walking, talking load of problematic emotional baggage that needs to be analyzed and solved, you shouldn't speak to a psychoanalyst. But what if the psychoanalyst is not a fellow guest at the cocktail party? What if the psychoanalyst is the voice of consciousness inside your own head, and what if the subject of analysis is invariably your Self? You can't excuse yourself or walk away from the analyst because the analyst is you and wherever you go. *There you are!*

Hyperconscious Rumination

> *Oh, this terrible second me, always seated whilst the other is on foot, acting, living, suffering, bestirring itself. This second me that I have never been able to intoxicate, to make shed tears, or put to sleep. And how it sees into things, and how it mocks!*
>
> —Alphonse Daudet[5]

Have you heard of "doomscrolling"? The dreadful phenomenon is born of the unholy marriage of the news media's penchant for reporting bad news on a 24/7 news cycle and the "infinite scroll" function on digital news web pages. The bad news never ends; it just keeps on coming. "Bad news," by the way, is anything that elicits a fear response in the consumer, fear being the neurological antecedent to anxiety. Because our brains are hardwired by millions of years of evolution to be "hyperaware" of threats in our environment, our brains are constantly on the alert for potential threats, even if the threat is 10,000 miles away and is in no way posing an actual threat to you or your loved ones. Remember, the brain engages directly with its media environment, and the media environment is not necessarily a physical environment, which means that a perceived threat gleaned from one's media environment is experienced by the brain as if it were a real threat in one's real environment. The brain has been evolving for millions of years to engage in real environments. The digital environment, which is virtual rather than real, is a brand-new environment for our brains on the evolutionary timescale, which explains why our brains and minds are so ill-equipped for adaptation to this brand-new virtual invisible environment and why books such as this one are so necessary.

Bad news elicits our fear, evoking a reaction, but because the fear is of a virtual rather than palpable threat, our physical fear cannot be sublimated into a physical reaction. The physiological signs of fear are present—quickened heartbeat, moistened skin, dry throat, hyperventilation, and so forth—but the body has no outlet for all of this increased arousal because the "fight or flight" instinct cannot be resolved in a physical act of fight or flight. Instead, the increased arousal just festers, devolving into a lingering anxiety, defined eloquently by Julian Jaynes as *"the knowledge of our own fear."*[6] The digital newsfeed captures our attention and imprisons it, casting us into the role of the blind media consumer, addicted to his media but unaware of the reason or the resolution because there is no resolution, just a never-ending cycle of reaction, a perpetual state of dread and doom.

Why is doomscrolling so common when it's so expensive in terms of time and attention, while it rewards us with absolutely nothing other than anxiety and depression? Although awareness of what's going on in the world is (arguably) important for most people, hyperawareness of everything that's going wrong in the world and the constant reminders about everything that's going wrong in the world (the same bad news over and over again) provides nothing but anxiety simply because we physiologically react to the news of wildfires in California and floods in Mississippi, but there's precious little we can actually do about it. Like Alexander DeLarge in *A Clockwork Orange* (1971), we're strapped to our seats with lid locks forcing our eyes open and focused on the screen filled of horrors in front of us. But the straps are invisible, and the lid locks are held open from inside of our own brain. The "blind consumer" is imprisoned by his own media, a "captive audience" in the kingdom/cage/theater of his own mind.

Pay attention for one moment to the voice inside your head, the voice of consciousness, and how it speaks to you in perpetuity. It won't shut up. No matter how hard you try, you can't turn consciousness off because consciousness is an independent agent in the mind controlled by no one, not even oneself. With great effort and practice, you can learn to silence the inner voice via meditation. (Or you can simply go to sleep and garner the same effect.) Unfortunately, most of us need to be conscious most of the time to survive. Complete detachment, for the average working stiff like me, is not an option. Yet how can we work when our external media reels us into a never-ending reactionary cycle of doom, and our internal media (the primary environment) not only clutters our attention with anxious thoughts and dreadful cogitations, but it criticizes us, mocks us, and derides us for the anxious depressive feelings and behaviors that consciousness itself is responsible for?

Clinical psychologists and psychiatrists have compiled a list of a variety of cognitive traits that they argue are symptoms of anxiety and/or depression. They are, indeed, symptoms but not of a disorder of the brain or mind. They are the "consequences of consciousness," the negative self-destructive thought patterns we naturally fall into when we're locked into our primary environment, the wall of words inside our own heads. First on the list is "**perseveration**," the tendency to continue to behave or think in a certain way, even when the stimulus for that behavior or thought patterns have ceased to exist. Doomscrolling is the epitome of perseverative behavior because we go on to the digital news page to quickly see what's going on, but then we persist and persevere in the process, well after the usefulness of the task has been exhausted (and well after our minds and brains have been exhausted as well). At the same time, we can conceive of perseveration itself as the "internal doomscroll function" within our own heads, the cerebral prison cell that locks us into a mode of thinking or being that is as self-destructive as it is inescapable. A computer, after all, can be turned off with the press of a button. The brain has no such button, nor does the mind. We cannot consciously turn consciousness off, making consciousness itself a perseverative behavior.

The process of perseverating specifically on our fears and stressors, playing the endless and futile game of imagining how to control and predict an unknowable and uncontrollable future is referred to as "hyper-reflective consciousness," "hyperconsciousness," or "hyperawareness." **Hyperconsciousness** is a cognitive trait that is very strongly associated with anxiety and depression. In my model, hyperconsciousness is the actual root cause of anxious depression. The mind's endless obsession with future-oriented stressors is the toxic element in the primary environment, the serpent in the garden that will not let us rest, with its interminable questions, challenges, and eternal doubt. Hyperconsciousness is the eternal quest for certainty in an uncertain world, a futile and self-destructive path that leads us only in circles, getting us nowhere, and killing us with stress as we proceed. A natural result is a chronic state of **"meta-anxiety"**—anxiety about our own anxiety—worrying about the fact that we worry too much. If ever there was a mouse running on a treadmill, getting nowhere but scurrying at full tilt, it is the average person in the modern world pursued by our own constructed demons, dashing full speed ahead toward our own doom.

"Rumination" refers to a state of mind in which we perseverate reflectively on the things that are lacking in our lives. It tends to draw us backward into our own personal history, where we haunt like ghosts the ruins of our past failures, brood on our own regrets, dwell on the things we never had, and wallow in our own misery. In essence, it's a personal pity party with one host and one guest, who are one and the same, and the only hors d'oeuvres are stale slices of humble pie, washed down with the bittersweet taste of our own tears. The distinction between hyperconsciousness and rumination is vague, just as the distinction between anxiety and depression is vague. They are both perseverative thought processes. They both epitomize left hemispheric engagement, as the focus on the subject (oneself) is deep and sustained. In its function as problem solver and solution finder, the left hemisphere puts our own identity under the microscope, scrutinizing the self to detect every single flaw or defect. When the self itself is the subject of scrutiny—when your very heart and soul is deconstructed by your own mind—the process itself is self-destructive, and it never ends. At no point will you ever "find yourself" in this endless and futile process of introspection because you're looking in the wrong place. **You are not your mind. You are not your consciousness.** These processes are just the media for your thoughts, media that drive your attention away from reality and into abstraction so that you become a problem to yourself, a puzzle that you cannot solve because there is no puzzle to begin with. Stop trying to "find yourself," and then you'll discover the underlying truth of your existence—that whatever you do and wherever you go, there you are.

The illusory distinction that psychiatrists make between "hyperconsciousness" and "rumination" has nothing to do with the processes themselves because they are clearly one and the same. Ruminating over one's own foibles is being hyperconscious of the self; and being hyperconscious about future stressors is merely ruminating about the future rather than the past. The illusory distinction has only one purpose—to distinguish between anxiety and depression—a distinction that's not only unnecessary but also obfuscating. On a basic level, every term I mention and every term in the field of psychology is merely a construct (a metaphor) used to represent a psychological phenomenon, such as a behavior pattern or a state of mind. The terms aren't real; they're just models to help us understand ourselves a little bit. When the terms overlap to the point of absurdity, they're no longer apt metaphors because they no longer serve the purpose of elucidation. Rather, they cloud the issue, making things seem much more complicated than they really are. Hyperconsciousness and rumination are the same thing, and they both result in thoughts and feelings related to anxiety and depression because on the same level, anxiety and depression are basically the same thing. To simplify, I'll just say that hyperconscious rumination—the curse of consciousness—is the primary cognitive cause of anxious depression.

The Tyranny of the Anxious

The road to success is paved with anxiety. Few people, if any, succeed without trying. The fear of failure is a very basic form of anxiety that motivates us all. When anxious depressive thought patterns prompt us to try harder to avoid failure and succeed, they play a vital and healthy part of our mental engagement with the world. When anxious depressive thoughts persist even after the work is done—when it *perseverates*—it becomes self-destructive. Oftentimes, hyperconscious rumination is so corrosive to our sense of self that it has an effect that opposes rather than supports its basic function. When our negative thoughts about ourselves injure or wound our sensitive egos, we fall into despair, a place of hopeless helplessness, where we doubt our ability to accomplish anything. This doubt, in turn, creates a fissure between thought and volition. Rather than thinking, "I will run five miles today" and then doing it, we doubt ourselves—"*Can* I run five miles today?"—and then we ruminate perseveratively in that doubt ad infinitum until the day is over and all that's left is the shame of inactivity. Our mind defeats our will before our body even has a chance to try. This is the point where the thought process that ideally motivates us becomes unmotivating. This is the point of dysfunction, what psychiatrists label "disorder."

The flip side of the coin are the overly motivated people—you know the ones, the people who work three jobs simultaneously to succeed at a level so high that they haven't a moment to appreciate and enjoy their success at all. The workaholic, the overachiever, the type A person who is never satisfied with himself, never able to step back and appreciate a job well done because the job never ends, nothing is ever good enough, and "appreciation" itself is an unproductive mindset. These people, driven by their own anxious depressive doubts and fears, never stop running because they're afraid to stop because stopping in and of itself represents a person who is simply a human *being*, while they can only perceive their own value when they are moving forward—a human *doing*. Of course, the people get very far but toward what end? If life is perceived as a race, then the finish line is death, so what's the rush? Our incredible brains and our even more incredible minds have created a race of beings so incredibly powerful that we have the ability to destroy the entire planet, and we're doing it right now. But with all this dominance and power, even as the undisputed masters of the world and everything in it, we've become an acutely fearful species, either hiding in fear, terrified of our own shadows or perpetually running, terrified at the very notion of slowing down. I call this modern species of hominid "**Homo nervusus**"—an inherently anxious-depressive creature—dominated and motivated by chronic self-dissatisfaction and its own imagined and manufactured fears.

The first type of anxious depressive—the one so stymied by their own self-destructive thoughts that they can barely function—is a staple of the psychiatric couch. Indeed, the psychiatric industry could not exist if not for the hundreds of millions of barely functioning anxious depressives who fill the treatment schedules. Ironically, the other type of anxious depressive, the workaholic who can't slow down for one moment for fear of momentarily not succeeding, is the least seen in psychiatric circles. Why? Because this person is a "success" and success is not a "disorder." It's more than likely that the person sitting in the chair facing the psychiatric couch, the psychiatrist herself, is, in fact, this other type of anxious depressive—truly, the blind leading the blind. In this modern world, "identity" is no longer a thing within us but a thing *about* us, a superficiality that we digitally project outwardly via social media. When identity is worn outwardly as a badge, a symbol of success and status, rather than experienced inwardly as a personal sense of self-acceptance, we see the reversal of values that afflicts all of Homo nervusus, whose motto has become, "Winner takes all," or "The one with the most toys wins," or "Winning isn't everything; it's the *only* thing." When success itself, rather than the fruits of one's success, becomes the primary motivator, we create a treadmill existence for ourselves in which self-acceptance must be bought with material possessions. This self-acceptance, however, is fleeting, as are all possessions. If one can only accept oneself if one is achieving, the moment of success provides only a moment of self-acceptance before the treadmill starts running again, with us racing away atop of it, desperately chasing that next achievement, all for that treasured moment of self-acceptance, which slips away as soon as it's experienced. Furthermore, when the social structure we all live in is dominated by the people who are most motivated by the need for certainty and control, we create a system in which the most anxious people are in charge of everything and everyone, a "tyranny of the anxious." Go to any success-oriented workplace, and you'll usually find that the person in charge is the most anxious person there, not because of the pressures of being the boss but because to become the boss and to keep climbing up the ladder, one must constantly be pressuring oneself and others as much as possible. As a former clinician and a psychology professor for over 20 years, I personally know my share of psychiatrists and psychologists, and I can tell you the bitter truth—they are no less anxious or depressive than you or me—and in my experience, it was their own anxiety that drove them through medical school and grad school and all the other hurdles and mazes that made them a "success." "*Uneasy lies the head that wears a crown,*" not because of the crown itself but because of the head that earned the crown.[7]

When neuro researchers want to study how the brain attends to certain stimuli, they hook up all their neurosensors and get a measure of the subject's brain in its "resting state," the state of mental engagement prior to the administration of the stimulus. The paradox is that a full picture of mental activity reveals that the brain as a whole is actually more active and engaged in its "resting state" than it is while it's engaged in a specific mental task. This finding is so universally true that neuroscientists have pitched the term "resting state" (since the brain is by no means restful when not focused on a specific task), replacing it with the term "**default mode network**" (DFN). What is the brain/mind doing when not engaged in a specific task but is in its default mode? You guessed it. The brain is engaged in hyperconscious rumination. This is the default mode that our brains fall into whenever it's not otherwise engaged in a specific task.

The DFN is actually much more active than specific task engagement because specific tasks often require only a small or specific part of the brain, while hyperconscious rumination is a "whole brain" affair, as it requires access to both long-term and short-term memory, and the voice of consciousness itself is heavily language dependent, and language is one of the most "expensive" cognitive functions processed by the brain in terms of the expenditure of mental energy and resources. Because the DFN is a process of hyperconscious rumination, neuroscientists have also dubbed it the "me network," as the task at hand is the analysis and deconstruction of the self, the process of finding a solution to the problem of "me," a process that will never end because "me" is not the problem; the problem is the process of self-scrutinization itself. As you might have guessed, the researchers found that their subjects were significantly "less happy" when their brains were in the DFN as opposed to when their brains were engaged in a specific task. In doing so, the researchers stumbled on the most brilliant and simple solution to anxious depression that anyone has ever stumbled on. If simply engaging your mind in a specific task makes you happier because it draws your mind out of the hyperconscious ruminative state that we tend to linger in when not otherwise engaged, then the key to happiness is simply to engage your mind in something other than hyperconscious rumination. In other words, *change your behaviors, and your thoughts will follow.*

The Joy of Self-Experimentation

How do you know the limits and capacity of your own thought processes if you've never tested them? The purpose of a **thought experiment** is to test a theory by thinking your way through it from beginning to end. The thought experiment utilizes the most advanced virtual-reality simulation technology known to Homo nervusus: the human mind. Consider the dream state for a moment. Reflect on how *real* it seems; note the density or richness of experience, the intensity of the psychological material being explored, and the ease in which we fall into the role of both subject and observer of our own dream world. Many researchers believe that dreams are unconscious thought experiments that our mind runs when conscious thinking is subdued during sleep. Dreams are virtual simulations of hypothetical real-life situations. They allow us to explore our possible futures and the consequences of our actions within them—they allow us to learn from our mistakes with the benefit of not having to live through the actual mistakes. Although some would say that a drawback of the dream-thought experiment is that we don't consciously remember the outcome or even the experiment itself, I believe that this forgetfulness of our dream experiments is by design. It seems that we only really "know" something when it seeps down into our unconscious mind and can be experienced intuitively, without the burden of conscious focus. Consciousness, as you may have noticed, tends to run us around in circles and is not quite as clever as we think it is. Our most important life lessons are learned at night while we slumber, in our dreams. Not consciously remembering those lessons are key because if we did, we would surely deconstruct and psychoanalyze those lessons to death, stripping them of their vitality and their inherent uninterpreted meaning (yes, I'm looking at *you*, Dr. Freud).

The most famous thought experiments have been in the field of theoretical physics, as the thought experiment literally allows the physicist to reimagine the universe as it would seem if it followed the mathematics being invoked by the experimenter. The physicist molds the shape and form of the universal dimensions in her mind and then inhabits those theoretical dimensions for as long as it takes, exploring the unreachable distances of time/space within the safe and secure realm of inner space. Galileo's Leaning Tower of Pisa experiment, which demonstrates that two objects fall at the same speed regardless of their mass, was a thought experiment. He never actually did it because the same principle could be demonstrated by dropping two objects off the side of a desk—there's no need to go to the top of the tower. Galileo just explained the thought experiment in reference to the tower so it could be more easily visualized by his students at the University of Pisa. Einstein's theory of relativity was born out of multiple thought experiments involving trains speeding toward a distant point and men falling out of windows. Most notably, Einstein's thought experiments were based on visual-spatial designs that he imagined, allowing him to explore time/space visually and intuitively rather than relying purely on logical-mathematical symbols. (It's well known that Einstein, ironically, was not particularly good in math. His visionary theories were just that—thought experiments based on visual-spatial imagination.) When Stephen Hawking lost the use of his hands due to ALS, his inability to write out long calculations and proofs by hand forced him to fall back on the more intuitive visual-spatial approach used by Einstein. Stuck in a wheelchair 24/7, unable to speak or to move any part of his body save his eyes and one thumb, Hawking conducted his most revelatory experiments within the confined kingdom of his own mind. In that virtual space, he inhabited geometrical patterns of time-space dimensions that even Einstein couldn't imagine.

The primary benefit of conducting a thought-based self-experiment is that like a dream, the process is completely "virtual," making the cost extremely low, the process itself quite convenient, while the sheer scale of the experimental designs that could be imposed are unlimited. In the concluding section of each chapter in this book, I'll be introducing a variety of self-experiments for media mindfulness and balancing. In a sense, the book itself is a thought experiment. You are both the experimenter and the subject, the constructs of media mindfulness and balancing are the independent variables (the methods being tested), and the dependent variables (the things that change as a result of the methods) will be your mental, physical, emotional, and spiritual health.

Flipping the Interrogative

Language-based consciousness is a questioning machine. All day long, it poses questions for us to answer. Most are simple: *"What time is it?" "Did I remember to charge my phone?" "Was I supposed to pick up the kids from school today?"* Some are not so simple: *"Should I quit my job?" "Am I happy in my relationship?" "What's the point of living?"* The question-making machine keeps churning, regardless of the answers it may receive. It's a function of the problem-seeking/solution-finding process of the left hemisphere. In the toxic primary media environment, the questions will never end, so it's best to just escape the environment when you can. While in the primary environment, though, here's a little flip that may help you channel the question maker's queries into useful eye-opening insights. I call it "flipping the interrogative" or more simply, **"flipping the W."** Every time you ask yourself a question, flip the interrogative word in the sentence (usually the first word of the sentence, usually starting with "W," i.e., where, what, when, why, which, who, how, etc.). This is a free association task. Immediately flipping the W to a random other W must be done *without* thinking or conscious reflection. The flip must be automatic. The process, like any other projective measure, such as the Rorschach (inkblot) test, allows for an unconscious association to be projected onto a random but controlled stimulus. More simply, our true feelings are likely to be revealed when we trick the mind into expressing itself without the sophistry of conscious deliberation.

Flipping the W on a question related to one's media technology is invariably going to pose the question to yourself in a way that you never considered before. So the next time you ask yourself ***"Where's my phone?"*** remember to immediately flip the W, and now you'll have some much deeper and more fundamental issues to ponder other than the location of your device, such as:

What is my phone? What exactly is this device that it should have such a central position in my daily life?

How is my phone? How exactly does my phone serve me? Are there ways in which *I'm* actually serving my phone by responding instinctively to its every beck and call? How can I make sure that my phone is my own "servo-mechanism" rather than the other way around?

Who is my phone? Who exactly is this thing that's forever calling me, texting me, notifying me, demanding my attention? It's not my child, but it demands as much if not more attention than my child. When I don't have it, I miss its presence. When I lose it, I feel I must find it immediately. Who is it that it should have such a strong hold on me? Is this thing my friend or my enemy? Is it servant or master? Is it brother, mother, secret lover? Whom does it serve? If not me, then perhaps I should just turn it off when I'm not using it lest the phone flips itself and begins using me.

And most important, *Why is my phone?* Why exactly is my phone such a necessity? (I can remember a time when it wasn't.) Why is it my *constant* companion? Does it really need to be on all the time, or is that just what Google, Apple, or Samsung require of me? The result of the thought experiment, the result of asking all these introspective interrogatives in response to the fairly simply question "Where's my phone?" is the somewhat unexpected answer, "I don't care where it is right now because I'm better off without it." If losing your phone throws you into an existential crisis, perhaps the resolution is not found in finding your phone but in accepting its temporary loss and existing without it. Obviously, Google, Apple, Samsung, and the other technocrats are heavily invested in each one of us being existentially linked to our phones at all times, but if it's all the same to those folks, I'll turn my phone off when I'm not using it so it will stop being such a tiresome nag, bothering me and interrupting me all the time. Invoking the "power of off" reminds me that I'm the master, and my phone is the servant. It makes me happier, more engaged in the real world, and it saves the battery too. If your phone asks you "why" you're turning it off, just tell it to go flip itself!

Chapter Four

Logical-Mathematical Media
The Twin Demons of Time and Money

What is a number that Man may know it? And what is Man that he may know number?
—Warren McCulloch

What then is time? If no one asks me, I know. If I wish to explain it to one that asks, I know not.
—Saint Augustine of Hippo

There's a counting instinct in humans that's intuitive and highly adaptive. When we see multiple objects, we automatically get a sense of "how many" or "how much" there are by detecting patterns of quantity in visual space. Mathematics, when paired with its natural partner visual-spatial thinking, is intuitive, effortless, and fun. Most puzzles and games, especially card games, board games, and many video games, rely on a combination of mathematical and visual-spatial processing, and we engage in these activities for fun. Then why do so many people not only dislike math but also viscerally hate it, and actually fear it, when exams are involved? The problem is that we teach math wrong in schools, which is why so many of us grow up hating math rather than loving it, developing an abiding aversion to the entire field. Mathematics—in its simplest, broadest, and therefore most correct definition—is the study of patterns of quantity. Mathematics, in its simplest and most natural form, is processed and expressed freely using visual-spatial designs that capture the patterns of quantity in a way that is completely intuitive. When we begin the study of mathematics as children, the process is visual-spatial. Teacher shows us five apples, he takes two away, and then we figure out the difference using both our counting instinct and our intuitive ability to detect patterns of quantity in space. Shortly thereafter, the teacher replaces the five apples with a logical-mathematical symbol ("5"), he replaces the physical action of subtracting three apples with another logical-mathematical symbol ("–"), and he replaces the remainder with two more symbols ("=" and "3"). Although this process seems harmless enough, great harm is actually being done.

By replacing the real with the symbolic, the actual with the virtual, the physical with the metaphysical, we take mathematical thought out of the ground of our real-life experience and place it squarely in the realm of figurative, abstract, logical thought. In short, by replacing the visual experience of math as patterns of quantity, with the symbolic representation of quantity using abstract arithmetical figures, we functionally take mathematical thought out of the grounding right hemisphere and situate it in the figural attention of the left hemisphere. In doing so, we take a mode of engagement that's inherently fun and make it anxiety provoking and cognitively painful.

We know very well that people in general, and children in particular, understand patterns of quantity better when they're presented visuographically rather than numerically. A graph is much easier to understand than a long string of numbers and logical symbols. The point of teaching arithmetic (the use of symbols and operators that denote quantity) in schools is to give us a written language that denotes mathematical thinking in symbolic form—a useful skillset to be sure. In that sense, arithmetic serves the same function as literacy. When we learn to read and write, we take the language sounds that we know intuitively through oral language and denote them symbolically using alphabetic letters and grammatical symbols. When we learn arithmetic, we take the patterns of quantity that we know intuitively through visual-spatial processing and denote them symbolically using numbers and operators. In both instances, the intuitive is replaced with the computational or deliberative, a neurological shift from right to left. Learning to read and write establishes the primacy of the "inner voice" of consciousness, just as the words you're reading at this moment can be heard clearly in your own mind. Without literacy, it's quite possible that most of us would not hear our thoughts as words but rather experience them via another medium, such as images, sounds, smells, tastes, and so forth.

Because written language stands on the shoulders of oral language and because we acquire oral language so incredibly quickly and early in our lives, literacy does not degrade our use of oral language because our ability to speak and understand is firmly established by the time we begin grade school. If anything, literacy complements oral language. Not so with math. Even though the visual practice of identifying patterns of quantity in space is established in early childhood, it does not reach the same level—or even the same dimension—of our practice of oral language. Language is such a dominant and overwhelming cognitive force because its acquisition is hardwired in the brain, acquisition happens extremely early, its influences are dispersed widely across the brain, and then on top of that, we spend thousands of hours deliberately training children to objectify their oral language in the form of literacy. That's why so much of this book is dedicated to countering the overwhelming and overrepresented influence of language over the mind (the primary media environment).

A parallel can be drawn between the acquisition of language and literacy in children and the acquisition of math and arithmetic, but overall, the metaphor is not apt. To have a level of visual-mathematical sophistication similar to a small child's mastery of oral language, the child would have to see patterns of visual quantity at the level of an Einstein or Stephen Hawking. Language is that complex. Unlike language, math is not hardwired in the brain, beyond our instinctive and intuitive approach to patterns of quantity. We're quite aware that forcing children to process math symbolically rather than visually is cutting against the grain in terms of their natural thought processes. However, in schools, the importance of learning the "alphabet" of math in the form of arithmetic takes precedence over the actual understanding of math as a field of study. Since arithmetic is not intuitive and since it cannot stand on the shoulders of a well-established mode of engagement similar to oral language, we get stuck at the arithmetical level of math for most of our school years and never actually proceed to the point where mathematics actually does become more about recognizing patterns of quantity in space. We have precious few Einsteins and Hawkings because we insist that children in schools master what they're not naturally good at (symbolic math) before they can proceed to what they're actually good at (visual math). We call children "backward" when they fail to learn math, yet the manner in which we teach math to children is entirely backward. Where else in life do we commence with the abstract, complicated, and difficult and then proceed to the more pragmatic, simple, and intuitive? Only in the backward space of the obsolete classroom. What's more, even though the digital age provides us with excellent tools for visually displaying patterns of quantity in ways that are more natural and intuitive for children to grasp, we still insist that children focus on ancient obsolete methods of learning math, such as memorizing multiplication tables, crunching repetitive numeric calculations by hand, and other rote methods that we know don't work but practice anyway. To quote McGilchrist, *"We are busy imitating machines!"*

My concern at the moment is not with the population of schoolchildren being forced to hate math but with you in particular and how math affects your particular mind. Math should not cause you anxiety, but it does so in many ways. We know that mathematics in its natural and intuitive state is relaxing and fun, which is why we spend so much of our time playing games and doing puzzles based on quantity pattern recognition. (Tetris, solitaire, and chess are my personal favorites.) We also know that math can be soothing and calming. How do you trick your mind into not worrying about tomorrow so you can fall asleep tonight? You count sheep, or you mentally review the stats of your favorite athletes, or you count the number of trees as you envision your backyard—any counting process that draws you into a repetitive and predictable rhythm of thought can be soothing and calming, like a hypnotic trance or a one-pointed meditation—the perfect antidote to hyperconscious anxious depression. So when does math cause anxiety (outside of the classroom)? When the primary media environment utilizes mathematical thought as a form of rumination on two specific constructs—money and time—we find ourselves locked in a cognitive prison cell of our own anxious depression.

The Commodores of Attention

> Money has an important function which it shares with writing: it replaces things with signs or tokens, with representations, the very essence of the activity of the left hemisphere.
> —Iain McGilchrist[1]

Attention has always been a commodity in one form or another. A hunter must "pay" attention to her quarry lest she lose it. The attention she "pays" to one prey is attention drawn away from another prey. She must make the right calculations about where and when to "pay" attention to ensure that her attention payments are efficient and well spent. Likewise, your boss or your job pays you for your attention. The fact that I and many of you work at home a lot of the time (especially in the post-pandemic world) demonstrates that our job pays us to "attend" to our work; we don't actually get paid to "go to work." The modern "attention economy" merely demonstrates explicitly what we already know implicitly: our attention has value, and anything that is valuable can be commoditized (perceived as a commodity that has monetary value).

Corporations commoditize our attention by selling bits of it to advertisers. Whether it's a commercial on TV, a pop-up ad on a web page, or a billboard on a highway, every moment of your attention has already been predicted, estimated, and commoditized. The modern attention economy didn't create the commoditization of the mind, but it certainly made it ubiquitous, more insidious, and more invasive. Whereas the robber barons of old capitalized on the resources that fueled the industrial age—oil, coal, timber, and so on—the modern robber barons capitalize on the single resource that fuels the information age—our attention. The new generation of industrial tycoons mine our minds for the fuel that fires the engines of the attention economy. They are the Mark Zuckerbergs and Evan Speigels—the *commodores of attention*—who transfigure each second of our attention into advertising revenue and then sell our attention back to us in the form of products and services that we don't even know we need.

Money Is a Medium

> Money talks because money is a metaphor, a transfer, and a bridge.
>
> —Marshall McLuhan[2]

When something is commoditized, the essence of that thing changes. The commoditized apple is now "produce," the commoditized cow is now "beef," the commoditized person is now an "employee" or a "slave," while commoditized sex is "prostitution." Commoditization takes a subject out of the realm of personal relation with whole objects and real beings (the grounding realm of the right hemisphere) and transfers it into the deconstructive realm of quantified objects or beings (the abstracting realm of the left hemisphere). But money itself is no object. (It is, of course, a symbol, a metaphor.)

Before the existence of money, services and goods were related directly to the people who provided them. A cow was worth a cow, an apple was worth an apple, and so on. You could trade 30 barrels of apples for a cow, but that didn't change the essence of the apples or the cow. By replacing the real with the virtual, money disconnects that relation, creating a sense of detachment from the real goods and services that the money symbolically represents and, in turn, creating a different perception of the relationship between the people in the community. The person grasping the dollar may have no sense of the services or goods that the dollar signifies. In grasping the dollar, one can conceive that the dollar is "mine" in complete abstraction without directly relating it to another person through services or goods. In creating the abstract detached sense of "mine" and "mine alone," money creates greed and avarice and thus becomes the "root of all evil." When money becomes digitalized into electronic numbers, it becomes even more abstract and thus severs us even more from the people and goods it represents. Only a person who perceives money in a completely abstract sense can, as CEO of a corporation, pay himself a $100 million salary in the same year that he lays off 10,000 workers. Only in complete abstraction could he rationalize that he somehow works 4,000 times harder than his average worker so that he deserves to be compensated 4,000 times more than his average worker despite the fact that his entire existence depends on the goods and services provided to him 1,000 times daily by the same average workers who are somehow unlike himself.[3]

However, the most insidious effect of commoditization is on how we view ourselves. In the ceaseless one-pointed meditation on money that so many of us find ourselves locked into much of the time, we degrade human relations into money-making ventures. "Arrangements," "situations," and "agreements" replace real relationships. We degrade our worldview into a monetary judgment, avoiding any position that isn't profitable. Ultimately, we degrade ourselves into money-making machines.

The Medium of Existence

> But at my back I always hear,
> Time's wingèd chariot hurrying near.
> —Andrew Marvell[4]

We can all remember a happy vanished time when we were very young and time did not seem to exist. Other than the nightly nuisance of "bedtime," we never felt the pressure of time beating down on us as it does now. Once, it was fine to dream the day away playing and doing whatever we felt like. Then the serpent entered Eden; the construct of time invaded our spotless minds. Gradually, time took on a new and somewhat sinister connotation. There was "a time for this" and "a time for that." One mustn't do *this* when it's time for *that*. There's also "no time for that today," sorry. Suddenly, there was precious little time for anything. Our recently enslaved minds bent to the task of doing things "on time." The abject horror of not being "on time"—the terror-laden construct of being "late"—arose as an ever-present specter of the mind. With so much to do and so little time to be, we became "human doings" rather than "human beings."[5] Our enslavement to the patriarchal master Father Time was established but not complete. Only when the twin demons of money and time are conjoined in the magic "ring" of the modern "attention economy" does the mental enslavement become absolute and entirely inescapable. The ring is a looping chiasmus—*time is money* and *money is time*—a closed circular reference that forms a chain around the mind and our behavior.

When time itself is commoditized ("time is money"), it immediately adopts the primary feature of a commodity, its perceived scarcity. Now we must think twice before "spending time" on anything lest we commit the cardinal sin of "wasting time." There's certainly "no time to lose." Time in its uncommoditized form is an interpersonal and intrapersonal medium of engagement—**the medium of our existence**—the dimension in which we live "in the moment," spending "quality time" with our loved ones or just with ourselves. In the attention economy, we can no longer "spend time" freely without cognitive dissonance, as in the background we *"always hear, Time's wingèd chariot hurrying near."* The intrapersonal and interpersonal take a back seat to the linguistic and logical-mathematical, who construct time by deconstructing it into a collection of seconds, minutes, hours, days, and so forth. Time, a metaphysical concept, has been objectified by the left hemisphere's way of attending into a physical quantity that could be measured in duration. **Time as duration** is an objective, quantifiable, physical commodity that could be spent, saved, or wasted. The result is a perpetual state of "time anxiety"—a conscious awareness of the incessant ticking of the clock, the constant fear at every moment that we may be "losing," "wasting," or even "killing" time.

The Evolution of Time

> *Time was not handed down from Heaven.... Time is a word invented by Man. If it has puzzlements connected with it, then whose fault is that?*
> —John Archibald Wheeler[6]

In the long history of everything, there have been three distinct revolutions in the way that we perceive time. The first such "timequake"[7] came about as a direct result of the birth of consciousness. Nonconscious animals live in one-dimensional time. They don't have the cognitive/intellectual wherewithal to ruminate on possible future occurrences or on "remembrances of things past."[8] They're stuck in one dimension of time, the present because the experience of three-dimensional time—the past, present, and future—cannot exist without a conscious internal narrator keeping tabs on the timeline of our life story. Consciousness of three-dimensional time was the first "timequake." It gave us history and it gave us the future, which humanity faithfully enclosed within the elaborate framework of mythology.

Our primordial ancestors needed no sense of time beyond the rough estimates provided by the sun, the moon, and the seasons. Time, as such, was circular, just like the heavenly orbs. Similarly, time, like the heavenly orbs, was "cyclical," as it followed the predictable cycles of the orbiting heavenly bodies and the seasons they foretold. The second timequake occurred as a direct result of the Agricultural Revolution. It has been referred to as a shift from "cyclical" time to "linear" time.[9] For the hunter-gatherer, life was centered on the migrating herds, which traversed the earth in a cyclical fashion, based on the recurring changing of the seasons. The farmer's life was similarly centered on the cyclical rotation of days and seasons. Cyclical time is grounded in the experience of nature from the viewpoint of someone living *within* nature. It assumes a somewhat comforting worldview in which everything that is happening has happened before and will happen again (as in Mircea Eliade's "myth of the eternal return"). This is comforting because no matter how bad things seem, it can't be the end of everything because everything is eternally reoccurring. Everyone who dies will be reborn. Every lost love will be refound in a different form or in a different place. Every bad day will dusk, only to reborn in a new morning. Time is felt as an inherent aspect of nature, which in every way imaginable is all-encompassing and eternally recurring, like the globe of the earth itself. The past and the future were inextricably linked in the never-ending cyclical return so that the future was not a mystery but a predetermined extension of the past, prompting Stephen Hawking to ask the "timeless" question, *"Why do we remember the past but not the future?"*

The Agricultural Revolution, beginning around 12,000 years ago in the Near East, heralded the need for agronomic calendars and almanacs to ensure the proper "timing" for sowing and reaping. The calculations required for calendar-making signified the first merging of time and the logical-mathematical mode of engagement. A calendar assumes a linear direction of time: day follows day, week follows week, month follows month, year follows year. Linear time is abstract and symbolic, represented by numeric and alphabetic symbols and divorced from the recurring cycles of nature. The shift from cyclical time to linear time changed the conception of our "medium of existence" drastically, thus changing our existence drastically. Linear time assumes either a specific beginning or end point, or an extension into infinity, not a circular recurrence. Instead of all things being reborn, all things die—the *end*. The soul, rather than being reborn, goes to heaven or hell for all eternity—the end. Linear time marches forward relentlessly, never looping back. Linear time, rather than being the progenitor of life (Gaia, Mother Nature), becomes the devourer and destroyer of life (Cronus, Father Time), who bears witness to the end of all things: "*I am come as Time, the waster of the peoples, ready for that hour that ripens to their ruin*" (*Bhagavad Gita*).[10]

Timequake #3

Thus, though we cannot make our sun stand still, yet we will make him run.
—Andrew Marvell

Linear time gave birth to the construct of time as duration, the objective measurable commodity that is both precious and limited. Time as duration, in turn, dethroned nature and the heavenly orbs as the gods of the medium of our existence. The image (but not the spirit) of cyclical time is evoked in the form of the analog clock, which was modeled on the sundial. The analog clock is circular, giving us the sense that time and therefore the world is a cyclical phenomenon, repeating itself perpetually at the 12th point of return. Nevertheless, the clock is an abstraction from nature, not a representation of nature, as McLuhan mused: "*The clock dragged man out of the world of seasonal rhythms and recurrence, as effectively as the alphabet had released him from the magical resonance of the spoken word and the tribal trap.*"[11] Both the image and the spirit of cyclical time are completely lost when the digital clock enters the picture.

The digital clock stretches time out vertically, transfiguring the circular recurrence of the clock into virtual numerals that move perpetually forward. No sense of return resides within the digital clock because even when the 12th point is reached, the numbers continue forward with a new designation indicating progression (the lettered sign "a.m." switches to "p.m."). And even at the second passing of the 12th point, at midnight, there is no sense of return because yet another designation indicates progression (the numerical date changes). The gradual phasing out of the 12-hour clock in favor of the more practical 24-hour clock ("military time"), which is happening as I write, marks another step toward the digitalization and linearization of time. Military time is completely detached from nature. It doesn't even acknowledge the most basic time distinction that all creatures on earth instinctively recognize: the difference between night and day. Rather than an eternally recurring sense of time, we have an eternally *forwarding* sense of time.

The intense anxiety surrounding the potential chaos of the Y2K bug that gripped the digital world as the new millennium approached was an indication of how locked-in modern society has become to this notion of digital time constantly moving forward. If time, even on a purely digital level, somehow defied this forward direction for a moment and actually stepped backward, many feared that the world as we knew it would come to an end. Notice how many indicators of time—clocks, calendars, computers, phones, and so forth—are in each room of your house. The medium of time has become so pervasive and invasive that it has become both the "medium" and the "message" of our existence to the point where we cannot tell with any degree of certainty do we exist in time, or does time exist in us?

Digital Time

> How should we be able to know if some agent could double the speed of all events in the world? We could discern a great loss of richness in experience.
> —Henri Bergson (1911)

In the digital age, everything seems to be moving so fast because the perception of time is that it's always "running out," like sand in the virtual hourglass. In this brave new world of instant everything, we don't feel the positive effect of technology freeing us from time-consuming chores, giving us more time to live. The effect, of course, is quite the opposite. Instant everything, this "brand-new world of allatonceness,"[12] just means that we now expect everything instantly and we have to hurry up and get it done before our time is up. Time has been co-opted by the tyranny of the anxious, which wields it as a whip, forever lashing at our backs. Now that information is passed along, quite literally, at the speed of light, we expect all things to come to us at the speed of light. We have to process and pass along our information without the luxury of completely perceiving it, much less understanding it. The promise of technology is a myth. Patience itself has become an obsolete construct.

> From our division of time into uniform visualizable units comes our sense of duration and our impatience when we cannot endure the delay between events. Such a sense of impatience, or of time as duration, is unknown among non-literate cultures.[13]

The medium of existence in the digital age is experienced as a perpetual state of ceaseless urgency. We're always painfully aware that "time is running out." We rush through our lives with unprecedented haste, *doing* so much but *being* so little. As Henri Bergson predicted over a century ago, technology has doubled the speed of everything. This doubling is experienced not so much as a quickening of experience but as a *"great loss of richness of experience."*

How does a filmmaker quicken her film? She "undercranks" the camera, capturing fewer frames per second. The time-lapsed images in the film will move in fast motion, but the film itself has lost much of its "richness" of imagery because fewer images are captured, and thus fewer images are perceived. In short, **when life speeds up, experience is diminished**. Our consciousness of time as the medium of existence is directly related to our experience of anxious depression. Notice how the experiences we have in life that feel "timeless" are also the experiences that either free us from anxious depression or help us deal with it. We have no sense of time while we're sleeping or dreaming, while we're having sex or falling in love, while we're immersed in experience, rather than analyzing or observing our experience. "Timelessness," when it's experienced, is equated with passion, ecstasy, inner peace, tranquility, serenity, and joy. In fact, the only way Homo nervusus can "return" to a state of timeless bliss is to reject (if only temporarily) the shackles and whips of time as duration and embrace the nonlinear construct of time as the subjective, unobjectified, and uncommoditized medium of existence.

Future-Oriented Thinking

> *The fool, with all his other faults, has this also: he is always getting ready to live.*
>
> —Epicurus[14]

We spend eternity in the passive state of thinking about what we're going to do and planning it out to the minutest detail. "*Life is what happens to us while we are making other plans*," as Allen Saunders wrote in 1957 (his words were slightly modified and made famous in the song "Beautiful Boy" by John Lennon). By the time we're ready to act, we've run out of time, energy, patience, motivation, interest, or volition. We think that planning is active and expressive, but it's actually passive and receptive. We're simply sitting back and receiving the thoughts from one side of our brain and then deliberating on those thoughts and passing them back over again. In other words, we're just bouncing our thoughts up against a wall. Deliberation feels better than rumination because we fool ourselves into thinking that we're being proactive, but at the end of the day, after all the calendar notes and preparation notes and all of the various lists and memos are drafted, what have we actually accomplished? The lack of any real action points to the truth. Deliberation is a receptive/active mode, just like rumination. Because we make believe that deliberation is expressive/active, it can be more harmful than rumination because we think we're on the path to changing our lives to feel better about ourselves, but we're actually just playing the same old game of denial, procrastination, and rationalization. Deliberation is the enemy of action; volition is its patron. So how do we stop deliberating, stop the endless planning and plotting and actually begin doing? The first step is to **change your behaviors, and then your thoughts will follow.**

The reason we get bogged down in the treadmill of perpetual planning and never doing is because our minds get stuck in the left hemispheric mode of analyzing life as if it were an algebra problem that could be solved using the right calculations. That's the left hemisphere's approach to everything—the problem-solving/solution-seeking mode of inquiry—which is great for algebra problems but bad for real-life problems, which don't necessarily have solutions. Life is a process, not a problem or a solution. The only way to handle a process is to live it and learn from it. Approaching the process of life as if it were a problem that could be solved once and then everything will be perfect forever is about as harmful an approach as thinking that your problems will never be solved, so you shouldn't even try. In both cases, the entire approach is founded on faulty logic, and so they're both destined to result in unhappiness and chronic dissatisfaction. The left hemisphere takes a **future-oriented approach**, conceiving a hypothetical future scenario and studying it for pros and cons by process of deduction. Again, this is a great approach if you're solving math problems or if you're a detective solving a crime, but if we're talking about your life, the approach is ultimately self-defeating because you're not a math problem, and I certainly hope you're not a crime. Approaching life as if it were a puzzle to be solved and perceiving oneself as a problem to be fixed epitomizes the left hemispheric approach and leaves us in a state of anxious depression because the future will always be unpredictable—no matter how many lists we make.

The more we try to control the future, the more anxious we get. Like gripping sand, the tighter we hold onto it, the quicker it escapes our grasp. The only thing we can do, the only healthy adjustment is to let go and accept the fact that the future is unpredictable and life is not completely controllable. We have to force the left hemisphere to let go of its tight grip on a hypothetical but ultimately unknowable future and allow the right hemisphere to chime in and do what it does best—**ground us in the present moment**—releasing us from the terror and torture of constantly worrying about the future, a future whose shape is determined by the twin demons of the mind: money and time. How do we do that? Essentially, the process involves being mindful of the medium of thought we're engaged in and then deliberately balancing or adjusting our engagement by switching media or flipping modes. In other words, **change your behaviors, and your thoughts will follow.**

Balancing Logical-Mathematical Media

> *What may well be the most important distinction between the left and right hemisphere modes is the extent to which a linear concept of time participates in the ordering of thought.*
>
> —Dr. Joseph Bogen (1969)[15]

Thus far, we've focused on the media of thought that tend to cause anxious depression. First and foremost is the primary media environment of private verbal thought. Consciousness is the birthplace of anxious depression. I'm certainly not the first to note this phenomenon. In 1862, Nietzsche warned us that *"the growing consciousness is a danger and a disease."*[16] In 1864, Dostoevsky proclaimed, *"I swear to you, gentlemen, that to be overly conscious is a sickness, a real, thorough sickness."*[17] And in 1918, Max Weber revealed to us that *"the fate of our times is characterized by rationalization and intellectualization, and, above all, by the 'disenchantment of the world.'"* When the primary environment is ruminating on money and time, we get locked into the unending cycle of trying to control an uncontrollable future. To be clear, neither linguistic nor mathematical media cause anxious depression. Linguistic media engenders conversation with loved ones, pillow talk, story, poetry, lyric, and song. Only when linguistic media is channeled into anxiety-provoking hyperawareness of future-oriented fears or into depressive self-reflective ruminations on one's own deficits and failings does the media imprison us in cycles of dread and doom. Similarly, mathematical media engenders the fun of games and puzzles, the thrill of reaching the high score, the serenity that's found in the silent counting of sheep, and even the contentment of actually solving an objective problem. Only when mathematical media is channeled into the one-pointed meditation on time/money and projected into a future that we cannot accept as unknowable does the medium become self-defeating and harmful. Even though the problem is complex, the solution is simple. Just switch it or flip it!

If you find yourself bogged down in hyperconscious rumination, whether the focus is time, money, the future, the past, or anything else, you need to break yourself out of that cycle by switching to another mode of media engagement or flipping your mode of engagement from receptive to expressive. Remember, worrying about time/money and concocting all sorts of hypothetical plans to increase money or save time is not expressive, nor is it active, if it doesn't directly lead to action. These are passive/receptive ruminations that lead nowhere other than anxious depression. Flip into the active/expressive mode of the same medium. Play a video game, a card game, or a board game. Engage your mind in a puzzle. Engage in any task that allows your mind to be present in the moment and your body to be physically engaged in what you're doing. Otherwise, you'll remain detached and disengaged from the world, the captive audience of your anxious depressive mind.

The term "balance" tends to evoke the mental image of a simple two-pan scale. When balancing the eight modes of media engagement, however, the image of a two-pan scale will simply not suffice, not only because there aren't nearly enough pans but also because the construct of balance itself breaks down when so many variables are involved. The metaphor stretches too thin, so we must conjure another. We must dissolve the simple image of the scale into the much more grandiose image of an orchestra playing a symphony. Unlike the measurement on a scale, the aim of the orchestra is to play as one rather than to differentiate between two. The aim of the scale is to find visual balance, while the aim of the orchestra is to maintain aural harmony. And although the scale is designed for the measurement of an object or product, the orchestra is neither object nor product. An orchestra is a process, just as an environment is a process, just as life itself is a process. They are meaningful—and beautiful—but only when accepted and appreciated as the processes they are. When we objectify these processes into products or commodities, we strip them of their vitality, rob them of meaning, corrupt their beauty, and detach ourselves from the processes themselves, alienating ourselves from the very things that give life meaning and value. The world (following Weber) has become "disenchanted." That doesn't mean that you must be disenchanted too.

How to Live to 120

> *If I'd known I was going to live this long, I would have taken better care of myself.*
> —Mickey Mantle

I get this warning message from my 401k retirement account regularly: "*Will you have enough money to live on after you retire?*" The message is intended to scare me into allotting them more of my paycheck, and even though I can't afford to actually do that, the message's intention—to scare me into worrying about having enough money to support myself and my dependents when I'm old—is always effective. It scares me. If, when I see that message, I hate myself enough to click on the provided link, I will get more scary messages that are even more terrifying. The following message, for example, seems intentionally anxiety provoking in the classic "good news and bad news" routine: "*Thanks to gains in modern medicine, people are living longer, meaning more time spent in retirement than previous generations. If you retire at age 65, that time could add up to three decades or more—longer than you actually worked—and long after you've earned your last paycheck.*" The message is terrifying because it conjures at once Homo nervusus's two greatest concerns: the twin demons of time and money. On the one hand, I'm scared that "retirement" age is creeping up on me and I won't have enough cash to support myself and my dependents. Both time and money are scarce. *Ahhh!* Now I'm worried about time running out, making me anxious, and I'm also worried about not having enough money, making me depressed. The twin demons work well together, feeding off each other's fears in an unholy glut of dread and despair. The key to exorcising these demons from consciousness is by overcoming the irrational fears they evoke so you can stop ruminating on them and then switch or flip your media engagement to a medium that channels your mental energy into a healthier arena of thought. You can overcome the fears by identifying their irrationality, which can be accomplished by deconstructing the presumptions that the irrational fears are based on. Let's use the messages from my retirement account as an example:

"*Will you have enough money to get by after you retire?*"

Why do you presume that I will retire? Obviously, I have a "retirement account," so that does support your presumption, but my retirement account was set up for me by my employer and I had no choice in naming the account. The less obvious reason for your presumption is that you want me to retire so you can make me worry about retiring so I can give you more of my money to hold before I retire. Your business and much of the financial business of this country revolves around the construct of "retirement," which is a relatively new construct that is quickly obsolescing. Fortunately, my background in life-span developmental psychology has provided me with the necessary ground to place the figure of "retirement" in a properly grounding perspective.

For nearly the entire history of humankind, the average life span was below 40 years, making the notion of retirement itself completely unnecessary. Old age was extremely rare among our primordial hunter-gatherer forbears. It was more common in agricultural societies, but in those cultures, large families lived in the same farmhouse their whole lives, so "retirement" was never an issue because even after you got too old to work, you didn't have to worry about where to live or what to eat because you never had to leave your family home. Those concerns only arise when agricultural societies transform into industrial societies and work is transplanted from the household farm to the town industry. The industrialist employer will not support a worker who is too old to work, and families in industrial societies do not live in the family home their whole lives, so the fate of the old and enfeebled industrial worker became a concern in the industrialized 19th century. The early 20th century saw the dramatic and unheralded lengthening of the average life span, making the issue of the elderly industrial poor with no family support a major social issue for the first time ever. "Retirement" entered America's collective unconscious during the Great Depression, when the New Deal created Social Security as a government pension and set the age of retirement at 65, which, at the time, was the life expectancy of the average American.

Since then, the average life span has been increasing rapidly, with the current average at around 80. In the 21st century, average life expectancy will not only continue to rise, but it will rise quicker because the merging of medical science with digital processing power means that we can apply unbelievable levels of data processing and scientific ingenuity to the problems of curing or treating the conditions that cause death. Today, as I write this sentence, President Joe Biden declared that cancer deaths will be cut in half over the next two and a half decades—a projection based on real scientific data, not just an empty promise. We've not only mapped the entire human genome, but we've also decoded it and digitalized it into virtual models that will help geneticists and other scientists test every imaginable cure on every imaginable human condition in completely virtual simulations. For better or for worse, life will get longer, up to and reaching the point of 120 years, which, for various reasons, seems to be the upper limit of human life expectancy (at least for now). Americans born after the mid-1930s lived their lives presuming that they would work until 65 and then retire, creating an anxiety-provoking milestone in their future: *"Will I have enough money to live on after I retire?"* The stress is compounded by the feeling of money always running out, while time to retirement is also running out, while the average life span—and in turn, the total number of years of retirement—continues to increase. All of this stress about time and money related to old age, retirement, and death is largely constructed and unnecessary, and here are the reasons why.

First, **you should not plan on retiring because retirement is bad for you.**[18] I've been teaching a course on aging and human development for years and years, and the gist of the entire course can be summed up in the following aphorism: **"Use it or lose it."** The brain and the body function according to this simple rule. If you walk a good amount every day, your legs will be in good shape and will stay in good shape. If you don't walk at all, your muscles will atrophy, wither, decay, and in due time—sooner than you may think—you will lose the ability to walk. This is true for every physical and cognitive activity. If you don't use your brain to process a cognitive function regularly, that cognitive function will obsolesce, just like your ability to walk will obsolesce if you don't walk regularly. As we get older, our bodies and minds fatigue easier, which means that we need to push ourselves a bit harder to be more physically, mentally, and interpersonally engaged. Retirement encourages the opposite. Retirement encourages less physical activity, less cognitive activity, and less interpersonal activity. Sure, for the first couple of years, the fantasy of filling up each day with as much golf, fishing, travel, and other leisure activities does come true, but the "honeymoon phase" soon ends, and human nature takes over. Human nature determines that people are much less likely to do something if they don't have to do it for their survival. Getting up early to go fishing or golfing is a chore, so we do it less and less often. Traveling is a fun change of pace but also a chore in many ways, so it becomes less frequent. More time is spent at home doing nothing, and since "idle hands are the devil's playground," we begin indulging in more food even though we're not burning off the calories, and we drink more even though it worsens our deteriorating health. A combination of reduced physical activity and increased substance abuse and eating causes or exacerbates health problems in retired people related to obesity, diabetes, alcoholism, and dozens of other maladies. For most retirees, the "golden years" of retirement devolve quickly into a malaise of inactivity, which in turn devolve into the health problems that become the primary preoccupation of the retired old. The construct of retirement functions in direct contrast to the one thing we know for sure about the aging process—*use it or lose it*. In short, **retirement is bad for your body** because it lures us out of the healthy pattern of daily regular activity and into the extremely unhealthy pattern of daily inactivity paired with overindulgence.

Work is extremely important for us in nonphysical ways as well. In the postindustrial age, many of us have developed high-level cognitive skills for our work that engage the brain in very important ways. Simply retiring and abandoning the work that engages those cognitive skills without replacing that daily cognitive engagement with a similar level of mental work is probably the worst decision you can make in your life. *Use it or lose it!* If you stop thinking at a high level of engagement, you will lose the ability to think at that level of engagement; that's true of everybody, but it's especially true of the elderly, as their brains are already in the natural aging process of diminishing connectivity. As we get older, we need to work harder to retain the cognitive skills we've worked our whole life to develop, as those skills will keep our minds and brains healthy and in good use. If retirement doesn't lead directly into new daily activities that absolutely require high-level cognitive functions almost every day, our brains will very quickly begin to deteriorate, opening the door to diseases and disorders of diminished cognitive function, such as dementia. In short, *retirement is bad for your brain*.

If you're anything like me, your interpersonal relations are binned in different social silos. There's my immediate family at home, more distant family dispersed far and wide, my friends that I spend time with close to home, older friends dispersed far and wide, and then the people I relate to through work: colleagues, students, editors, and work-related friends. On a daily basis, I'm more likely to interact with work-related associates than friends or distant family. Retiring, therefore, means I will be disconnecting from the people who provide the bulk of my daily interpersonal engagement. If I don't replace those connections immediately with new ones that are just as meaningful, I will very quickly become socially isolated. This is what happens to retirees. They think that retirement will be a never-ending holiday of golf and travel and time with grandkids and friends, but it quickly devolves into the socially isolated ennui of a figure who craves engagement but who has cut herself off from the grounding environment in which most of us get the bulk of our daily interpersonal engagement—work. In short, **retirement is bad for your interpersonal and social health**.

In the postindustrial world, many of us spend our entire lives building up toward a professional career. From preschool through graduate school, we spend 20–30 years educating ourselves, and then in our careers, we spend another 30–50 years developing our professional selves until we reach a point of professional status and proficiency that feeds our ego. Although titles are inherently meaningless, the notion that you're at the top of your field, or that you have specific knowledge and abilities that are valued highly in your field, or that you're known by others to be knowledgeable and skillful in your field gives us a feeling of self-worth and personal esteem. We spend our whole lives working on ourselves to get to that level, and for what? To simply step down and abandon it when we turn 65? That seems absurd to me, but it's exactly what's expected of us. This is one of the hidden costs of retirement. When we think of retiring, we think of how nice it will be to be unburdened of the pressures of having to be the person who makes decisions or being the person that others rely on because of our specific knowledge or abilities. The unburdening itself is doubtlessly pleasant, but the unforeseen consequence of retirement is obsolescence. The moment you are no longer engaged in the work environment, you are obsolete, and quite suddenly, you realize that nobody in the world cares what you think, that your skills and knowledge are useless, and that nobody relies on you for anything. The resultant blow to your self-esteem is swift and devastating, leading to anxious depression and the self-medication that accompanies it. In short, **retirement is very bad** *for your intrapersonal health, your mental health in general, and your self-esteem in particular.*

In general, people begin their careers at the entry level, earning the entry-level salary, and then they proceed up the ladder, earning higher and higher salaries as they move up. In this model, we're making the most money we'll ever make at the time of our career when we're eligible to retire, even though the work we're doing at that time of our career may seem relatively easy, simply because we've been doing it for so long that we've reached the state of total mastery. It feels good to have total mastery of an important job, and it also feels good to make a lot of money. Why give all of that up simply to chase the illusion of a blissful retirement? Even though "Mr. 401K" bombards us with daily messages about making the right financial decisions in our life to secure a stable future retirement, voluntary retirement in and of itself is the absolute worst financial decision anyone could ever make. In short, **retirement is bad for you financially.**

I could go on and on about why retirement is a really bad life decision and why you should avoid it if at all possible, but I'm already way off the point. Our collective anxious depression about time and money is often evoked by the relatively new and ironically harmful construct of retirement, which is set up by modern society as a deadline for accumulating an unreasonably high level of financial security to fund an unnecessarily long period of unhealthy inactivity and self-indulgence that causes diminishing and deteriorating health in every domain of existence, while simultaneously incurring the total loss of one's primary income. Developmental science researchers have recognized and pointed out the ironic harmful effects of retirement in that it is directly associated with increased health problems, decreased physical mobility and activity, decreased socialization, increased isolation, anxiety, depression, and substance abuse, decreased financial security, diminishing cognitive abilities, and it increases the onset of dementia and other "age-related" disorders that should more properly be considered "disorders of disuse" because aging in and of itself does not necessarily cause these problems; rather, they represent the "lose it" end of the "use it or lose it" principle.[19]

How do we counteract the anxious depression evoked by retirement anxiety? Simple. **All you need to do is live to be 120 years old!** If retirement anxiety is evoked by an email from Mr. 401k telling you that your age of retirement is coming soon and that you will not have enough money saved to retire, you can just flip the whole construct of retirement and thereby tell Mr. 401k to go flip himself.

First of all, since I'm living to 120, my retirement age is actually *not* coming soon, unless I happen to already be well over 100 years old. My retirement account is rushing me toward an incredibly early retirement in my mid- to late 60s, when I already know that I'm going to live to 120. Why should I worry about retiring now when I'm going to live for another 70 years? The **anxiety about time to retirement running out is a false construct**, and I absolve myself of that false and harmful construct by deleting the email from Mr. 401k and not giving it a second thought.

Second, the warning that I won't have enough money to retire on is based on the false presumption that I will be retiring about *50 years before* I actually plan to retire, at around the age of 115. Since, due to seniority, my earning potential now is at the greatest it's ever been and will only continue to increase, I will make exponentially more money in the next 50 years than I have already earned in the past 30 years of gainful employment. Hence, the **anxiety about too little money for retirement is a false construct**, and I absolve myself of that false and harmful construct by deleting the email from Mr. 401k and not giving it a second thought.

Third, the warning about the need to save more money to account for my increasing life span is a false presumption that reveals its own falsehood in its premise. Mr. 401k's message to me explains that *"modern medicine"* is making *"people live longer,"* which *"could add up to three decades or more"* to my *"time spent in retirement."* Hold on a minute, Mr. 401k. If you're saying that I'm going to live three or more additional decades on top of my projected 80 or so years (let's make it an even five decades and round up to 120), then why on God's green earth should I retire at age 65 when I can be happily, healthily, productively, and gainfully employed for an additional 50 years beyond that age? It makes no sense, and only benefits you, Mr. 401k, so I will delete your email, forgetting about it and you, and you can keep the anxious depression.

If you're a good reader, you have some obvious questions about my reasoning, which I will address right now.

How do I know that I will be able to continue working past the age of 65 (or whatever arbitrary number established by the Social Security Administration, Mr. 401k, or myself)?

First of all, both work and the worker have changed since Social Security was created in the 1930s. The average worker is much healthier, even in old age, than the average worker in the 1930s, with a significantly longer life expectancy. Work, at the same time, has become exponentially easier, moving from the hard physical labor associated with industrial and agricultural work to the physically easy cognitive labor associated with informational work. The information age worker does not have the physical demands of the industrial age worker, while she's also much healthier physically than the industrial age worker, making retirement as a construct a somewhat obsolete, or at least obsolescing, idea. Meanwhile, our aging society keeps voting in policymakers who make it easier to continue working well into our 100s. It's illegal to fire someone due to their age, and it's also illegal to deny elders promotions or other opportunities for advancement due to their age. Age caps and mandatory retirement ages are now illegal for most professions. New laws also allow seniors to collect their full social security and employer pension benefits while continuing to work full time, with no limits on income, which makes it much more financially beneficial to avoid retirement until absolutely necessary.

Most important, *How do I "know" that I will live to 120?*

This one's easy: I *don't* know. I also don't know that I'm going to live to 77, the average life expectancy for an American born the year I was born. I might die at 87, or 67, or 97, or 107, or 57, or 117. At a certain point, the numbers become meaningless because it's all so arbitrary. Seventy-seven is the average number relevant to my age cohort, but that number is based primarily on 20th-century demographical information, and we're in the 21st century. As I write these very words, half the world is on fire due to global warming, and the other half of the world is under floodwaters due to the same reason, so how do I know that we're all not going to die in a year or two? You're right. I don't know. Neither do you. I could die tomorrow, and so can you. Neither Social Security, nor Mr. 401k, nor the surgeon general can assure you otherwise. The reason we're always worried so much about time and the future is because we have absolutely no control over them. I can die tomorrow, and that's terrifying, but it's also *liberating*. If I truly don't know when I will die or what my physical condition will be at any point in the next seven decades, then I can just pick a number that works for me, and that number will be my working number for my presumed age of death. What number should I choose, then? Should I choose the relatively arbitrary average number (77) based on out-of-date demographics that do not take into account the revolutionary advents in medicine that will surely expand life expectancy by decades in the 21st century and that also don't take into account all of the personal effort I put into making myself healthier than the average American male my age? That seems stupid, and why should I do something stupid? If my own anxiety requires that I choose a presumed death date, I'll choose the number that evokes the least amount of anxious depression, and that number, for me, is 120.

And here's the magic behind the trick.

Once you really accept the truth of your mortal existence—that you can die tomorrow, or 100 years from tomorrow, or at any point in between and you have no control over that—then you accept the fact that your presumed death date is a relatively arbitrary number, with the prime benefit being that since it is random and arbitrary, you can choose it yourself. The death date of 77 is as random and arbitrary as 67, 97, 57, or 117. You and I really don't know, and total acceptance of not knowing gives you

Chapter Four. Logical-Mathematical Media

the freedom to choose for yourself. If you choose wisely, you'll be generous with yourself and with your life, and you'll give yourself as much time as you want.

Think of it this way—It's your birthday! Everybody you know and love are here to celebrate your birthday. It's a party, a wonderful party, with love and happiness and joy all around. But when does it end? Well, it's your party, so it ends when you want it to end. So when do you shut it down? I don't know about you, but if it were my party, I'd plan to keep it going as long as I can. Is it likely to end sooner than I want it to end? Probably. Does that mean that I should presume it will end sooner than I want it to end and plan my whole evening accordingly? I don't see the reason behind that decision. Why presume the worst when you can presume the best? We live life in the moment, not in the past and certainly not in the future. Our future-oriented consciousness is always pressuring us to predict and thereby control the future, which is inherently unpredictable and uncontrollable. Therein lies the root of our anxiety. We cannot *not* predict because our brains are designed to do just that. However, we can accept the fact that Homo nervusus is a predicting creature, and we can adapt to that truth by taking ownership of our predictions and presumptions. So if I select 120 as my predicted and presumed death date, acknowledging that 120 is as good as any other arbitrary random number, I give myself the gift of a very long life. Every day that I live from that point on is another day in my extraordinarily long life. My longevity frees me from temporary anxieties about retirement and money that I can do precious little about right now. My longevity frees me from the burden of worrying about age. My longevity frees me from worrying about not having enough money for retirement because I'm not retiring for another 60 years at least. My longevity frees me from the modern scourge of FOMO[20] because I have 70 years to do all the things I want to do, 70 more years to do the things I may be missing out on this year. If I decide for myself that I'm living to 120, then every day of my life from that decision onward is a day in the life of a person who is living to be 120 years old, and every day of that life, I earn the existential benefits of a person living to be 120 years old, which includes freedom from the anxious depression evoked by the demons of time and money. My longevity is experienced as a real psychological feeling of time stretching out in front of me rather than time compacting in on me and crushing me. My longevity and its existential benefits are experienced every day of my life, whether that life lasts 70 more years or 70 more seconds.

Living to 120 years is a thought experiment. I applied it to my own thinking, and it was an eye-opening experience, and I did feel its effects as decreased anxious depression. Like all thought experiments, it's a mind game you play with yourself, thus the benefits, if any, depend on how you apply the rules of the game to your own thinking. If you accept the premise that life and death are generally not under your physical control—but your *thoughts* about life and death are psychologically under your mental control—then you can apply the 120-year death date to your life, and see how it makes you feel.

There's an old saying, *"You're only as old as you feel."* That's very true. To that sentiment, I would add, *"You're only as old as you believe,"* but let's not stop there. We can also say, *"You only live once, so make sure to give yourself the longest life possible."* The life we live is not determined by our date of death, just as it's not determined by our date of birth. The life we live is determined by the decisions we make in between those dates, and the most important decisions are the ones we make about our own perspectives on our own lives. If you're 20 years old and you decide that you'll live to be 120, then your life will benefit from the longevity of a 120-year-old's life for every day of your life, whether you live 100 more years or just 100 more days. The benefits of great longevity don't suddenly fall in your lap like a windfall on the day of your 120th birthday. In all likelihood, your ability to enjoy and appreciate your great longevity will be largely diminished by the time you reach the end of your life. The benefits of great longevity are available to you now while you're still young,[21] and you must take advantage of them now. Don't wait until you're 120 to enjoy all of the benefits of being a person who will live to 120! There's no benefit in waiting, only loss. Similarly, there's no benefit in shortchanging yourself with a presumed death date shorter than the maximum human life span, only loss. So choose to live to 120, and every day of your life from that choice onward will be blessed with the benefits of a person fortunate enough to live to the ripe old age of 120. And this is entirely true, regardless of how long you actually live.

Chapter Five

Nature
The "Ground of Being"

> *The world is too much with us; late and soon,*
> *Getting and spending, we lay waste our powers:*
> *Little we see in Nature that is ours.*
> —William Wordsworth[1]

Yesterday, my teenaged daughter casually mentioned that her friend needs to *"touch grass."* When asked what that means, she explained that when a friend is *"chronically online,"* a good friend tells them to *"touch grass"*—that is, to get out of the house, to turn off their phone—to experience the world and other people "IRL" (*"in real life"*), as opposed to limiting their experience to the virtual simulacra of life radiating from their phone. *"That's nice,"* I replied, not wanting to tell her at that moment that she desperately needs to *"touch grass"* as well. The fact is, we all need to *"touch grass."* "The world," indeed, *"is too much with us."* The screens we stare at all day are mirrors, reflecting our own narcissistic needs, anxious fears, and depressive ruminations back at us. Like Tommy in the classic album by The Who (and Narcissus too), we're transfixed by the uncanny image in the media mirror. How do we transcend the tractor beam of our own reflection? How do we snap out of the trance? How do we break the mirror without breaking ourselves?

Most American children and adolescents, as well as their parents, suffer from *"nature deficit disorder."* No, it's not an actual psychiatric disorder listed in the DSM, but the fact that you and I thought it could be is the point. Richard Louv coined the term in his book *Last Child in the Woods* (2005). The phenomenon could just as easily be referred to using my teenaged daughter's term of choice, *"chronically online."* There's a huge movement in the educational and developmental fields to reintroduce children to Nature to stem the plague of childhood obesity, childhood anxious depression, and the other horrific maladies afflicting our chronically online children. They all need to touch grass, but so do we. Telling the kids to shut off their phones and devices and go play outside while we remain fixated on the same phones and devices is the epitome of hypocrisy, which is at the root of the problem. Children see us as role models. They do as we do, not as we say. They inhabit the world we provide them, not the ideal world we wish existed. We created the toxic media environment in which they live. We provided the devices that detach them from the natural world of real people, places, and objects. Shouldn't it be our job to show them how to detoxify their media environments? If so, wouldn't the natural first step be to "touch grass" ourselves—to become good role models of media engagement for our children—so they could follow our lead?

The digital age presents us with an inverse state of values. Technology is revered while Nature is degraded. Technology, in fact, is killing Nature via global warming and other processes. Our response is to shake our heads and wish that we could do something about it. The fact is, we'd rather see the planet die than change our relationship with technology. *"The world is too much with us."* The indoor, sedentary lifestyle that most of us live in is not just unnatural; it's *antithetical* to the natural state of humanity, which is to exist within Nature, as a part of Nature, rather than outside of her. Just as verbal consciousness detaches us from our natural state of being, placing us in the role of the distanced and objective observer of our own identities, the media that monopolize our attention detach us from our natural state of being, placing us in the role of the distanced and objective observer of Nature, rather than a part of her. That's why we can't save the planet. We observe the Earth as it dies (as we kill her), and from our distanced vantage point, we objectively say, "What a pity. I wish someone would do something!" We cannot empathize with Earth because we do not exist in Earth. We exist in the ether—chronically online—*on* the Earth but not *in* it. The notion that the death of the Earth heralds the death of humanity doesn't hit home because we're so disconnected from Nature, from Earth, from humanity as a part of the natural order of things that we can't even understand that if the Earth dies, so do we. Some part of us believes that we're not just disconnected from Nature but *above* Nature—supernatural—like a disinterested "watchmaker" or a neglectful god. If technology is killing the planet, maybe it will rescue us? When the planet dies, maybe we can all just move to Mars?

The "Ground of Being"

> When we lose nature as a direct experience, we lose a balance wheel, the touchstone of natural law.
> —Marshall McLuhan and Bruce Powers[2]

Chapter Five. Nature

Alienation from Nature is in a very real sense alienation from oneself. Humans are natural beings. If, as most people believe, there's an aspect of humanity that yearns to reconnect with Nature, like a baby yearns rapprochement with its mother, then that aspect is fragmented in urban life. *An indoor life is disconnected from both the outer world and the inner self.* **Nature is the medium of life**—not just your life and my life—all life!

I'm not a religious man (despite the best efforts of a crack team of rabbis). To my chagrin, I lack the crucial ingredient of religiosity—faith. I do believe in spirituality, and I believe—following Carl Jung—that there's a spiritual drive in humans, an instinctive urge to transcend the individual self and commune with something larger than oneself. In his correspondence with Jung, Freud referred to the notion as an *"oceanic feeling,"* an illusion of transcendence, perhaps a primordial desire to remerge with mother, but he couldn't relate to it himself. Like Freud, I see illusion where others see divinity. Even the *"oceanic feeling"* has evaded me thus far, but there are moments when I do feel connected implicitly with Nature, and those moments are transcendent for me in their own way. Working, playing, and being in Nature reminds me of the deepest truth in life: that there is beauty in every living thing. Meditating on this truth as a gardener in my yard, my hands immersed in the good earth, I often feel that I'm digging into the "Ground of Being," Paul Tillich's name for God. Nature, in my philosophy, is the medium of all content, the vessel of all life, the ground to all figures.

Nature, of course, is an environment. You must be in it to be engaged, but if you're in it, you're automatically engaged. Unlike a medium that you need to focus on, such as this book or a video game, Nature doesn't necessarily have a focal point, as it's all ground. There's nothing you must "do" in Nature; you can simply just "be" in Nature. Being within her and feeling a part of her offers the ultimate metaphors for life and development. There are seasons for birth, growth, death, and rebirth. The falsehood that time is linear is revealed in the eternal circularity of Nature's cyclical design. There *is* eternal recurrence—I see it in my garden each spring! The rootedness of the plants in my yard and the inner direction toward home that my dog displays, reminds me that I must be rooted as well. I have a home, I have a garden, I have family, friends, memories, creations—the physical and interpersonal soil of my life. I'm grounded in the soil of my home and my relationships, just as solidly as a tree is grounded to one spot in the earth, and I mustn't forget or devalue that. The false promise of a totally rootless, mobile society—with families and friends dispersed widely across the globe, connected by Wi-Fi and airplanes—has left us schizoid, uprooted and rootless, desperate, sad, and alone. We seek company in reflections on a screen. We seek love in the ether. Nature reminds us that home is where the heart is. She grounds us in the reality that all life is physical, not virtual. Physical life cannot be so easily uprooted and dispersed. Physical life cannot thrive in the ether.

Lateral Development

> *May you have a strong foundation, when the winds of changes shift.*
> —Bob Dylan[3]

A tree, or any plant, provides the ultimate metaphor for development. The tree, first and foremost, must be firmly rooted in its home soil. Like a child in its early years, it must be nurtured and protected, so the roots can grow deep and spread wide. A deeply laid groundwork of roots will provide a broad foundation for *"when the winds of changes shift."* As the tree grows up, it grows out. Pruning should and must be done to keep the limbs balanced so the trunk won't split and to encourage new growth. Overpruning, however, causes more harm than good. In the arboretor's ardor to make the tree grow up straight and fast and taller than the rest, he often favors vertical over lateral development.

Vertical development is unidirectional. When applied to a tree, it involves pruning lateral growth (branches and limbs) to channel new growth in one direction—upward. When applied to a person, it means focusing your attention via education and profession into one field of study or practice. It is the narrow path of **specialization**. To succeed in this cutthroat world of cutthroats, we not only need an edge, but we must always be on the cutting edge of that edge. Specialization is the continual edging of the edge—eternal vertical development—forever edging to be taller than the rest. Specialization is where the money is, to be sure, but it's also where the anxious depression is. Specialization is a narrow tall tree.

The broad tree will eventually grow as tall as the narrow one, and it will be bigger, lovelier, more well rounded, and more stable for its broadness. In all likelihood, *"when the winds of changes shift,"* the tall narrow tree will uproot and fall, while the broader tree, with its deep and expansive root structure, will stand.

So too with the human. When we're young, our environment encourages broad, lateral development in the manner that I'm encouraging in this book. Yes, we require our kids to learn their letters and numbers, but we also encourage them to develop artistically and musically. We construct a home environment that nurtures strong interpersonal bonds with family and friends. We provide a spiritual or ethical framework for their intrapersonal development. We make efforts to see that they're not neglecting the physical development of their bodies, and in the interest of eluding "nature deficit disorder," we introduce them to Nature and reacquaint them with her whenever we can. Development is lateral and multifaceted by design, in the interest of constructing a broad foundation. Then, as childhood ends, so does encouragement in lateral development. By college, they're required to choose a major, with the expectation of specializing in that major in their education and career. Each forward step—the college major, the college degree, the graduate school degree, the professional career path—is another step toward specialization, another step of vertical development. In accordance with the displacement principle, focus in one specialized area of study will displace time dedicated to other areas of interest: sports, music, art, friends, family, inner peace, Nature, and so forth. This long narrow road toward the destination of becoming a highly specialized authoritative expert in a very specific field is perceived as the "road to success." Once again, specialization is where the money is, but it's also where the anxious depression is.

Let's say you specialize your attention on one field of study (i.e., accountancy) for an extended period (let's say 20 years) in which the bulk of your engagement is restricted to just one or two modes (mathematical and linguistic media). What are the chances that you will get sick of accountancy? You guessed it. The chances are 100 percent. The saturation principle dictates that anyone will get sick of anything if forced by herself or someone else to perseverate on that one thing indefinitely. That's just how the mind works. The principles at play—displacement and saturation—are very basic, and they apply to everyone. In focusing all of your attention in one mode of engagement, you displace the other modes of engagement, giving you even more time to specialize. However, when you've reached the saturation point in that one mode of engagement, you're out of luck because you have no broad foundation to fall back on. The tree that stands above all the rest is the tree that will fall *"when the winds of changes shift."* The "winds of change" are not just out there in the world—pandemics, economic recessions, war, turmoil, and so on. The winds of change blow in our minds as well. When our mind reaches the saturation point, we must respond because we have no choice. If you're locked into a pattern of existence that doesn't allow for lateral development because the foundation has been stripped, you're in serious danger. The average person in this predicament handles the pain and discomfort of saturation nausea with substances, both prescribed and otherwise. She lives on coffee, chocolate, and cigarettes, stimulants necessary to force the saturation-nauseated and fatigued mind to stay focused on the media it now finds old and abhorrent. She stuffs herself with food to fill the stomach and deaden the nausea. She drinks alcohol or smokes weed to quell her anxious depression in the evening, pops antidepressants to quell her anxious depression during the day, and pops sleeping pills to force her anxious depressive mind to sleep at night. She can do it, but it's a daily struggle, and the risk of falling—the risk of breakdown due to oversaturation—is a constant risk and concern.

The counterbalance to specialization in your field of work is generalization in fields outside of work. If your work is consumed with linguistic and mathematical thought, then Nature provides the perfect counterbalance in work and activities that require physical rather than cognitive tools. Whereas linguistic/mathematical work revolves around manipulating abstract lifeless symbols, natural work revolves around manipulating physical materials that are not only real but also alive. Whereas linguistic/mathematical work is sedentary and indoors, natural work is active and outdoors. Whereas linguistic/mathematical work causes unhealthy mental saturation exhaustion, natural work produces healthy physical exhaustion. Whereas linguistic/mathematical work drives us toward distant abstraction in our isolated kingdoms of mind, natural work draws us out of ourselves, out of our minds, and into the grounding inclusiveness of physical reality. Whereas linguistic/mathematical work is specialized labor, natural work is general labor that anybody can do, and that you should do too because it's good for your body, your mind, your heart, and your soul. Nature provides the perfect anti-environment to your toxic linguistic/mathematical media environment. She invites you into that environment with open arms. All you need to do is accept her invitation.

This is not a book on meditation, but the process does require "media mindfulness" in every area of life. Sometimes it's as simple as recognizing saturation nausea or saturation fatigue and realizing that you should switch media or flip modes of engagement. Sometimes it's as simple as realizing that overengagement in one mode (such as accountancy) is displacing engagement in another mode (such as interpersonal relations with family and friends). Other times, mindfulness is attained by a meditative process in which the hands and body are engaged, but the mind is relatively free. It's wonderful how liberated the mind becomes when the hands are busily engaged. It may have something to do with the left hemisphere's concurrent control of both the right hand and the function of verbal thought. The left hemisphere specializes in serial tasks, doing one thing at a time. It may be more difficult to "stay focused" on one line of thought when the left hemisphere is simultaneously busy directing our hands as they're focused and engaged in their own work. *"Busy hands and idle minds have knitted many a sweater; busy minds and idle hands have knitted many a brow."*[4]

Put more simply, the displacement principle is in effect when working with our hands, as focus in one area displaces focus from another. Put even more simply, *bury your hands in the ground, and your mind will soar to the sky.* And to put it simplest, **change your behaviors, and your thoughts will follow.**

Gardening provides me with my most protracted and elaborate form of mindfulness, a freeform one-pointed meditation on the Self, within the ground of Nature. The focal point of this meditation is the primary metaphor—the figure that symbolizes you to yourself. If it's a tree, or plant, or hedge, or a garden, so be it. That works for me, but you may need to find something else. The point is to immerse your Self in Nature to the point where everything in Nature can be seen as a metaphor for your Self—including your Self itself—as you are a natural being who exists in Nature as well. The ultimate goal would be to sense that "oceanic feeling" of total oneness with Nature that Freud acknowledged but found elusive himself (perhaps because he was too busy writing books). Regardless of where it takes you, as long as you achieve this meditation within the ground of Nature—the Ground of Being—you are communing with her and receiving her grace.

Subliminal Development

Gardening provides my mind with wonderfully apt metaphors for life and living. The lateral development of the trees and hedges I planted around my home represent my own lateral development in the eight modes of engagement. Even though I'm aware that the bulk of these modes of engagement will never earn a penny, I don't despair because I know that what I truly need is a life framed around all of the people and things that fill me up and give me joy—something that money in and of itself cannot provide. Gardening also makes me implicitly aware of the ongoing **subliminal development** in both my yard and my life. When I planted a hedge of shrubs, I was eager and impatient for them to grow. A couple of seasons passed, but they were still short. Then, around the third season after planting, the hedge began to grow much quicker, leaping upward and outward, seemingly all of a sudden! Did that really happen all of a sudden? Of course not. Nothing in Nature is sudden. Things only appear sudden when we don't see the underlying processes at work. *"To the blind man, everything is sudden!"*[5] The underlying process is the broad root structure developing subliminally—below the surface of the ground—which cannot be seen.

For the first two seasons, there was indeed a tremendous amount of growth, but it was mostly underneath the ground in the root structure.

Because we're blind to anything that's subliminal, we may fail to see the benefit of a seed that's planted in good soil with good sun and regular water. So, too, we may fail to see the long-term benefit of planting a hedge of shrubs in our yard, or playing an instrument on a daily basis, or engaging in some rigorous outdoor physical activity each day, or taking time each day to connect with family or friends. From one day to the next, in the short term, we don't see the development because it's subliminal. There's a lot going on under the surface that we're unaware of. Only in the long term do we see the tremendous benefits of a big, beautiful hedge that gives shade and privacy to the yard. Only after years of playing do we realize the tremendous joy of mastering an instrument through which your own personal music can flow. Only when we're sick or disabled do we realize the tremendous importance of daily rigorous physical activity. Only when we're sad and alone do we regret not making daily connections with family or friends. The benefits of broad development in multiple (eight) modes of engagement are lateral and subliminal. They don't seem obvious and they don't stand out because they compose the "ground of our being" rather than the figure of our attention. They don't earn us a penny and they're expensive in terms of time, but they have the prime benefit of making life worth living.

Gardening relies on the twin virtues of patience with oneself and faith in natural processes. When we plant a tree, we must first have faith that the tree will grow. Then we must have the patience to allow it to grow without losing faith. If this is ostensibly true for the tree, why is it so difficult to be patient with ourselves, and why is it so hard to have faith in our own eventual growth and development? Once again, the "medium is the message." The "ground of your being" is composed of all the things that you engage in that make you you—family time, time with friends, your creative musical, artistic, or linguistic expressions, and so forth. The "figure of your attention" changes from moment to moment, but in terms of hours of engagement per day, the most expensive engagement is likely to be your work. Because we tend to focus on the figure of our attention—our profession—we also tend to be blind to the ground of our being, which includes our profession but also includes much much more. The figure of our attention is more noticeable because it's a specialization, so its development is vertical, it grows quickly and in one direction. Although professional development is crucial for survival, the process can easily become blind to the need for development in other areas of life, especially when those modes of development are unseen because they're happening laterally and subliminally rather than vertically. The purpose of mindfulness is to be aware of the underlying subliminal and lateral developmental processes that we tend to ignore when focused on making money or saving time.

You Can Learn a Lot from Your Dog!

There are many physiological benefits to personally walking your dog (or doing something physical with another animal, such as a cat or a horse) at least once a day. It's good for you and it's good for the animal. The emotional benefits of communing with a nonhuman fellow being for a while are also quite clear. We love our pets, and we feel loved by them in return.[6] You may be surprised by the innate wisdom of "dumb animals." The consciousness they lack (the curse they're blessed to not have) leaves them directly connected to an instinctive and intuitive approach to life that's much more intelligent than our own. You may wind up wondering, who's the "dumb animal" after all?

The first thing I learned from my dog, Daisy, is that she has a different sense of time than me. **Dogs have no sense of "time as duration."** Dogs have an internal clock that tells them what they should do based on instinct, associative memory, and whatever psychosocial conditioning they developed individually. In other words, they don't "know" it's time to eat; they just feel hungry. They feel it's time to take a walk when the opposing urge rises. If they feel sleepy, they go straight to sleep without any struggle to turn off consciousness. Simple as that. Dogs are much better at figuring out what they want because there are no figures—no symbolic representations such as words—involved in their thought process. Blissfully ignorant of consciousness and its consequences, they don't consider, deliberate, reconsider, redeliberate, and ruminate their lives away. They just trust their feelings and do. *Why don't we?*

When I need Daisy to walk faster because I want to go home, I get frustrated with her because she's in no particular hurry, and I feel like she's "wasting my time." *Why are we in such a hurry all the time? Is everything really so urgent? What is it that I'm hurrying to get back to anyway?* Even as I stroll in Nature with Daisy the hound, I see how she revels at each present joy in her surroundings, while my thoughts race ahead to tonight, to tomorrow, to next week. *Why are we so stuck in the cobweb of time? Is it our tangled web of words that entwine us? Why can't I disengage from the symbolic representations in my head and just enjoy a nice walk in Nature with my dog? Why must my mind always be in the future rather than remaining grounded in the present with my body and my dog?*

Getting frustrated with a dog is essentially getting frustrated with yourself because it forces you to reflect on your own expectations, which are directly tied to your own anxieties and generally reducible to one of the twin demons: money and time. Dogs don't get frustrated with money or time. Money is no object to dogs, and they don't understand symbols. Dogs do get frustrated in the interest of time but only because their "masters" disrupt their natural rhythms with our ridiculous constraints. They have to beg to go outside, beg for a walk, beg for a meal, beg for everything. I'd be frustrated too. *But wait. I am frustrated. But why? I have no masters. Or have I? The demonic masters: money and time.*

Are you aware that most "pet" dogs can't even go outside of their master's domicile unless the master physically opens the door for them, and even then, they get held by a collar and a leash? How absurd to keep a natural creature away from Nature. To keep a natural creature tied down to one spot, indoors, insular, and reticent rather than outside, active, and exploring. What a crime against the natural creature! What a crime against Nature herself. *Yet are we not natural creatures ourselves? If so, why do we sequester ourselves indoors, staring at screens all day long? Why have we divorced ourselves from Nature? She did us no wrong. Quite the contrary! At least let us attempt to reconcile. A good first step may be to learn how to love and respect Nature from creatures like Daisy, who haven't forsaken her.*

A dog's primary sense is smell. Simply knowing this fact is a wonderful walking thought experiment. Why must she turn around 12 times in a circle before peeing? (My dog, that is—Daisy.) I can't possibly know why because I have absolutely no personal metaphor to apply to my dog's primarily olfactory "way of attending" to the world. It's like I'm trying to understand the inside of someone else's mind, which I can't possibly do because my only experience is the inside of my own mind. Like Plato's cave, I can see only the shadows and reflections of other people's experiences, not their actual experiences because I cannot experience being inside their minds. I cannot possibly know why Daisy needs to turn around 12 times before she pees because I can never truly know Daisy's mind. **And so it is with every other living thing on Earth!** I cannot possibly know you; I can only know my reflections of you, the metaphor of you that I construct to understand you. So what have I learned from Daisy in this instance? *Does Daisy worry about what other dogs are thinking?* No, she's primarily concerned with the smell of their pee. *Should I be concerned with what Daisy is thinking?* Absolutely not, because I cannot possibly conceive of what she may be thinking (an olfactory meditation). Any guess that I may have regarding her "thinking" is just me projecting my own thought process onto her. By extension, *should I be concerned about what other people are thinking (especially their thoughts about me?).* Obviously, I should not. If I cannot truly know what others think about me, then the whole process of wondering what others are thinking about me is just a futile and pointless exercise in narcissistic projection. *So why do we humans waste so much time and energy trying to know what other people are thinking about us when the task itself is futile and pointless?* Daisy just keeps getting smarter and smarter, doesn't she?

Chapter Five. Nature

Relating to Nature as a "Thou" Rather than an "It"

Spirit is not in the I, but in the space between I and Thou.
—Martin Buber[7]

You may have noticed that I've referred to Nature in this chapter as a capitalized proper noun, as if she were a person or a goddess, following the classical characterization of the construct as the archetypal mother of life. There's more to it than that. I wanted to drive home the notion of true personal relation with Nature and all of her children. Following Martin Buber's famous distinction, if we relate to Nature as another person rather than as an inanimate object or a purely physical thing—as a "Thou" rather than an "it"—then it would naturally follow that we will treat her with love and respect rather than exploiting and neglecting her. By meditating on the relationship between I and Nature and realizing ("real-I-zing") that it is the same relation between I and Thou, we relate to the medium of life as a child to its mother. Only then do we realize how much we love her, how attached we are to her, how much she loves us, and how completely and utterly dependent we are on her. Furthermore, when we relate to the medium of all life as a Thou, we must naturally include ourselves within her, "lest we deny that we're even alive! Only then, through complete subjective identification, could we truly feel the pain we're causing her rather than relying on feeble thoughts and concepts. Only then could we truly feel the pain in ourselves when we're disconnected from Nature. How is this "I-Thou" relationship with Nature conceived and engendered? Simple, just walk your dog every day, do you own gardening and yard work, and in general, make an effort to reconnect with Nature as much as possible, all the while keeping your mind open to the metaphors found in Nature that you can personally relate to. In short, *change your behaviors, and your thoughts will follow.*

Chapter Six

Music Therapy for Your Self

All art constantly aspires towards the condition of music.
—Walter Pater

I fell in love with music in my early teens. By my mid-teens, listening to music wasn't enough. I felt compelled to make my own. In retrospect, I believe that after immersing myself in music constantly for years, I'd reached the saturation point in terms of receptive-passive music, and I needed to flip into the expressive-active mode. (If I'd only understood the process then, I could've written this book 35 years ago and saved myself [and possibly you] a lot of trouble.) By the time I went to NYU for college, I was a declared music major. My immediate response to being a music major was self-consciousness. I went to a small yeshiva[1] from kindergarten through high school, where music was not in the curriculum. Being a self-taught musician with no background in music theory, I was overwhelmed by all the talented and educated musicians in the program, and I felt inadequate. Everybody in the program, from student to professor, was very competitive and judgmental. I think I know what it feels like to be dyslexic, at least a little bit because my abilities to sight-sing and read notation were excessively slow, and I repeatedly failed those exams, which was a blow to my ego.

But at my back I always hear, Time's wingèd chariot.... Deciding to be a musical professional is a critical choice for a young person because the music industry is entirely youth-oriented, and there's a rigid timeline for success. If you haven't made it by your late 20s, you're basically not going to make it, at least not as a professional musician. That was a tremendous amount of pressure on our very young and narrow shoulders, and we took it out on each other in the form of hypercompetitiveness and hypercriticism. I soon despaired at my ability to measure up to my peers. I was also disillusioned with the music industry in general. I fell in love with music because it was so accessible, so inviting, an open doorway to my stifled adolescent emotions and lonesome soul. The music industry, to the contrary, was entirely inaccessible, uninviting, and the door was decidedly shut. I was attracted to music because it made me feel good, but the competitiveness and criticism made me feel bad. I realized that even though I still loved music, I wanted no part of the music industry, which seemed to corrupt the very essence of what I loved about music in the first place. My distaste for any form of self-commoditization probably arose at that time in my life.

It was my great fortune to have discovered the field of music therapy at NYU. I volunteered at the Nordoff Robbins Music Therapy Clinic and witnessed firsthand how Clive Robbins and his colleagues used music to connect with autistic children in miraculous ways. These children, who absolutely did not speak a word ever, came to the clinic and *sang* with Clive Robbins. Furthermore, in the therapy sessions themselves, there was never any sense of competition or criticism. The point of the music therapy session was to musically connect with another person. The quality of the session was based on the quality of the connection—the level to which the client is able to open up musically and express himself—while the quality of the music itself was inconsequential. There were no judgments, no critiques, no right or wrong notes. Music therapy was about expression, acceptance, and the joy of sharing a musical experience. I was hooked!

There was no undergraduate program in music therapy at NYU, so upon the advice of a professor in the graduate department, I became a psychology major in preparation for my application to the master's program in music therapy. (Yes, that's how I was drawn into the field of psychology.) In due course, I earned my bachelor's in psychology and then my master's in music therapy from NYU. At the simplest level, "music therapy" is simply any form of therapy that's conducted via the medium of music. When applied, music therapy is the practice of helping people connect (or reconnect) with their musical selves. Music therapy is NOT about passively listening to music. *Nobody needs a therapist to make them a mixtape.* Music therapy is an active-expressive experience. It's particularly useful in helping people express themselves within a therapeutic setting in ways other than talking, making it especially useful in the treatment of children with autism and quite relevant for our aim in this book—finding engagement in a medium that circumvents, stifles, or redirects verbal thought. As a music therapist, I can attest to the fact that when someone does adopt the practice of making music for their own joy and expression, the results are overwhelmingly therapeutic.

After completing my degrees and becoming a certified music therapist, I worked in the field for a few years but found it difficult to make a living. There were no full-time jobs in music therapy. (In retrospect, I probably should have looked into that issue before completing my academic degrees.) One could string together a bunch of clients as a private practitioner, but that life was very hard—lots of commuting to various homes and offices, lots of billing issues, lots of hustling to get clients, no benefits, and not much money. One could also get a gig in a special education school, a mental hospital, or a nursing home as a teacher or therapist who specializes in music therapy. I tried all three. The problem there is that you get to do maybe three or four music therapy sessions a week, and the rest of the time you're doing casework, lesson plans, file work, assessments—stuff that had nothing to do with music and stuff that I had no personal connection to. (This was back in the 1990s, so maybe the field has changed.) I became disillusioned with clinical work and went back to school to earn my PhD in developmental psychology from Cornell University. I've been a writer and a psychology professor ever since, transitioning from developmental to media psychology. I still consider myself a music therapist, and recently, I've gotten back into the field on a very part-time basis. I find that I enjoy doing music therapy a lot more with others when I'm *not* doing it for a living. My former and present clients aside, my primary client has always been my Self, and it will always be my Self. Even when I was a 13-year-old boy seeking solace in music, I hadn't the foggiest notion what music therapy was or that it even existed, but I was practicing it on my Self all the same.

The Corruption of Music by Modern Media

> But whereas, in the case of language, there is considerable emphasis in the school on further linguistic attainments, music occupies a relatively low niche in our culture, and so musical illiteracy is acceptable.
> —Howard Gardner[2]

Music predates language ontogenetically, in the development of the individual human brain, as well as phylogenetically, in the evolution of the human species. Singing was the evolutionary precursor to oral language.[3] Similarly, singing is an integral part of linguistic development in infants and toddlers because music appreciation precedes language comprehension. The preverbal infant's brain is more receptive to music than to language because music is nonsymbolic. It affects us emotionally without the need for decoding or analysis. Adults intuitively leap into singsongy falsettos when "speaking" to babies. In fact, we don't speak to babies at all; we *sing* to them. Obviously, they can't understand a word we're saying, but they seem to like the tune. Far older and far more deeply ingrained than spoken language, music is the only true "universal language."

When school begins, song gives way to speech as music is co-opted by the classroom as a tool for learning literacy. The first song we're required to learn in school is the "ABC song," a string of phonetic symbols that has no meaning other than the sounds and signs themselves, but the melody—lifted from "Twinkle, Twinkle Little Star"—is easy to learn, and we all seemed to like the tune. When music itself is taught, we generally begin where we should—with the natural and the intuitive—first in sing-alongs and then on to a chorus. Singing is intuitive and requires no training at all. Eventually, schools do what they were built to do. They replace the intuitive with the calculated, the oral with the written, the natural with the notional, and the real with the symbolic. We "learn" that to *play* music, we must be able to *read* music, thus the bulk of engagement and attention is directed toward musical literacy and music theory, the ability to read and write music. It's no surprise that schools handle music in the same way that they handle language. When schools came around, well before the age of industrial machines and electronics, the only way to experience music was to sing or play it yourself or to be with someone who is singing or playing. Thus every home, and every person in those homes, was musical, as music is universally adored and needed. When not provided to us, we have no choice but to provide it ourselves. Schools presumed that oral language was naturally taught and reinforced at home, so their job was to build written language atop the shoulders of oral language. Similarly, schools presumed that natural music (aka "folk music") was learned and reinforced at home, so their job was to build written music atop the shoulders of natural music. This is where it all went wrong.

With the advent of industry and electronics, music could be heard via phonograph and radio. One no longer needed to create one's own music because music was written by musical specialists (composers), expressed by musical specialists (professional musicians), recorded by engineers, and mass marketed by corporations. In its utilitarian function as the factory of tomorrow's workforce, the education industry handled music as if it were just another vocation that students could be trained for. Music in schools was focused on training potential musical professionals and specialists. Nobody presumed that natural music would be lost if not reinforced in school because its parallel—oral language—was not at all threatened by the focus in school on the written word. The problem is that the oral language/music metaphor is not particularly apt in our society. Although we all must be orally expressive to be functional as a worker, we don't necessarily need to be musically expressive to function as a worker (though it helps tremendously). It was the advent of the new media of electronic recording and broadcasting that really stuck the knife into the heart of "natural music." This single media "enhancement" was one of the biggest tragedies that ever befell humankind because it began the process of obsolescing natural music in the home and in the Self.

Music, the universal language that speaks directly to the soul, was stolen from the average person and handed over to the musical specialists, transferring the task of soothing our own souls to the hands of others. Electronic media has transformed much of humanity from a species of expressive-active musical performers into a species of receptive-passive music listeners. The recording industry created the music "star," casting the rest of us, by default, into the constellation of passive listeners sitting in the audience. The loss of personally expressed music in the life of the average person is a key factor in the evolution of our species from Homo sapiens (the wise ape) to Homo nervusus (the sad and worried ape). The only music experienced in my school growing up were the Hebrew prayers, hymns, and Jewish spirituals we sang in temple. Those group sing-alongs are the only things I miss about school and the only religious ritual that ever gave me a sense of connection with something outside of myself. I miss them. If I ever find myself in a temple or a church service, it will be because I want to sing with others again and feel that connection to something bigger than me. To a very large extent, my only conscious connection to any feeling of spirituality has only come through music and singing. On a related note, I have a peculiar fascination with the world wars, and I enjoy watching documentaries about them. On many occasions, I've heard former soldiers recalling their war experience, saying that while they, of course, don't miss the war and the fighting, they do miss the singing because what else is there to do when marching all day than to sing with your comrades and express the beauty of shared humanity even in the profoundest depths of human hatred and self-destruction.

At a certain point in life, the music lover must decide if she wants to "specialize" in music by turning it into a career—a "musical identity crisis." If the career path is chosen, she must necessarily curtail other modes of engagement to focus on music. This displacement automatically destabilizes her balance of media engagement. Music, once a source of solace, comfort, and inner peace, when commoditized becomes a source of stress, disappointment, ennui, and anxious depression. Self-medication may ensue as a means of coping. If the career path is not chosen, musicianship as a form of personal expression may be abandoned forever. The personal loss of the most natural self-soothing endeavor known to humankind will, by default, result in stress and anxious depression. Self-medication, once again, may ensue as a means of coping. This dichotomizing process, in which each of us either specializes in music performance or not, turns our species into a population consisting of a tiny percentage of musical performers and creators on stage and in studios and an overwhelming majority of music listeners sitting in the audience. This dichotomy need not exist. Although commoditization cannot be totally avoided for the person who wants to make music her career, it can be minimized via mindfulness of the need to balance any mode of engagement—especially the one we rely on for money—with all of the others. For the vast majority of us who don't need to commoditize music to have it in our lives, there's no good reason to abandon or never engage in the joy of musical expression. There is a "bad reason," however.

Silencing the Inner Critic

> *Music therapy, to me, is music performance without the ego.*
> —Jodi Picoult

The passive role in any medium—the role of consumer of media content as opposed to producer—promotes a critical stance. The mind likes to stay busy. If it's not busy expressing and creating, it's busy listening and critiquing. As long as you aren't actually creating the music, it's quite easy to sit back and deconstruct it. Everyone's a critic! We've become a species of fans and nonfans, defining our musical identities by our likes and dislikes rather than our own musical expressions. This critical stance is the deathblow to creativity for one's self, for if one is to judge one's own musicianship by the same critical standards that we hold for recording artists—the 0.001 percent of the population who is gifted or lucky enough to make a living through their music—then our own music will always rank low and seem flawed and amateurish at best. Not only are we judging ourselves by comparison to the best of the best of the best, but we're also judging our homemade off-the-cuff music to the music produced by dozens of professional musicians, arrangers, producers, and engineers, working in state-of-the-art studios, with unlimited chances to retake each track until every sound is exactly perfect. No regular person's real natural music could ever measure up to this comparison.

The parallel metaphor in a visual medium are the images of super-skinny models in fashion magazines with their perfect hair and perfect skin and abnormally thin bodies. Supermodels don't look like regular people, and their images are photoshopped by editors to create the illusion of perfection. What is the effect of these images on adolescent girls who automatically compare their bodies to them? The effect is hyperconscious social comparison, body image rumination, resulting in anxious depression and, oftentimes, bulimia and anorexia. Comparing your voice to Beyoncé's and then saying, *"I can't sing like that; therefore, I can't sing"* is tantamount to comparing your body to Heidi Klum's and saying, *"I don't look like that; therefore, I can't show myself in public."* It's an extreme personal reaction to a form of irrational social comparison that's completely uncalled for and entirely self-destructive. It is, in fact, **the shadow of narcissism**. The narcissist says, *"I will appear, but only if my appearance is the best."* If the narcissist becomes aware that he is not "the best" or even on the same level as "the best," then his narcissism is wounded, and he will hide like a frightened turtle, refusing to appear lest his narcissism be further wounded. *Stop hiding your musical Self! Stop wallowing in the shadow of your own narcissism! Silence your inner critic so you can express your true Self!*

As little children, we sing and play music intuitively and freely because we're not self-conscious. We could care less about how we sound because that's not the point. The point, as all children know, is to have fun. (*Oh, the wisdom of children! How much we lose. How much we forget!*) When consciousness invades the mind, followed close behind by her ugly stepsister self-consciousness, we begin to judge ourselves. This process is aided and abetted by music "teachers" who may give us bad grades for music theory and criticize our ability to read and write musical notation. They make us feel self-conscious about our musicianship even though the stuff they teach has absolutely nothing to do with natural music as expressed by natural musicians since the dawn of humankind. All of my favorite musical artists never learned to read or write music, and they never had a problem expressing themselves musically and becoming rich and famous in the process. Nevertheless, our schools focus almost exclusively on musical literacy and music theory, displacing any opportunity for the experience of expressing natural music in its spontaneous and intuitive form. The result is that for the vast majority of us, musical education is actually a barrier to musical expression rather than a bridge. A very small minority of students will master musical literacy in grade school and go on to become professional musicians, composers, producers, engineers, and so forth. A similar minority of students will learn to express their music naturally and go on to become professional musicians in an idiom that doesn't require formal musical knowledge, such as rock 'n' roll, pop, folk, dance music, country, and so on. These people mastered natural musical expression *despite* their musical education in school rather than because of it. The rest of us wind up in "music appreciation class," typecast in the role of the passive listener in the audience, too self-conscious to actually express music and too critical of ourselves to even try.

There is no statement less true than *"I can't sing"* or *"I can't play music."* Have you ever heard a three-year-old child say she can't sing or play? I didn't think so. Have you yourself ever said the ultimate untruth, "*I can't sing*" or "*I can't play music*"? If so, are you less capable than a three-year-old child? Apparently so, but why? It's not that you can't. It's that you won't. And why won't you? Is it the tyranny of self-criticism, the inner critic who won't shut up? Is it the shadow of your own narcissism, the flawed presumption that anything you play must be equal to the music of the best of the best of the best? **Self-consciousness becomes the ultimate barrier to self-expression.** We limit our singing to solitary moments in the shower or the car, when we think nobody can hear us, and get super self-conscious if somebody does happen to overhear. Thus, the first step toward any practice of musical self-expression is the silencing and total disregard of the tyrannical, elitist, inner critic, born out of the passive listening role that the recording medium created. Your inner critic is restricting your voice and limiting your potential as a person. The truth is, although listening to music feels good, playing music *makes us good*.

The Primacy of Song

> *I don't sing because I'm happy. I'm happy because I sing.*
> —William James

It seems obvious, but sometimes what is obvious is also the least observable because of its invisibility. Singing is the most natural form of musical expression for humans, birds, whales, and any other creature with the capacity for song. Sometimes, when she's happy or excited, even Daisy the hound howls out a spontaneous little tune. Providence gifted us humans with the blessing of song because it provides us with a natural release from our anxious depression. When singing, language processing shifts dominance from the default mode in the left hemisphere to the right hemisphere, the primary seat of song and musical cognition.[4] This rightward shift makes it difficult if not impossible to hear the voice of consciousness in your head because singing requires the ability to hear your own voice while recalling words and focusing on their expression. In short, when we sing, our language function shifts to the more intuitive right hemisphere, while the left hemispheric channels normally used for conscious verbal thought become preoccupied with the lyrics of the song. The verbal thought that causes anxious depression is thus temporarily drowned out, releasing us from the constant burden of consciousness. **This single point is possibly the most important point in the book because it's so easily applicable to almost everyone.**

Everybody can sing. If you say you can't sing, you're lying to yourself. **Stop lying to yourself!** Everyone who can speak can sing. Children and infants do it easily and intuitively, so why can't you? *Self-conscious much?* That's the curse of your anxious depressive mind, dictating to you what you can and cannot do. Don't stand for that! If you can speak, you can sing. If you can't speak, then I sympathize, but you can still channel your musicality through an instrument or another medium. Some of the greatest musicians are mute and many blind. *What's your excuse?*

Pure (nonvocal) music bypasses the verbal thought system altogether, connecting directly to our emotions. That's why *"all art aspires to the condition of music"* because no other form of expression cuts to the quick of our emotional being so instantaneously as music. Have you ever noticed that a certain song or melody can instantly bring you to the point of tears just from hearing a few notes? Vocal music (singing) obviously calls on verbal processing, but the process is completely unlike that of verbal thought. Verbal processing in song is a right hemispheric task, and the right hemisphere attends to the whole experience rather than focusing on specific details and searching for discrepancies.[5] When we sing, we naturally feel language as a part of a musical experience, and our attention is directed toward the overall patterns of sound being created and how your song fits within those patterns. The "figure" of the melodic vocal part is at all times "grounded" in the entire harmonic and rhythmic musical experience, grounding us as beings in the experience as well. When we're grounded in an experience, we're in the present moment, the moment in which life actually happens—as opposed to our normal state of consciousness—in which our mind is always decidedly unpresent, preoccupied with hyperconscious future-oriented anxieties or depressive ruminations on the past. *Music and song ground us in the present place and the present time.*

Admittedly, the process of stifling verbal consciousness via song works better if you sing while playing an instrument because doing two things at once (singing and playing) engages your attention twice as much as doing just one thing. In the previous chapter, I mentioned how keeping your hands busy frees your mind. In no medium is that truer than in music. When my hands are busy playing chords and notes, my voice and language functions busy singing lyrics, my memory fully engaged in recalling lyrics, melodic lines, and harmonic chord changes, and my mind and body fully engaged in the instinctual counting process known as "keeping rhythm" or "staying in time," I cannot simultaneously engage in linguistic hyperconscious rumination. This is displacement principle 101. Occupy the left hemisphere entirely with tasks that make you feel good, and then it will be unable to continue to make you feel bad. Put more simply, **change your behaviors, and your thoughts will follow.**

If it sounds difficult to learn how to sing while accompanying yourself on an instrument, you're right, and that's the entire point! Fully engaging your mind to the point where verbal consciousness does not exist is difficult. People who practice Zen meditation work for years and years on the task of "silencing the inner voice" and, even then, aren't always successful. It takes practice, patience, and commitment. Nobody said that balancing your media engagement was easy. (I certainly did not.) Anything worthwhile takes effort. The more worthwhile the endeavor, the more effort required. If you're not interested in putting some effort into rearranging your media engagement in general—and rearranging your relationship to music in particular—then you should put down this book right now because it will not help you. Only *you* can help your Self. This book may guide you in the process, but the motivation and the commitment must come from you. As the old joke goes, *"How many therapists does it take to change a light bulb? Only one, but the lightbulb has got to want to change."*

Fortunately, if you do truly want to change, applying some basic principles of music therapy to your Self is incredibly fun and liberating. The work is joyful. There's no drudgery involved, and if there is, that means you're doing it wrong. If you do it right, you will experience significant decreases in your anxious depression immediately (while singing or playing), and you'll also experience significant decreases in your anxious depression the rest of the day. *"Music hath charms to soothe the savage breast."*[6] The cathartic release of pent-up emotions and stress that music naturally facilitates is visceral and tangible—you will definitely feel it—and the feeling is both powerful and empowering. You'll also experience an increase in self-esteem and personal satisfaction if you get in touch with your musical self and express it. In the past, you experienced the benefits of music passively, in a secondhand way, via reception. When you begin to experience music expressively, you double the experience because you're now both the performer and the audience of your own music. The doubling of your musical experience doesn't merely double your benefits; it multiplies them exponentially because human beings are naturally musical creatures, and the reward for getting in touch with a part of your natural Self that's been stifled and repressed since childhood is a huge release of creative energy—creative energy that was always there but never accessed because the door to that part of your Self was locked. That locked door is most likely to be the most toxic aspect of your toxic media environment. Allow your Self to unlock that door, and you will see how your media environment will detoxify itself of its own accord. To requote Joseph Campbell: *"When you follow your bliss ... doors will open for you where there were no doors before."* And to requote Bill Indick: **"Change your behaviors, and your thoughts will follow."**

Technology Is Your Assistant, Not Your Friend

The easiest and funnest way to reconnect with your musical Self is to sing and play along with your favorite songs and albums. This is a great first step that never ends. I still do it all the time. As a teenager in the analog (predigital) age, I would play along for hours to audiotapes and records of my favorite artists and bands, like Pink Floyd, Led Zeppelin, The Stones, The Beatles, Lou Reed, Bob Dylan.... You get the idea. It was always rather tricky to set the tape or record to the exact spot I wanted and then to quickly get my hands back in playing position while also keeping my paper notes with lyrics and chords placed in front of me as well. Quickly rewinding the tape or resetting the needle was always a challenge (God forbid I scratch the vinyl!). It was also a chore to get the lyrics and the chords, either figuring it out myself or searching in music stores for songbooks. Nowadays, it's really so much easier. I merely ask Google to play whatever song or album I want to play along with and presto! The music from my YouTube Music profile immediately plays without me having to touch anything, so my hands are all set to go. The chords and lyrics to any song I want to play are immediately accessible via the internet through websites like E-chords.com, and a laptop or tablet works great as a digital replacement to the old paper sheets and songbooks. These digital enhancements make singing and playing along with your favorite artists incredibly easy and lots of fun. However, as with all digital media enhancements, there's a hidden danger.

Playing along to prerecorded music is easy and fun and it sounds great too. In fact, it's so easy and fun that you can very easily fall into the trap of only singing and playing along with your favorite recordings and never seeking out fellow musicians to play with in person. ***Don't play with yourself and pretend that you're playing with a friend.*** Digital media is so immediate and so immersive that it often fools us into thinking that we're interacting with real people in real time when we're absolutely not. Every medium is a mirror. The more sophisticated the medium, the more it fools us into thinking that it's a window to other people, making us less able to perceive that what we're actually experiencing is merely a reflection of ourselves rather than the presence of real others. When I'm playing along with a John Lennon song, in my mind, I'm playing with John Lennon, but in reality, I couldn't possibly be playing with John Lennon because the man died over 42 years ago! Obviously, I'm just playing with myself while fantasizing that I'm playing with John Lennon. That's perfectly fine—great, in fact—but dangerous. At what point does the fantasy replace reality? At what point do I replace the natural human need to express and commune musically with another person with the fantasy of digital interaction that feels almost as good, sounds good if not better, and is instantly accessible whenever I want it? The enhancements that digital media provide also obsolesce the media that precede it. Playing in real time with real others in real space is a real interpersonal musical experience. Playing along to a recording by yourself is real, but if you think it's an interpersonal experience or if you're using it as a substitute for an interpersonal experience, you're not only fooling yourself, but you're using the digital medium as a barrier to interpersonal musical development rather than a bridge. Digital technology is a wonderful assistant, but it is not your friend. **When digital technology begins to take the place of real friends, it has, in fact, become your enemy.**

The Errorless Field of Play

> There are no mistakes in jazz. You're always a semitone from salvation!
> —church joke

When practicing as a music therapist, I stumbled upon a technique that most natural musicians employ in their playing and most music therapists utilize in their work. (The same techniques are avoided by music educators and professionally trained musicians because they would be considered "cheating," as if such a preposterous construct could have any relevance outside of the classroom or studio.) Children naturally love music and want to be engaged as much as possible. They want to sing, dance, and play instruments as well. Problem: How can you facilitate instrumental musicality in a child who does not know how to play an instrument? Solution: Set up an instrument in such a way that whatever the child plays, it will sound good. I refer to this technique as the "errorless field of play." A musical stage is set in which the client can fully engage with a musical instrument without first having to learn how to play the instrument. This technique works incredibly well in the music therapy setting, and I also used it when playing music with my kids when they were little, and I still use it when practicing music therapy for my clients and especially when I use it with my primary client—my Self.

We begin with a very simple nonharmonic rhythmic acoustic instrument, such as a tambourine, a maraca, or a hand drum. Because the instrument is nonharmonic, we don't have to worry about ever playing the wrong note or chord because there are no notes or chords. The tambourine can just play on or against the beat, a rhythm instrument that could be employed as simply or as complex as you want. Rhythm, like the melody of a song, is intuitive and natural. Even infants have a basic sense of rhythm. In fact, all living creatures have an internal sense of rhythm or "time." If I set up an errorless field of play with a child and play a song on my guitar, we are now engaging in a fully immersive interpersonal music experience. The child provides the melody by singing and the rhythm by tapping the tambourine. I provide the harmony via the guitar chords and by singing along. The band is playing, and they sound great!

Music therapists know the next step implicitly well. The child, hearing and seeing the guitar, will naturally approach with curiosity and reach out to strum the strings. I've actually seen music teachers in classrooms and musical performers at children's parties push children away from their instrument when they attempt to touch the guitar. Such a response would be sacrilege in music therapy! Music is a bridge, a medium for interpersonal expression. It should always be open, accessible, and inviting. The child should be encouraged to approach and play, so why is she pushed away? Because the child's "interference" will result in dissonant chords and notes. Here we see the teacher/musician placing the importance of the *sound* of the music over the *experience* of the music. Rather than adjusting the guitar so it will sound good when played by a child, the child is pushed away, negating her basic instinct to explore and play the instrument and disengaging the potential interpersonal connection being made through the music.

Music is a medium, and every medium creates an environment. When there's conflict between a person and the media environment containing her, which variable should be adjusted? You guessed it. The media environment should be adjusted to fit the child rather than the other way around. Pushing the child away from the guitar is the "other way around." Inviting the child into the shared experience by adjusting the media environment—that is, by retuning the guitar—is placing human needs above the restrictions of the environment. Classrooms, as a rule, function the "other way around." The child is forced to fit the restrictions of the environment, and if external pressures aren't enough to make her fit, more invasive measures, such as "medication," will be employed to *make* her fit. This approach is antithetical to the principles of music therapy as well as the principles of media mindfulness and media balancing.

Whether it's the untrained child approaching the guitar or an untrained You, the guitar is imposing at first. First of all, most acoustic guitars have steel strings. It actually does hurt your fingertips to hold the strings in chord positions, and it takes years to develop calluses that buffer the pain. It also takes years to develop the finger strength to play chords well on a steel string acoustic guitar, and it also takes a while to learn those chords as well. The irony of a perfectly tuned guitar is that if you strum it open, with no fingers pressed down on the fretboard, it sounds awful. "Standard tuning" on the guitar and most other stringed instruments is designed to be the most efficient for playing in every key with other instruments. This is a tuning designed for professional musicians because it's rather difficult for a novice player to make a nice sound out of it. Nevertheless, all guitarists initially learn to play in standard tuning. Go figure. All guitarists eventually realize that there's more than one way to tune a guitar. The tuning pegs aren't adornments or accessories; they're crucial parts of the instrument, providing the musician with the ability to change the sound of her instrument and the manner in which it's played. Any nonstandard guitar tuning is called an "alternate tuning." These tunings are generally "open-chord tunings" so that if you strum the strings open, without any fingers on the fretboard, a big beautiful rich chord is heard. A child or a novice can strum to their heart's content and never strike a dissonant chord or wrong note. This is a beautiful, easy, and simple way to begin playing the guitar. I'll break it down into steps:

1. To begin as a novice, get a nylon string guitar rather than a steel string guitar. Classical guitars have strings made of nylon (formerly catgut) rather than steel. The tension on classical guitars is also looser than the tension on steel strings. As a beginner, strumming on a classical guitar will not hurt your fingers, and it will be easier to form your initial chords because of the looser string tension and the wider spacing on the fretboard. Music therapists, as a rule, use nylon string guitars rather than steel strings because the former is much more inviting and accessible to children or other clients who want to physically explore. Many guitarists in nonclassical idioms play primarily nylon string guitars because they prefer both the sound and the feel of them over steel strings. Willie Nelson, Jerry Reed, and José Feliciano are just a few examples. In time, you're likely to move on to a regular steel string acoustic guitar, but for the beginner, nylon strings are definitely the way to go.

2. Tune your guitar to an open-chord tuning, such as an open D tuning. (You can find easy instructions on the internet.) Now you can strum the open strings and make a beautiful sound (a D chord) just like that! I advise getting a digital tuner because learning how to tune by ear is a skill in and of itself, but you can leapfrog over that obstacle with a tuner.

3. After practicing your strumming on the open strings, use the internet to find the fingering for a chord in that tuning, such as a G chord. Once you can play that chord, you can play two chords because the open strings alone form a chord on their own. Also, it's likely that

you can just take the fingering you used to create your second chord and simply slide it up the fretboard to make additional chords.

4. Now that you can play two or three chords on your open-tuned nylon-string guitar, find a song that you like that only has two or three chords (such as almost every folk, pop, country, and rock song). Look up the lyrics and chords on the internet, tell Google to play the song, and then you're in business! Just sing and strum along. Pretty soon, you'll be singing the melody, strumming the harmony and rhythm, and tapping the beat with your foot. Full musical engagement! By applying another simple device—a capo—to your guitar's fretboard, you can change the pitch of your guitar, so that by using just two or three chord fingerings, you can play a simple song in any key, just by sliding the capo up or down the neck of the guitar.

5. The next step is never ending. Learn new chords and new songs. Learn how to play in other open tunings, and eventually, learn how to play in standard tuning. Learn other instruments using the same or similar technique. And most important, find some real people to play music with. *"Learn to play a musical instrument, and you will always have a friend."* Ultimately, the best friend you'll make through music is your Self!

There are many other ways to set up errorless fields of musical play. Any instrument with a tuning peg can be tuned to an open tuning and made easier and simpler to play in the same general vein as the process laid out above. Harmonic percussion instruments like xylophones and glockenspiels have removable bars, so with just a little bit of know-how, you can set up simple chords or pentatonic scales on these instruments, making it impossible to hit a wrong note. The piano or keyboard is not easily retunable, but it's super easy to find errorless fields of play on that instrument too. You just need a very peripheral understanding of what a musical scale or key is.

For example, the instrumental jam in the song "Any Colour You Like" on Pink Floyd's classic rock album *The Dark Side of the Moon* (1973) has just two chords: D-minor-7 and G-major. The jam is played at a rather slow, loose, and extremely basic blues-rock groove that any novice familiar with rock music can easily slide into. For Rick Wright, the keyboardist, the jam is an errorless field of play. All the white notes on the keyboard are in key, so as long as he doesn't hit a black note, he literally cannot hit a wrong note, while the groove is so loose and free that it's almost impossible to play anything out of time. The errorless field of play is like free play for the musical brain and body—anything goes—so you can let yourself go and not even think at all about what chords or notes you're playing.

Chapter Six. Music Therapy for Your Self

Once ensconced in an errorless field of play, you will always be playing "in tune" and "in time." Pretty soon, your hands are just playing of their own accord, and you're not thinking at all about D-minor-7 or G-major. In fact, you're not thinking at all; you're just listening and feeling and expressing in pure sound, intuitively matching the movements of your fingers on the keyboard to the sounds you're hearing. The complete freedom of the errorless field of play, also called a "free jam" or "free jazz," is incredibly liberating, allowing Rick Wright to go all out on his various organs and synthesizers, conjuring some incredibly weird and wonderful sounds, without the possibility of hitting a wrong note.

A similar approach was used by Marvin Gaye in the song "Inner-City Blues" from his classic soul album *What's Going On?* (1971). The song is a slow, infectious groove based on two chords: D-sharp-minor and G-sharp major. They're the same two chords as "Any Colour You Like" but up one half-step on the piano. So as long you play all the *black* keys, you can't hit a wrong note. I've seen Marvin (on the internet) play that album on stage, and unlike most of his other concert performances, he's playing the piano while singing throughout because he wrote all of the songs himself on the piano. Marvin, however, was not a trained pianist. Like me, he was self-taught, as are most folk musicians, rock and soul musicians included. So he set himself up an errorless field of play on piano so he can play along freely while singing and never have to worry about playing out of key. The album features a number of errorless fields of play, the most recognizable being the vocal bridges in the title song—*What's Going On?*—where the chords modulate down to A-minor-7, and the backup singers harmonize in a heavenly gospel chorus as Marvin lets loose with some marvelous soul scat. The scale matching the chord of A-minor-7 on the piano includes all the white keys. Marvin could just sing freely and focus on the sounds in his head, while letting his hands do whatever they want as long as they stick to the white keys. The errorless fields of play that Marvin created for himself in these, the most personal and heartfelt songs of his brilliant career, led to the very natural and loose grooves developed out of the free jams in the studio, which gave the album its heart and soul.

Finding and setting up errorless fields of play for your own musical expression will allow you to transcend the obstacles of formal music theory and musical literacy, as well as the obstacles of developing basic musicianship on an instrument, so you can dive on in and freely engage yourself in a musical media environment. Eventually, with time and practice, you will develop beyond the simplicities of the errorless field of play; but like Rick Wright and Marvin Gaye, you will never outgrow them, just like you will never outgrow the natural pleasure found in a simple song.

Music Therapy for the Musically Dyslexic

More advanced methods for your self-directed music therapy practice can be explored but not here. (Perhaps I should write a book specifically on this topic?) I consider myself a "musical dyslexic" because my reading comprehension for musical notation is very low, which means that I can't just look at sheet music and play the notes because it would take me way too long to decode the notation while also trying to play in anything close to the time signature of the musical piece. In short, I can read music but very slowly—so slow, in fact, that it's too burdensome for me to play music in the literate fashion. Decoding the notation is such a difficult process for me that it takes all the fun out of playing music, becoming a frustrating chore. The errorless field of play and other techniques are compensations I developed to overcome my musical dyslexia. Just as a regular dyslexic prefers spoken language to written language, musical dyslexics prefer natural music to written music. In this sense, the overwhelming majority of musicians could be considered musically dyslexic (or musically illiterate), just like the overwhelming majority of people in the world were illiterate before the advent of socialized education. The thing about dyslexics is, *we can read*, just very slowly. Also, we can learn to read more efficiently, but that process too proceeds *very slowly*. I started to try to learn to read music in my late teens and didn't get too far, but I kept trying because I was passionate about music. Now, over 30 years later, I still can't read too well, but I'm a pretty good musician anyway. Also, I've adapted my playing to compensate for my musical dyslexia. The errorless field of play is just one of those compensations.

When playing piano or guitar, I generally just play the chords rather than the written notes. After 35 years of playing them, I know chords very well and I can play them intuitively. Even with sheet music in front of me, I'm only looking at the lyrics and the chords, not the actual notes. If I'm singing, the melody is played by my voice, while the harmony and rhythm are played in the chords, and that's the most you can get out of any musical expression—melody, harmony, and rhythm—full musical engagement. However, there are some musical pieces that I play that do involve a bit of actual reading. For instance, I love the music of Satie. His *Gymnopédies* and *Gnossiennes* for the piano are so beautiful and hypnotic. Playing them really gets me into a meditative state of peace and tranquility. The tunes are very very slow, and the melodies are simple, so I took the sheet music and used my basic knowledge of chords to note the chord to play in each measure. When I play Satie, I'm playing mostly chords, not the actual notes on the page. I know the melodies well, so I can play them a bit my memory, and the notes on the page give me a good clue because I only have to look at the one very top note on the notation to get the melodic notes, while ignoring all of the other notes, and just intuitively playing the chords. The rhythm in these Satie pieces is not just mournfully slow, but it's a dreamy, pensive, almost trancelike state, which means I can slow down as much as I want or need to and not fall out of time with the piece because the time of the piece itself is so open and dreamy. Essentially, I'm improvising, something that all musicians do. My improvisation is very simple, requiring almost no musical training or musical literacy. Nevertheless, it sounds good, and every time I play the pieces, it sounds better. Most important, I'm enjoying myself while I learn rather than learning in hopes that one day I might enjoy myself.

So if you're musically dyslexic or a musical illiterate like I am, give yourself a break. First of all, don't force yourself to practice sight-reading until you're anxious and depressed and frustrated. This is a path that you will eventually abandon because it's no fun and it doesn't evoke the joy of music that's hidden behind the notes. Second, give yourself compensations that will allow you to get to the joy of music that's hidden behind the notes without having to actually read the notes. Humans have a great instinctive memory for melody, so singers can usually sing by ear without reading the actual notes. To accompany yourself, just learn some chords and play. Can't do that? Start with one chord. You can play a lot of great songs with just one chord. Harry Nilsson's "Coconut Song" (1971) is just one that comes to mind. The entire song has just one chord (C7). Once you learn that one chord, you just need to learn one more (F7), and you can play Joe Cocker's "Feelin' Alright" (1969) as well as dozens of other great two-chord songs. Once you know two chords on the guitar, you can use a "capo" to play simple songs in any key. Then add a third chord to your repertoire, and a fourth, and so on. Like the trees in your yard, development may seem slow at first because there's so much lateral and subliminal development going on. Keep at it, and then one day, you'll be surprised at how good you sound, just like you're surprised when you look out the window one spring morning to see a tall hedge of trees in full bloom where a row of saplings once stood. "*Wow! I did that!*" is your natural response, and the associated feeling is pride.

Just be patient, build on the skills you have, and keep on developing. Soon, you'll find the "errorless fields of play" can be expanded on incrementally. If you play only the white keys on the piano, for instance, you're in the key of C. That's the most basic errorless field of play. If you sharpen just the F note, adding just one black key and removing just one white key from your field of play, you are now playing in the key of G. Every time you learn a new song in a different key, you're adding another modified errorless field of play to your repertoire. In essence, a "modified errorless field of play" is just a musical key that you mastered while circumventing the traditional route of mastering music theory. Musicians take these shortcuts all the time, and they make up their own as well. Composer Irving Berlin initially could not read music and knew how to play piano in only one key (F-sharp major). He bought a piano that could be adjusted so he could play in other keys. The modification was basically like a guitar capo but for the piano. And that's how music therapy for your Self works. Start simple; progress at your own pace; employ compensations, devices, and tricks to get past obstacles; trust your intuition; and follow your bliss. You will never regret making a new best friend out of your musical Self!

Musical Time Is Not Time as Duration

> *Music is, indeed, time made free of temporality.*
> —George Steiner[7]

We've all experienced the phenomenon of "musical time" as it differs from our normal experience of time, as measured by the duration of hours, minutes, and seconds on the clock. Maybe you were listening to music and got so immersed in it that you "lost track of time," thinking only a few minutes have gone by when it was closer to an hour. This is a normative experience for everyone. Musicians, however, experience the freedom of musical time in a much more immersive way because they're not just listening, but they're expressing. The listener is engaged and attending to the medium. **The performer *becomes the medium*.** Only when you yourself are the medium you're expressing, only when you are *inside* the musical environment, rather than listening to it from the outside, can you feel the full effect of becoming completely unaware of time as duration, as you're entirely immersed in the parallel dimension of musical time. Seconds fade into minutes, and minutes into hours, as those hallmarks of normal time are eclipsed by the beats and meter of the music you're playing, the musical time that you're inhabiting. George Steiner expressed it more poetically than I ever could:

> *We can say that music is time organized, which means "made organic." We can say that this act of organization is one of essential freedom, that it liberates us from the enforcing beat of biological and physical-mathematical clocks.* **The time which music "takes," and which it gives as we perform or experience it, is the only *free time granted us prior to death.*[8]

In musical expression, we find relief and release from both the tyranny of conscious thought and the prison cell of time as duration. Music is the great liberator. That liberation is felt most completely when experienced with others. When I'm playing music with friends, we're all playing "in time." We're playing in the same rhythm of the song we're sharing, and we're also sharing the extraordinary experience of musical time together, as we create it together. This is where my own articulacy breaks down because I cannot express the joy of that feeling of **collectively transcending time** with my friends through music in mere words. "*Where words fail, music speaks.*"[9] You'll just have to experience it for yourself.

Playing with versus Playing Out

> *Learn to play a musical instrument, and you'll always have a friend.*
> —Ronnie Lane's Uncle[10]

Unless you're a musical specialist seeking a career in music performance, "playing out" at bars or other venues is fun and exciting but completely unnecessary for the purposes of music therapy. I've done it myself a few times, and it is indeed fun because you and your bandmates are so much more invested in sounding good, but there's obviously an element of narcissism involved whenever your goal is to be up on stage in the spotlight. If you're up there on the stage alone, narcissism is probably the primary motivator, as you're certainly not getting any of the interpersonal benefits of music therapy, up there in the spotlight, all by your lonesome. If you're on stage by yourself because you're trying to make a spare buck or a living out of playing music, that would have to be considered "careerism," which was a dirty word for the folk musicians of the early 1960s, who believed that music should be shared and enjoyed for its own inherent value. The musician's dream is to make a living out of playing music, to become a "professional musician," so she can tell her boss to "take this job and shove it." Careerism in music is commoditization, and it's the biggest danger for anyone who loves to play music and wants to share it with others. My advice in this chapter is directed at the person who wants to use music as a means to personal growth and expression, not at the person who seeks financial gain, recognition, or a career.

When we're simply playing with our friends in somebody's basement, garage, or living room, we're experiencing all of the cognitive, emotional, and interpersonal benefits of musical expression. This is the fullest and most rewarding form of music therapy for your Self. The drive to take that intimate interpersonal experience and capitalize on it by going on stage in front of an audience will only detract from the therapeutic benefits of the process. Once again, playing out is fun, and if you can do it without making it a big hassle, it's totally worth it. I'm talking about the occasional gig at the corner bar for your garage band, or the occasional folk duet at the local open mic, or the occasional set at the local piano bar. These gigs, if not motivated by commoditization or narcissism, are extensions of the musical experience you're already enjoying, and they can become beneficial motivators to continue your therapeutic musical practice with friends. In my personal experience, these types of gigs are rare and hard to come by. Usually, you need to travel to a gig, which means a lot of equipment to haul, possibly a van to rent, time and money spent driving, hotel rooms, and so forth. In other words, it's a lot of schlepping around for very little reward beyond the benefits of simply playing music with friends.

If you're thinking about finding musical satisfaction and expression by playing out by yourself as a solo musician, I suggest you press pause for a moment and explore your motivations. First of all, music evolved as a form of communication, and its primary force comes to the fore as a means of communication, especially for emotional content that cannot be expressed through words alone. Musicians communicate to each other via the common medium of music. It is at heart an interpersonal experience, meant to be experienced with others, though we mustn't undervalue the private intrapersonal experience of playing music for your Self. As such, where does playing music all by yourself on a stage in the spotlight come in? You're right, it doesn't. Explore your motivations, and excise any motive that's rooted in narcissism (the need to be admired), as well as any motive that's rooted in money (the desire to become a pro). Once you become honest with yourself and your motivations, you can liberate yourself of these unholy goals and simply enjoy the process of sharing music with your Self and your friends without the pressure of having to "do something" with your music. The drive to always "do" something is your anxious depressive mind telling you that it's not OK to just "be" musical; you must "do" something to show off and profit from your musicianship. In other words, you must be a "human doing" rather than a "human being." Why can't you allow yourself to just have this one part of life for your own personal enjoyment and pleasure? Why must everything be framed in the form of an ambition, an achievement, a goal, a money-making venture, a public relations event for your personal social media brand, or an accomplishment that can be displayed to others? Why can't you just allow yourself to enjoy the process and reap its benefits?

It's no secret that anxious depression and self-medication is so common among professional musicians as to be thought of as an "occupational hazard." You might say that playing music all the time might be a risk factor for anxious depression, in which case, you would be completely wrong. Playing music relieves anxious depression; it doesn't cause it. What causes anxious depression is a mindset driven by the twin demons of money and time that convert into the narcissistic needs to be perceived as talented and successful. These narcissistic needs exist in all forms of expression, not just music. However, they take on a more sinister tone in the case of music.

For many if not most of us, music is the one medium of engagement that consistently evokes peace and harmony within the Self. When this sanctuary is defiled by the need to make money, the anxiety of a deadline to "make it" as a musician, or the narcissistic need for external acknowledgment (fame), the one safe and pure place we had to go is no longer safe and pure. In fact, anxious depression is multiplied exponentially by the inevitable experiences of rejection and failure that any expressive artist with careerist goals is bound to experience. The thing that should make everyone happy, especially for the musician, becomes something that makes her worried and sad. The thing that relieves anxious depression becomes the primary source of anxious depression. The thing that most of use as a release and a break from the chores of everyday life and labor becomes a chore and a form of labor. In short, "playing out" is unimportant in terms of the benefits of your music therapy, and it's more likely to draw away from rather than complement your personal music therapy practice.

To sum up, *"playing with" is all important, while "playing out" is not important at all*. The last time I played out, the whole time I was thinking, "*I'd rather just be hanging out in my living room and playing with these guys, rather than going through all the trouble, simply to play the same tunes with the same fellows but in a strange place with a few strangers watching us.*" Playing out is unnecessary and probably counterproductive in terms of music therapy. "Playing with," however, is exponentially more important, and it's a great aim for anyone pursuing the practice of music therapy for your Self.

The Medium of the Soul

> *Music can lift us out of depression or move us to tears—it is a remedy, a tonic, orange juice for the ear.... Music is not a luxury, but a necessity.*
> —Oliver Sacks

You may find it odd that I'm insisting you practice music therapy on your Self even if you're not a "musical" person. After all, to each her own, right? Not right. *I think it odd that you think my insistence is odd*. Music is the universal language, the language that predates language by hundreds of thousands of years, the language that can conquer the consequence of language (consciousness). Music speaks directly to the soul. The construct of "music therapy for your Self" is why I wrote this book, and I strongly believe that it's the strongest argument in this book. Howard Gardner—endowed chair of cognition and education at Harvard, recipient of the MacArthur "genius grant," and all-around clever fellow—granted music a place of honor among the eight noble intelligences that define humanity. So according to *his* model, if you're not in touch with your musical intelligence, then you're not firing on all eight cylinders. There's a part of your Self that's misfiring, and it's limiting your potential and negatively affecting your mental health. If you don't take my word for it, at least have some respect for Dr. Gardner.

You also may have noticed that I've been capitalizing the word "Self" in this chapter. This is not a case of spellcheck gone psycho. The spelling is a reference to Jung's construct of the "Self," a symbol that represents the balancing of all aspects of one's identity and personality within one frame of orientation. Jung's construct will be featured more prominently in the next chapter, but it's entirely relevant for this chapter (and all the others) as well. A balanced Self requires that we get in touch with each part of our own identity, especially the parts that may be repressed or just forgotten, such as our musical expressivity. The experience of "wholeness," of being a fully functioning individual, can only be attained when all the parts of the Self are acknowledged, expressed, and in balance.

Music Withdrawal

> *Without music, life would be a mistake.*
> —Nietzsche

Last summer, I hurt my finger catching a football. The splint on my right middle finger made playing piano or guitar impossible for a couple of weeks. I didn't notice how grumpy and surly and altogether anxiously depressed I got after about a week or so without playing, but my family sure did. I was suffering from music withdrawal but why? After all, I was still listening to music. Like many Americans, I drive a lot out of necessity, and I *desperately* need my tunes while driving. The environment of the road is so tense, so filled with time-as-duration-obsessed stressaholics driving like maniacs that I need my music to balance me out and keep me sane. So why was I experiencing music withdrawal even though I listened to a fair amount of music each day? By now, you should know that the answer has to do with the expressive and passive modes of engagement. Each mode is different, and each fulfills its own function in its own environment. Listening to music buffers my environment from external stressors, but performing music actually expresses and releases my internal stressors. *I need both, and so do you.* It wasn't until I actually sat down at the piano and started playing that I realized just how grumpy I was and how closely that grumpiness was linked to my musical expression withdrawal. The moment I began to play, my mood elevated sharply, as did my energy level and focus, and I immediately felt happier and less stressed out, and that feeling lasted the rest of the day. I haven't missed more than a day or two of playing music since then, regardless of the shape of my fingers.

The individual with no personal form of musical expression doesn't feel the overt effects of musical expression withdrawal because she saturates herself with passive musical reception so frequently during the day and night. Only after a period of musical *reception* withdrawal would somebody truly feel the overall effects of music withdrawal because she'd actually be experiencing withdrawal from all forms of music. As a thought experiment, I encourage you to engage in an experimental period of total music withdrawal. It will be more difficult than you think, especially because music often comes to us from sources out of our control and we cannot shut our "earlids" because we don't have them. You may find yourself being drawn to the music coming from a nearby house or car, like Odysseus drawn to the Sirens, but you must resist for as long as you can bare it. When you finally can't bear a life without music for one moment longer, create your own music rather than turning on the radio or stereo. If you prepared your reentry into the musical dimension well (possibly with a preset errorless field of play), you will be in for a pleasant surprise. You will discover the basic truth of music—that it flows naturally from inside of you—if you only give it a chance. External sources of music saturate our senses to the point where we forget that basic truth. We become dependent on them, even as that dependence masks our need to lend expression to our internal musical source. Realizing that basic truth and finding ways to reconnect your Self with the internal wellspring of music inside of you is the ultimate reward of self-directed music therapy.

Balancing Musical Media

Whereas the visual ideal for objects is a sense of balance, the musical ideal for sounds is a sense of harmony. So rather than asking, how does your musical engagement fall into balance with your seven other modes of engagement, I will ask, how does music "harmonize" with the rest of your life? In four-part harmony (as in a barbershop quartet), harmony is attained when all four voices are heard clearly, with each separate voice sounding distinct yet with the overall effect of all four voices blending into one. Does music play this role in your life? Is your own distinct voice heard, or are you just listening passively, afraid to join in? If your voice is heard, does it harmonize with others, or are you just playing with your Self? Although playing with and for your Self is a key part of your **intrapersonal** music therapy practice, it's easy to fall into the trap of making it your only form of music therapy, which is unnecessarily limiting your development as a musician and your development as a person. To truly communicate and connect, your musical expressions must eventually become **interpersonal** as well as intrapersonal.

Does your music channel your **body movement**? The focal point of physical activity when playing an instrument is your fingers, drawing blood and mental energy away from the head and toward the hands. This is why playing music (rather than just listening) is the perfect remedy for a headache, or for saturation fatigue, or for anxious depression in general. It also wards off arthritis and other ailments of the joints and muscles, especially in the hands. Music gets the blood running, and it gets you out of your head and into the arena of real physical sounds, movement, objects, and actions. When we're passionate about playing the music we love, we really get into it, and it's a physical workout that makes you huff and sweat. If you don't get a physical rush out of playing, then you're not really putting your whole Self into it. Find different music to play, a different instrument or a different style, and most important, find friends to play with. That's the surest way to reignite the passion in your musical expression. It's also a great way to integrate music into your interpersonal life and to widen the range of your interpersonal experiences.

In song, we integrate **linguistic** and **mathematical** media in ways that are much more natural and intuitive than our usual modes of engagement. Lyrics are linguistic, but the words themselves are poetry, and the use of language in song is much more impressionistic, flowery, and romantic than our normal everyday use of language in which the ideal is precision and clarity rather than beauty and harmony. Song is based in the grounding right hemisphere in which language is intuitive and metaphorical rather than the left hemisphere's way of attending in which language is used to form an argument or express a specific point. *Music doesn't have a point; it just is.* Similarly, there is math in music, found in the division of beats into measure and meter. The math in music is both obvious and invisible because it's intuitive, bringing us back to the basic counting instinct hardwired into our brains. If we're doing it right, we feel it rather than think it, and we experience musical time as a much-needed respite from our normal everyday experience of time as duration. Music can also bring us closer to Nature, and it can inspire visual-spatial imagination as well, but I don't wish to belabor the point. Harmony should never be forced. Find a way to harmonize music in your life, and you'll find that the other modes of engagement will naturally sing along. After all, music *is* the universal language.

Chapter Seven

The Body
Medium of the Self

> He who uses machines does all his work like a machine. He who does work like a machine grows a heart like a machine. He who carries the heart of a machine in his breast loses his simplicity. He who has lost his simplicity becomes unsure in the strivings of his soul.
> —Zhuang Zhou (4th century BC)

Here's something that, by a random fluke of timing, happened a few times. I go out to mow the lawn, and as I do, I see my neighbor with his gym bag getting in his car to go to the gym at around the same time that the landscapers arrive to mow his lawn and trim the hedges. In other words, he's driving to the gym to exercise, as he simultaneously pays these men to get great physical exercise by mowing his lawn and trimming his hedges. Seems inefficient and wasteful, but that's life in suburbia. Not for me, however. Not anymore.

YoDEM

During the pandemic, I was involuntarily furloughed from my university. Money was tight, and I was looking to cut corners. I also had much more free time than usual, and I was beginning work on the book you're currently reading. It was a stressful time for me, laced with high-potency anxious depression, so it seemed like the perfect opportunity to test my theory of media balancing on my Self, and that's just what I did. You're reading the results of that test. The decrepit state of my body made it crystal clear that I needed to balance my bodily kinesthetic mode of engagement by increasing my physical activity. The most obvious choice would've been to go to the gym more, attend more yoga classes, maybe hire a trainer, but quarantine culture and no money put the kibosh on those options. I therefore resolved to "do it myself." Not just the exercise and the yoga—*everything*. I declared a **"YoDEM"—a "Year of Doing Everything Myself."** As a practice in self-dependence and mindfully integrated bodily kinesthesia, I resolved to make physical movement a daily part of my life. I don't use the term "exercise" in this chapter or in my life because "exercise" is something we do specifically for our bodies. "Exercise" is not an integrated experience. The reason why we often put ourselves on "exercise regimes" that we quickly abandon is because these regimes are not integrated into our lives, so it's easy to forget about the regimes or blow them off, especially if the unintegrated regime adds to our already busy schedules and expensive lifestyles. Going to the gym requires taking time out of our day to get there, the "exercise" itself, returning home, and so forth. Gym memberships are expensive, and if you're not going to the gym anyway because it's too much of a schlep, cutting the membership is an easy way to cut an expense, and there goes the "regime." However, if much or even all of your bodily kinesthetic engagement is integrated into your daily lifestyle, playing a role that's integral and necessary, rather than supplemental and optional, it will be difficult or even impossible to avoid or blow off daily physical engagement. That's where YoDEM comes in.

My pandemic situation meant that I had to fire the landscapers who came weekly to mow the lawn and trim the hedges. But I had a lawnmower, I had a hedge clipper, I had two arms and two legs. There was no reason on God's green earth why I couldn't do those things myself, so I did. At the time, I thought to myself, *"If you can't mow your own lawn, you don't deserve to own a house"*—a non sequitur that nonetheless helped me think of homeownership as more than just paying the mortgage. Homeownership, like body ownership or baby ownership, does not come with a "manual" on how to do it, but it does come with a "manual work" requirement that cannot be hired out for someone else to do, either physically (in the case of your body) or psychosocially (in the case of your baby). A long time ago, when my kids were babies, somebody mentioned a certain celebrity whose wife recently had a baby. That celebrity raved about his joyful "quality time" with the baby, how he loved to cuddle and play with him, but he admitted that he didn't change the baby's diapers, feed him, dress him, bathe him, or do any of the chores associated with infant care. My mother, confused, commented, *"What does he do with the baby—play chess?"*

Her point was well taken. We make an interpersonal connection with our baby by taking care of him, and that care is hard work. The work can be joyful, even transcendent, but it is, no doubt, hard work! Thus, we encounter the most basic truth of existence. Anything that is worthwhile is going to take effort because the "worth" that is gained is attained "while" you are putting in the effort. We get to know and love our baby by changing, feeding, bathing, and dressing him. We play with him too, but "quality time" is not determined by how much you personally enjoy the time together; it's determined by the quality of the engagement and the frequency and consistency of that engagement. To apply the metaphor, I loved my house and my yard, but I never truly felt that love until I stopped paying men to take care of my house and my yard and began doing it myself. Once I became physically integrated in the daily care of my home, I became more emotionally invested and I felt the love as a true connection to my home. I also began to feel that my home loved me back, not in a psycho haunted house way but in the only way a home can show love. The hedge of trees and shrubs I planted grew tall to blanket my family and me in lovely shade and privacy. The flowers I planted in the garden bloomed just to please me with their beauty. The rooms I painted indoors looked so much nicer and warmer, displaying their gratitude toward me in their splendor. In short, by channeling my love into my home, I truly fell in love with my home, and the love I feel in return (admittedly a psychological projection) feels great all the same.

During my YoDEM, I started doing *all* of my own yardwork, and I never stopped and never regretted it. Mowing my own lawn, trimming my own hedges, weeding my own garden brings me back in touch with Nature and with the land. I often feel like a farmer working his own soil because the primal connection between a person and the land he lives on is physical and can only truly be felt with your hands in the dirt that's been irrigated with your own sweat. I feel this primal connection with my home primarily when I'm working in and around my home. I don't feel it when I'm merely living or occupying my home.

It occurred to me, while working in the yard, that just as the body is the physical medium for everything about ourselves that we could label "the Self," our home is the physical medium for our physical bodies and the "selves" residing in those bodies. More simply, just as the body is home to our Self, our house is home to our body. By extension, our home isn't merely a physical place and structure; it's an integral part of our psyche that must be included in our understanding of our Self. The roots we grow in our home are both physical and metaphysical, as our home becomes one of the primary symbols of our own existence. As such, taking care of our home personally and physically—just like taking care of your own body and your own baby personally and physically—is the key to experiencing this transcendent bond between home and homeowner. The bond is transcendent because it allows us to transcend our normal understanding of love and affection so that it could be experienced between a person and a place rather than exclusively between a person and another person. The bond, furthermore, is experienced physically through real manual labor. Hard work is hard (go figure), but it's great for the body and liberating for the mind. The harder you work on your home, the more you will love your home and the more your home will love you, as demonstrated in the beauty and comfort she provides to you in return.[1]

In his utopian novel based on behaviorist principles, *Walden Two* (1948), B.F. Skinner prescribed "*one or two hours of physical work each day as a health measure.*" This seems to be a common theme in utopia stories—the utilitarian agrarian ethic of physical labor—the notion that everyone who lives on the land and partakes of the bounty of the land must, in return, work the land. The common requirement of every person, regardless of sex, age, or status, to work the land if physically capable to do so is the ethic that keeps each member of the community connected and functioning at the same level and invested in the same common purpose in the same place. The same principle could be applied to every person in every place.

The Kitchen Sink Paradox

My YoDEM was a great success and a primary motivator for writing this book. I also learned a lot about what I can and can't do and what I enjoy and what I hate. Yardwork, as I mentioned, is something that I love to do (but only in my own yard). Any work that gets me outdoors is much more preferable to indoor work, as it gets me in touch with the naturalistic media environment, which liberates my mind and energizes my body. Physically, I can work longer and harder when I'm outdoors. Indoor work is much less preferable. Simple indoor household chores like doing the dishes, vacuuming, laundry, and so forth aren't much fun. I do them because they need to get done. I found a trick for making these simple chores much less burdensome. The trick is by no means new or original, and I'll mention it a little later in this chapter. One specific thing I learned was that I'm not a very good plumber. The plumbing jobs I took on in my house became comedies of error in which a simple job became a very long and complicated job because every mistake I made ballooned into bigger and bigger ones that had to be fixed. I hate plumbing, I suck at it, and that's OK. That's something that I know about myself now, so I won't force myself to do plumbing work; I'll just call a plumber. Media mindfulness and balancing is not about forcing yourself to do things that you hate (banging square pegs into round holes). It's about configuring the holes in your environment so that your own naturally shaped pegs slip in of their own accord. There is, of course, a paradox in this philosophy that I call the "kitchen sink paradox."

The kitchen sink broke during the pandemic, toward the end of my official YoDEM. I had already experienced my plumbing epiphany, letting myself off the hook for any plumbing job bigger than a clogged drain, so I called a plumber. Problem: I couldn't find a plumber to come to my house to fix the sink because of the pandemic. I would have to wait a few weeks, or do it myself. *Ever try living in a house with kids and no kitchen sink?* I sucked it up and did it myself. The work was hard and miserable. I made mistakes. A job that would've taken a plumber a couple of hours took me nearly a week. I bashed my thumb a bit and almost cried, not out of pain but out of frustration. Finally, I got it done! The sink looks fine and works fine. It's not a work of art; it's just a sink. Every time I use it, though, I feel pride. There's a certain satisfaction that can only be attained by doing something you hate, doing it even though the work sucks, you suck at it, and it's really hard. Doing it so long that it makes you want to cry. Doing it not because you want to do it but simply because it must get done. Doing it for your family, your home, and your Self. That specific sort of satisfaction is specifically avoided when we let ourselves off the hook from doing things we aren't good at and simply don't like doing. But it is that specific sort of satisfaction—seasoned with your own blood, sweat, and tears—that has a taste sweeter than honey. It is the kitchen sink paradox. **Sometimes you have to do what you hate to feel the love.**

My greatest achievement (beyond the kitchen sink) was psychological, attaining both a physical and metaphysical connection with my home that I didn't have before. Prior to my YoDEM, I lived in my home. That's still true, but now, as an added benefit, ***my home lives inside of me***. The daily physical activity—planting, mowing, weeding my yard—as well as painting, fixing, and installing things inside my house—was fantastic for my body. I lost a lot of weight (about 40 pounds), and physically, I haven't felt or looked better since my twenties. My house has never looked (or felt) better either.

The Benefits of Generalization

My YoDEM also broadened me as a person. If you consider the life of a farmer or a hunter-gatherer, their work is the work of a generalist, a dilettante. A farmer may plough the fields on Monday, but on Tuesday, she may be a carpenter mending a fence; on Wednesday, she may be a painter painting the barn; on Thursday, she's a shepherd tending and shearing her sheep; on Friday, she's a cowhand branding her cattle. In short, humans evolved to do many jobs. **Modern society and the media technology that fuels it has turned us into a species of specialists.**

The modern professional works in an office all day, cut off from Nature and from anything that isn't specifically related to her specialist job. The specialist's mind and body are confined and reduced to a unimodal focus on a single mode of engagement. It is this critical imbalance in both physical and mental engagement that sows the seeds of anxious depression in our imprisoned minds and bodies. For me and probably for most of you, yardwork and physical labor in and around the home is antithetical to the kind of work you do for your career, and that's exactly the point! We need to move away from specialization, which is lucrative but also limiting and deadening to the body, mind, and soul. We must embrace generalization, engaging in tasks that allow our bodies and minds to explore new and different modes of engagement. Furthermore, this generalized engagement must be completely integrated in our daily lives. It can't just be another gym membership that you'll eventually cancel, another yoga class that you'll blow off, or another exercise regime that you'll give up. If your yard looks like crap because you haven't mowed the lawn, guess who needs to mow the lawn? The work may seem like drudgery at first, but give it time. Eventually, you'll feel the connection between you and the land you work. You will definitely feel the physical benefits that daily manual labor engenders—your body will feel better, look better, and work better. A true human being is not a specialist but a generalist, a creature that can adapt to any environment and master any task. She can do anything and everything she puts her body and mind into, including the kitchen sink.

Man versus Machine

Another curse that arises from modern technology is the mechanization of both work and play. We fly over the water in speedboats rather than paddle in canoes. We fly over the snow in snowmobiles rather than ski on skis. We fly over the road on mopeds rather than peddle on bicycles. Machines make these modes of engagement much easier and much faster, but do they enhance the actual experience or detract from it? Henri Bergson argued that when we *"double the speed"* of an event, *"we discern a great loss of richness in experience."* The moped gets us there faster, and it sure is fun, but what are we missing out on compared to the slower bicycle? The physical aspect is certainly lost because effort is diminished to the point of nonexistence. The visual aspect is lost, as the scenery blurs into a hazy background with any specific figures passing by too quickly to really appreciate. Certainly, any sense of peace and quiet that could be experienced from a nice bike ride is lost, replaced with the loud invasive buzz of the engine. On a deeper level, that sense of oneness that is achieved when we are completely integrated with a simple person-driven mechanism, like a bicycle or a canoe, is lost when the mechanism is replaced with a fuel-powered machine like a moped or a speedboat. When the arms and legs that propel the mechanism are replaced by engines and gears, the mechanism becomes a machine, and the unity of the experience is divided into two parts: person and machine. When we displace our own personal engagement in an experience by placing a machine in between ourselves and the thing we're engaging in, we experience a level of disconnection from that experience, "*a great loss of richness.*" When we displace the vast majority of our direct physical engagement with machines, we grow "*a heart like a machine,*" we lose our "*simplicity,*" and become "*unsure in the strivings*" of our "*soul.*"

Let's not forget the landscapers, painters, dog walkers, and all the other folks we pay to do the physical things we can and should do for our Selves. One reason we hire landscapers and painters to do our physical work for us is because they have better machines than us, which is why they can do the work much quicker and much more efficiently than we can. If I was mowing your lawn, I would want to use the biggest and best lawnmower available so I can get the job done as quickly and efficiently as possible. However, I'm not mowing your lawn. In fact, you can't pay me enough to your mow lawn.[2] I would never mow anybody's lawn other than my own, for the same reason I would never walk anybody's dog other than my own. Me mowing my lawn is me maintaining an existential connection that I've developed with my yard and my home, just as me walking my dog is me maintaining the interpersonal connection I've developed with Daisy. There are personal reasons why I engage in that labor that make the labor itself both meaningful and joyful. Those personal reasons disappear when the lawn or dog are not my own. Therefore, I will not pay someone else to do those jobs for me, even if they have better machines than I do and even if they can do a better job than me. The more we pay people and machines to do our work for us, the more disconnected we become from the work itself and the more blind we become to the hidden meaning and connections behind that work, and in this way, we become more "*unsure in the strivings*" of our "*soul.*"

Yoga

Yardwork and home maintenance/improvement are great and efficient ways to experience bodily kinesthetic engagement in a way that's integrated with your life as a whole. Not everybody has a yard, though. Not everybody has a house. Not everybody owns their own home, making substantial DIY work impractical, especially in a small apartment. I get that. I've lived in many small, rented apartments in my day. You may need to find other ways to experience bodily kinesthetic engagement. Maybe the gym is your best bet, or jogging, or walking. Whatever it is, find it and do it to balance and integrate the bodily kinesthetic medium of engagement within your life. However, bodily kinesthetic engagement in and of itself must be balanced. Think of it in terms of mode flipping. Music, for example, has both a receptive and an expressive mode. We need to experience both modes to achieve balance in that one medium of engagement. Bodily kinesthetic engagement, however, doesn't have receptive and expressive modes. We can say that the body must be active and that the body must also rest, but that's not even close to the same thing. The body resting is not the body engaging receptively; it is the body disengaging. We need a different metaphor.

In traditional agricultural societies, farmers break their backs working in the fields all day. They do 10,000 forward bends each day, as they plant and plow and reap, but they never do any backward bends to correct for those forward bends. This is just one example of how doing one form of labor—whether it's working in the field or staring at a screen—creates an imbalance within our body and/or mind. Yoga arises as the perfect counterbalance to physical labor and as the perfect metaphor for the construct of both physical and mental "balance." Regardless of your work (unless you're a yogi), most people's bodies are completely unaligned and unbalanced because we work in a very unbalanced way. Whether it's the 10,000 forward bends of the farmer, or the 10,000 hours we spend hunched over our laptops and phones, we must correct that imbalance by mindfully engaging in a practice that stretches our backs backward and realigns our posture and muscles so that we may be appear like the descendant of Homo erectus, as opposed to Homo hunched-overus (a first cousin of Homo nervusus).

Like yardwork, yoga isn't for everyone. I'm just using the term "yoga" as a blanket term to refer to any mindful practice of bodily kinesthetic engagement that counterbalances our engagement in one mode (e.g., yardwork) by engaging in stretches and postures that reverse and realign the body in the opposing direction. In the same vein, for most of us, our right arms, legs, hands, and feet are generally stronger than our left because of the right-handed bias that most of us have (a by-product of our left hemispheric-dominant brains). Yoga practice is designed to balance the body in both the forward-backward and lateral dimensions, but there are other practices not called "yoga" that do the same thing. You can call it whatever you want, but if you don't do it, your body will pay the price in terms of back pain, poor posture, reduced flexibility, stiffness, muscle pain, and other maladies. I do yoga and I like it a lot, but that doesn't mean it's necessarily right for you. I also like yoga as a metaphor because we all intuitively relate the practice to the construct of "balance," which is the central metaphor in this book.

Am I saying that you have to go to yoga class? No, but it couldn't hurt, at least in the beginning, especially if you're a novice. In the previous chapter, I went to some lengths to explain how you can integrate musical expression in your life without suggesting once that you should go to music class or take lessons. Do you have to get a guitar teacher to help you learn guitar if you've never played before? No, but it couldn't hurt. I refer to you in the singular, but you are plural, so I can't give blanket suggestions for everyone for everything. Ultimately, we all need to find ways of engaging that are right for each one of us, which means you will eventually need to become the master of your own mindfulness practice. Does that mean you don't need personal instruction? Not at all. It just depends on who you are and how you work. The point of any mindfulness practice, whether it be media mindfulness, meditation, yoga, or whatever, is self-determination—to become the master of your own mind. How you get there is up to you. More important than how you get there is the *practice* of getting there—the intention of direction and a firm commitment to that intention. As every yoga teacher is required to say at regular intervals, *"It's yoga practice, not yoga perfect."* You may never become Master Yoda, the total master of your mind and all its capacities, and that's OK. As long as you're on the road to getting there, you're on the road to salvation.

Returning to the question *"Do you need to go to yoga class?"* I went to yoga class on and off for about 20 years, sometimes regularly several times a week, sometimes not at all for years. When the pandemic hit, classes were canceled, so I stopped going. When my YoDEM commenced, I knew I had to do yoga to counterbalance all the yardwork and other physical labor and activity I was doing. It occurred to me that if I've been going to yoga class for over 20 years and still haven't mastered the subject yet that I was probably going to class for reasons other than to learn that subject. In other words, after 20 years, I knew how to do yoga. I really didn't need to go to class. Yoga class was more of a security blanket for me, a familiar situation that made me feel comfortable. That's perfectly fine, and there's absolutely nothing wrong with that. For many yoga "students," the practice is a combined interpersonal, intrapersonal/spiritual, and bodily kinesthetic experience. I realized in my YoDEM that for me, at that time in my life, the practice was primarily bodily kinesthetic, which is also perfectly fine. I began practicing yoga at home and found that I liked it more and did it more consistently that way. It's cheaper, there's no schlep, and I also practice a specific type of yoga that's done in a heated room and I prefer to control the heat, so that works out better for me as well. I still go through "dry spells" of not doing yoga for weeks on end, but those are literally "dry" spells because when the weather is dry, I prefer to take my bodily kinesthetic time outdoors in the nice weather. Rainy days are Nature's way of telling me that I should do yoga.

As for you, you can let Nature tell you when to counterbalance and stretch, or you can figure it out for yourself. I can suggest, but I will not prescribe. In addition to finding counterbalances to physical engagement in one direction (the forward bends and muscle exertion of yardwork), through physical engagement in the opposing direction (the backward bends and stretching of yoga), we must also balance our physical engagement in terms of the experience itself. Yardwork, housework, chores, and home improvement are all well and good, but they are work. You must find a physical counterbalance to that work in a physical activity that you do purely for fun. For me, it's trail biking, though I also love regular biking, hiking, and body surfing in the ocean. Those activities work for me but not necessarily for you. You have to find out what works for you for yourself. The main thing is setting your intention and then committing to that intention with action. In other words, **change your behaviors, and your thoughts will follow.**

This book is full of suggestions. I have a specific suggestion, but it's certainly not for everyone. This is something that I do in response to mid- to late-afternoon saturation fatigue to help me balance my engagement in various media and modes of engagement and to facilitate a switch or flip from the deep-focused left hemispheric mode of attending I need for book writing and academic work to the more intuitive, holistic, and grounded way of attending fostered by the right hemisphere. This "mind flip" isn't timed in any way, but it usually feels right at around 4:20 p.m. If this is a suggestion that you're not interested in hearing, please stop reading and skip to the next chapter.

OK, you've been warned.

Stop! You're Smoking Weed Wrong

I was conflicted about writing this section because marijuana is a drug, and like all drugs, it can be misused, overused, or abused. I don't want to suggest that people use a drug that could cause them harm, especially in light of the fact that my negative attitude toward some of the psychopharmaceutical drugs prescribed by psychiatrists has already been expressed in a previous chapter. I'm not a hypocrite. I'm not here to say that some drugs are "good" and others are "bad." I can only speak to my own experience. I am a "recreational" marijuana user and have been, on and off, for over 30 years. I've found wonderful benefits in the proper use of the herb. Just as it would be wrong to suggest something that is potentially harmful, it would also be wrong to not suggest something that is potentially helpful. Furthermore, when I see people using this wonderfully helpful herb in ways that are potentially harmful to themselves, it makes me want to stand up on a platform and shout at the top of my lungs, "*Stop! You're smoking weed wrong!*" So, like it or not, here I go. If you don't like weed and you don't want to learn about its potentially helpful psychoactive effects, then don't smoke it and skip to the next chapter. For those of you who are still reading and especially for those of you who use marijuana, listen.

If you're a "stoner," you're smoking weed wrong.

If you're "self-medicating," you're smoking weed wrong.

If you're smoking to disengage from the world, you're smoking weed wrong.

If you're smoking because you're bored, you're smoking weed wrong.

Now that I've covered the wrong ways to smoke weed, let me explain why these ways are wrong, and also, let me cover the right way to smoke it.

Why Are You Smoking Weed Wrong?

> *Cannabis is one of the safest therapeutically active substances known to man.*
> —Francis Young, DEA Chief
> Administrative Law Judge[3]

In general, I don't suggest that anyone use a drug unless they're intrinsically knowledgeable about what the drug is, where it comes from, how it's made, how to use it, and the history of its use and effects on both the societal and individual levels. For these reasons, I'm able to tentatively suggest the potential use of marijuana, while for the most part, I can only warn people against the use of prescribed psychiatric medications for anxious depression.[4] Let's go through the reasons one by one.

What is a drug like Prozac? Fluoxetine (better known by its trade name Prozac) is a substance created and manufactured by pharmaceutical corporations. You need to be a chemist to understand the chemicals involved in making the drug. You cannot make your own Prozac. You also need to be a neurologist to really understand its effect on the brain, though even neurologists aren't quite sure how it works. Neurologists are aware that the anxiolytic and antidepressant effects of the drug are primarily placebo effects, so nobody really knows what, if any, actual benefits are experienced from the drug itself, not even the psychiatrists who prescribe it, the companies who make it, and especially not the people who take it.

What is marijuana? Marijuana is a plant that's been cultivated by human societies for thousands of years. It's easy to grow, and many people, including myself, grow their own. The psychoactive effects of marijuana, such as stress reduction and mood enhancement, are demonstrably real and have been enjoyed by hundreds of millions of people for thousands of years.

Where does a drug like Prozac come from? Prozac and its cousins are produced by multiconglomerate pharmaceutical corporations, the same companies that have been inculpated in the opioid epidemic, considered by some lawmakers to be a conspiracy to deliberately addict hundreds of millions of people around the world to synthetic opioids via the false marketing of drugs like Oxycontin as "safe and nonaddictive" opioid substitutes. The same companies were responsible for addicting millions of people to amphetamines ("speed") in the mid–20th century, which were marketed as "safe and nonaddictive" "pep pills" or "diet pills." When doctors were forced to stop prescribing amphetamines to their patients for the purpose of weight loss and energy gain, the dearth in the marketplace for "speed" precipitated the invention of synthetic amphetamine—"methamphetamine"—a drug so addictive and harmful that it has afflicted our society like a scourge ever since its invention. Prozac and its cousins are marketed by pharmaceutical companies as "safe and nonaddictive," claims that are patently untrue.

Where does a drug like marijuana come from? It comes from my backyard, where I grow it myself.

How is a drug like Prozac made? Pharmaceutical corporations make it. The process itself is so complicated that you need to be a chemist to understand it, and the drug itself cannot be synthesized outside of a laboratory or produced in quantity outside of a modern pharmaceutical factory. Large parts of the synthesis and manufacturing process are "trade secrets," known only to the chemists and the higher-up executives in the corporations.

How is a drug like marijuana made? I plant a seed in a pot of organic soil, adding rainwater and providing sunlight until it matures. In the late "flowering" phase, I add a teaspoon of organic molasses to the rainwater. When fully mature, I harvest the plants, dry them, and then clip off the buds and cure them in glass mason jars until they're ready to use.

How does a drug like Prozac work? Prozac is an SSRI, which means it blocks the reuptake of the neurotransmitter serotonin in neural synapses, artificially increasing the presence of serotonin in the brain. SSRIs are prescribed to patients in accordance with the theory that anxiety, depression, and other conditions are caused by a deficit of serotonin in the brain. This theory has been thoroughly disproven many times by many researchers. Most people working in the field admit that for the vast majority of people taking SSRIs for mild-to-moderate anxiety and/or depression, the primary benefit they're experiencing is a placebo effect. That means that in terms of a real clinical effect for most patients, Prozac and its cousins don't work at all.

How does a drug like marijuana work? There are two psychoactive chemicals in marijuana: CBD and THC. They both affect the brain and the body by binding to cannabinoid receptors that are located primarily in the brain. Although it's difficult to know exactly what's going on in the brain at any given moment, we know that the THC chemical results in the psychoactive mood elation and other associated symptoms linked with the feeling of being "high." The CBD chemical has no psychoactive effect on cognition, but it does induce a feeling of physical relaxation, linked with the feeling of stress reduction and being "mellow." These are demonstrated effects that have existed in practice for thousands of years. Marijuana works and not by placebo effect, which is why we've been growing and using it for millennia.

What is the history of the use of a drug like Prozac and its effects on both the societal and individual levels? Prozac was synthesized about 50 years ago in a corporation laboratory as a product that could potentially be profitable. Eli Lilly and Company were looking into maximizing product sales by marketing the same drugs they were already manufacturing for new consumers. Specifically, they discovered that their drug, diphenhydramine (better known by its trade name Benadryl), which was marketed as an antihistamine, consistently evoked the side effect of drowsiness. They could profit off that side effect by marketing the same drug under a different name and calling it a "sleep aid." It was that successful double-branding of the same drug that motivated the experimentation that resulted in the synthesis of fluoxetine (Prozac), which was initially marketed toward women exhibiting the symptoms of premenstrual dysphoric disorder (PMM). At the time, this was a controversial condition, not yet accepted as a real "psychiatric disorder" because it transfigured the common physical condition of "premenstrual syndrome" in women into a diagnosable psychiatric condition—essentially translating a physical condition of the body into a neural problem within the brain. In fact, the primary reason why PMM was added to the DSM was due to the pressure that the pharmaceutical corporations placed on the psychiatric industry to market their new drugs. Eli Lilly was criticized vehemently, in fact, for overtly and unethically pressuring the psychiatric industry to create the official diagnosis of PMM and then encouraging psychiatrists and doctors to diagnose the condition broadly and prescribe SSRIs for its treatment. Eli Lilly was justly accused of "inventing the disorder" for its own benefit and then overaggressively marketing their cure for the disorder by advertising it directly to doctors and patients alike in aggressive ad campaigns for prescription drugs whose like had never been seen before but since then have become commonplace.[5] Since then, the pharmaceutical corporations experimented with other populations and found that the predictable placebo effect evoked in women with PMM was also evoked in people complaining of anxiety, depression, and associated maladies. Guess how quickly the same drug was rebranded and remarketed to individually address each of the many syndromes that the placebo effect can moderate? Each newly named drug featured a new and increasingly more aggressive marketing campaign and a new way of capitalizing on our own miseries and fears.

Pharmaceutical corporations have also been severely criticized for marketing SSRIs as being completely safe and harmless when they are clearly not. SSRIs have many side effects and interaction effects which are often quite serious, permanent, and even deadly. *"Serotonin syndrome"* in particular is a *"predictable consequence of excess serotonin on the central nervous system"* caused by the overuse of SSRIs.[6] Symptoms include high blood pressure, increased heart rate, autonomous nervous system agitation including tremors, sweating, diarrhea, as well as dangerously high fevers, seizures, excessive muscle breakdown, and the potentiality of death. Despite all of the unethical practices and criticisms, SSRIs are still being prescribed to hundreds of millions, while the corporations themselves—immune to criticism or government censure—reap record profits each year. If all of this is making you nauseous, by the way, it's probably not media saturation but merely disgust with the level at which the psychiatric and pharmaceutical industries have conspired to not only pathologize every aspect of human behavior and experience but also to profit directly off the everyday pathologization of normality by conspiring to get us all hooked on psychoactive drugs that they prescribe and sell, even as the industries themselves simultaneously lobby the government to keep less harmful and less profitable substances like marijuana illegal to eliminate the competition.

What is the history of the use of marijuana and its effects on both the societal and individual levels? Humans have not been planting, cultivating, and using marijuana for thousands of years just for the hell of it. We've been growing and using marijuana for thousands of years because it gets you high and mellows you out, two effects that have literally been documented for thousands of years and experienced peacefully without fear of overdose, deadly complication, or physiological addiction by hundreds of millions of people. Although, like any substance, marijuana can cause harm because the substance is self-administered, there's far less chance of falling prey to the illusion of the placebo effect or to other harmful effects and conditions that occur when we take a substance that we don't understand and have no control over in terms of origin, production, prescription, acquisition, dosage, or medication regime. In short, **we place ourselves in the role of "victim" when we give over power and control of our own mind and behavior to so-called experts in the psychiatric and pharmaceutical industries**, whom we blindly trust and obey, despite the clear evidence that these industries only exist to profit off our own misery by first convincing us that the problem is in our brains rather than our environments and then by getting us hooked on substances that are functionally no better than the "snake oil" sold by the patent medicine salesmen of old.

The Marijuana Mind Flip

The primary benefit of marijuana (in my honest and humble opinion) is to facilitate a shift in thought processing. Upon ingesting the drug, I immediately sense a change in cognition. I personally relate this change to a shift in hemispheric dominance from left to right. Carl Sagan made the same attribution over 50 years ago in his Pulitzer prize–winning book *The Dragons of Eden* (1977) and also framed it poetically within the following metaphor:

> *Our awareness of right hemisphere function is a little like our ability to see stars in the daytime. The sun is so bright that the stars are invisible.... In the same way, the brilliance of our most recent evolutionary accretion, the verbal abilities of the left hemisphere, obscures our awareness of the functions of the intuitive right hemisphere, which in our ancestors must have been the principal means of perceiving the world.... Marijuana is often described as improving our appreciation of and abilities in music, dance, art, pattern and sign recognition and our sensitivity to nonverbal communication. To the best of my knowledge, it is never reported as improving our ability to read and comprehend Ludwig Wittgenstein or Immanuel Kant; to calculate the stresses of bridges; or to compute Laplace transformations.... I wonder if, rather than enhancing anything, the cannabinols (the active ingredient in marijuana) simply suppress the left hemisphere and permit the stars to come out.*

Marijuana affects the whole brain. Since activation in any neural region could reflect stimulation, inhibition, or disinhibition in that region as related to stimulation, inhibition, or disinhibition in any corresponding region on the other side of the brain, it's often impossible to know with any accuracy what's really going on in either side of the brain. Sagan's hunches about lateralization may or may not have been correct, but the observable effects of marijuana clearly favor right hemispheric ways of attending. My own similar attribution has not yet been verified by neurologists. It may be overstated or even completely wrong, but the *feeling* of being on marijuana certainly corresponds with the "ways of attending" attributed to the right hemisphere by researchers and scholars of the mind and brain such as Iain McGilchrist and his many colleagues.

Sagan published an anonymous essay under the name of "Mr. X" in his colleague Dr. Lester Grinspoon's influential and seminal book *Marijuana Reconsidered* (1971). In the essay, Sagan explains how marijuana helped him get in touch with his artistic and musical sides, as well as how he experienced both interpersonal and intrapersonal insights while "high" and how he experienced more intimate connections with both nature and his body while experiencing the effects of marijuana. Even though he admitted to having the occasional deep insight or "out of the box" idea in his dominant media—linguistic and mathematical—the primary benefits that he noted for himself were found in how marijuana helped broaden him in the areas that were not his dominant media of attention, ways of attending that he'd been repressing, suppressing, and displacing most of his life to focus on science, math, and academic writing.

When I smoke weed, I feel an immediate shift from a focused, calculating, and analytical mindset to a more open, intuitive, and holistic point of view. Rather than seeing my world as a problem in search of a solution, I see my world as an environment in search of an inhabitant—a distanced, discrepancy-minded, problem-solving way of attending shifts to an integrated and integrating way of attending. Rather than focusing on what's wrong, I become more accepting of what's right. If we think of our general way of attending during business hours as left hemispheric in its tendency to narrowly focus on problem-solving tasks, the "flip side" to that mode of attending would be the more holistic and integrating right hemispheric approach. This, in essence, is the "marijuana mind flip." It's just another one of the many examples of "mode flipping" suggested in this book.

On a purely cognitive level, the marijuana flip helps my mind escape the cage of hyperfocus that I deliberately lock myself in for the purpose of work. It frees my thoughts by widening and loosening the associations that I permit my mind to follow and entertain. As a result, my really good ideas (associations) usually emerge shortly after 4:20 p.m.—after I've turned off my computer—as I'm playing the piano or guitar, gardening, biking, or walking Daisy. That's why I always carry a pen and notepad (if I don't forget). Similar experiences are universal, not necessarily attributed to the marijuana flip, but to the switch from conscious focus to unfocused intuition. Intuition is "knowing without thinking," such as having a sudden insight that gives us a new perspective. Wittgenstein noted that our best thoughts always come to us within the context of *"the three Bs: the bed, the bath, and the bus."* The mind, when deeply focused, falls prey to "**inattentional blindness**," the inability to see anything outside of our myopic frame of focus. We're unaware of anything we're not attending to. Flipping to a mindset that's by nature less focused and more open is the key to experiencing the cognitive "breakthroughs" that only come when we're thinking (to recall a tired old cliché) "outside the box." To think outside the box, one must first exit the box. The marijuana flip, I've found, facilitates this necessary box exodus. Marijuana isn't required for this flip or even necessary. I like it, that's why I use it. You don't have to. It's just one of many suggestions.

The "Rules" for Properly Smoking Weed

> *A little learning is a dangerous thing;* **drink deep, or taste not the Pierian spring***: there shallow draughts intoxicate the brain, and drinking largely sobers us again.*
> —Alexander Pope

Sorry to harsh your buzz, dude, but if the notion of "rules" as applied to weed smoking brings you down, don't think of them as "rules" per se. Think of them as guidelines, suggestions, helpful reminders, or as a general philosophy, if that helps. Nevertheless, even though I use marijuana to flip my mind away from the rigid rule-oriented ways of attending, I also need some basic rules to govern my weed smoking so I don't fall victim to the many potentially harmful effects of the drug. The following rules apply directly to the four "wrong" ways of smoking weed listed above.

If You're a "Stoner," You're Smoking Weed Wrong

A "stoner," in my definition, is someone who's stoned most of the time. They don't necessarily smoke a lot, but they start smoking early in the day, way before 4:20 p.m. Why is "4:20" a thing anyway? For most people who work roughly nine-to-five-ish type jobs, 4:20 p.m. is a pretty good time to make the flip. It is for me, at least. If I generally get up before 8:00 a.m. and get busy writing and answering emails and generally doing left hemisphere work by 8:20 a.m., then by 4:20 p.m., I've reached saturation in that mode of thinking. There's literally no point in continuing with that way of working and thinking because I'd just be fighting my own saturation, fighting my own saturation fatigue, fighting my own inhibition energy, fighting an uphill battle against myself. I make sure that I've gotten done everything that absolutely needs to get done that day workwise by 4:20 p.m. so I could go ahead and flip and then transition to other tasks that are more amenable to a right hemispheric approach. I play piano or guitar, do some gardening, walk Daisy, do the dishes, ride my bike, maybe paint a watercolor. You get the idea. More often than not, I get a great idea at around 4:30 p.m., and then I'm right back on the laptop, but now I'm excitedly letting the ideas flow directly out of my brain and onto the screen in a stream of consciousness that I'll edit and revise the next day at around 8:20 a.m. Not all of those ideas are good. Many are just recasts of ideas I've already had or ideas somebody else had, but I forgot; some are silly, some absurd, some make no sense at all, but there's usually an unpolished gem or two in the mix as well—ideas that simply would not have occurred to me if the "doors" of my own cognition had not been wedged open wider.

The 4:20 rule is without a doubt the most important rule when it comes to smoking weed. (Obviously, if you have a different schedule, you should adjust the timing of your own personal 4:20 p.m. in relation to your own personal schedule.) Following the rule means you're using the drug for its most useful effect—the flip from left to right—and all that this flip entails. You're maximizing the worktime for your left hemisphere in the first eight to nine hours of the day, and then you're taking advantage of the physical and psychological benefits of right hemispheric thinking in the latter part of the day. The 4:20 rule promotes efficiency in both your productive work time and in your recreational ("re-create-ional") leisure time—the time when we recreate and reground ourselves through the integrated and holistic approach of the right hemisphere. Most importantly, following the 4:20 rule means you're not a stoner. You're not always stoned, retreating from the world and the stressors within it. To the contrary, you're fully engaged in the world every day, up to the point where you decide that it's time to step back and deliberately disengage for a while until the next day.

The 4:20 rule could be summed up in the notion that there's a time for smoking weed and a time to refrain from smoking weed, regardless of when your "personal 4:20" is set. One good reason to refrain until 4:20-ish is because of the inescapable law of physics: **Whatever comes up, must always come down.** If you get high in the morning, you'll be feeling low on energy by the afternoon—that is, you'll be "coming down" from your high.

You can take a long nap, but if you do that every day, you're productivity will suffer. You can speed yourself up with coffee or cigarettes or other stimulants, but that's a very dangerous cycle of drug dependence to initiate. You can just keep smoking so that you don't actually come down, but then you'll be stoned all day, and so much for productivity and the marijuana mind flip and all of its benefits. No, the easiest, simplest, healthiest, and most balanced way is to simply wait until 4:20 p.m. The wisdom of the ancients has always advised us that all things could be consumed but only in moderation. Moderation of consumption is implicit within the 4:20 rule.

The 4:20 rule also concretizes the very important notion that we should avoid smoking weed when the weed mindset results in inefficiency or frustration. This notion is so obvious that it becomes invisible, and we oversee it. We might say to ourselves, "This task is difficult" or "This task is time consuming," presuming that smoking weed will help us complete the task when it actually makes the task harder. Oftentimes, we presume that it's easier to get through something when we're a bit high when the opposite is true—something we may have learned from experience—but we still go ahead and smoke anyway, ignorantly taking the wrong road to get to the same place just because that road looks more scenic at the moment of decision. *Why follow a mirage that you know from experience is not there? Why fight your Self?* (Sometimes, admittedly, it's because we forget the lessons we learn while on weed, an issue I will address shortly.)

As a rule, 4:20 p.m. tells us to be mindful of when to smoke and when not to smoke, the latter distinction being the more crucial. For instance, I've found that smoking weed before yoga is (somewhat ironically) a very bad idea. Rather than mellowing me out, it throws me off my practice because my mind wanders rather than focusing on the postures. Yoga (at least for me) is not an intuitive state of relaxed unfocused-ness. Just the opposite. Yoga, for me, is an intense period of deep focus on my body and my Self, a one-pointed meditation on "balance" as both a physical goal and a personal quest. Balance has symbolic meaning for me on personal, professional, physical, and spiritual levels, and I meditate on that intensely during yoga. Lately, I've been meditating on how to incorporate the construct of balance into all eight ways of attending to the world, and it occurred to me—during yoga—that I should write a book about it. *Eureka!* I get some of my best logical and entirely self-evident ideas during yoga, and I'm never stoned when I'm doing it. Smoking weed totally throws me off my practice, so I never do it before yoga. (*Afterward*, on the other hand …)

If the purpose of smoking weed is to effect the mind flip from left to right, then what weed provides is contrast facilitation—the quick action of the drug effects a noticeable and stark contrast in our way of thinking before and after 4:20 p.m.—especially as it pertains to left versus right hemispheric thinking. The mind flip is useful only inasmuch as it facilitates this contrast. So let's say it's the weekend, and you don't work on the weekends (*lucky you*). If you're not forcing your mind to engage in the linguistic and mathematical media that causes anxious depression, then you really don't need the contrast of the mind flip because you're most likely doing the things that you find naturally relaxing and pleasing anyway. That means, in your case, you shouldn't smoke on the weekends because the 4:20 p.m. mind flip is only meaningful on workdays. If this applies to you, take a "weed sabbatical" on the weekends and on days when you're not working. A weekly weed sabbatical will establish that you are *not* a stoner, that you're not dependent on weed on a daily basis, and that you are in control of your weed use. If you cannot take a weed sabbatical for even a day, then you need to reconsider the role of weed in your life because you are dependent and possibly psychologically (if not physiologically) addicted to the stuff. If you deliberately refrain from smoking for a day or two on your weekly weed sabbatical (i.e., the weekends), then your mind flip will feel that much better on Monday at 4:20 p.m., I guarantee!

If You're "Self-Medicating," You're Smoking Weed Wrong

Weed is not an antidote for anxious depression. It may take those symptoms away temporarily while using it, but the fact that your anxious depression returns when the drug wears off means that the drug didn't cure anything; it just temporarily dispelled the symptoms. Anxious depression is a product of your media environment. The primary environment—verbal conscious thought—produces the hyperconscious rumination that envelopes your mind in anxious depressive thoughts. Simply flipping the medium of consciousness from left to right does not extract your thought process from the primary environment. You're still in the same environment, engaged in the same medium; you're just experiencing it in a different way. Because smoking weed does not switch your medium—it only flips the mode of that medium from left to right—you're still likely to feel anxious and depressed after smoking weed. It's happened to me many times. I was anxious and depressed, so I smoked weed and sat there, feeling high but still thinking the same anxious depressive thoughts. It's easy to wallow in your own anxious depression when stoned because it doesn't feel as bad as when you're not stoned, but you're still smoking weed wrong. The point of the flip is to use it as a launchpad to dive into another medium of engagement, one that will moderate, redirect, suppress, or stifle the hyperconscious ruminations that cause anxious depression. If you're smoking weed and then sitting idly in a chair or staring at a screen, feasting on the same poisoned thoughts that now taste slightly sweeter, you're not taking advantage of the primary benefits offered by marijuana, and you are most definitely smoking weed wrong.

You're also smoking weed wrong if you're getting too high some or all of the time, or (less likely) if you're not getting high enough. The two active chemicals at work in marijuana—THC and CBD—have different effects. THC gets you high, and you feel it more in your head, as it actively affects your cognitive and perceptive faculties. CBD creates a mellow feeling in your body, but you don't feel it at all in your head. That's why you can buy CBD products at any local convenience store, but you need a medical marijuana card to buy THC products in my state, even though marijuana was legalized quite a while ago. People who use marijuana for medical reasons tend to prefer higher CBD-to-THC ratios. That's because they're using it to manage pain, tension, or stress in their daily lives. They don't want to be high, but the mellow feeling in their body helps them get through their day, with none of the cognitive effects of THC and none of the side effects of commercial pharmaceuticals. Fortunately, you can grow your own strains of marijuana with seeds that are custom cultivated for their ratios of CBD to THC. If you like to get high and also feel mellow (the usual), then grow a plant with a relatively high THC content in proportion to the CBD content. If you want it the other way around, plant the high-CBD low-THC plant. You can even grow plants that have virtually no THC at all. The medical users prefer marijuana that's high CBD, low THC. Recreational users like it the other way around. As a consumer or someone considering becoming a consumer, you should be knowledgeable about the product and understand that there's not just one way to smoke weed. Smoking weed, if you opt for a high-CBD/low-THC variety, doesn't even get you high, and most people who smoke weed nowadays don't even smoke it; they vape it, use edibles, or a dozen other means of ingestion. I personally use a vaporizer with my ground homegrown "flower." I find the vapor less harsh on my throat and lungs, while the medium itself is much cleaner, as the vapor lacks the tar and other unhealthy ingredients found in smoke. So, technically, I don't "smoke" weed at all. If you think weed only gets you high and that there's just one way to do it, *you're definitely "smoking" weed wrong.*

There are two strains of marijuana, indica and sativa. Indica gets you stoned, while sativa gets you high in the sense that it energizes you. Indica is felt more in the head and is more associated with the couch potato effect of just lounging and engaging in media such as TV, video games, music, a good book, and so forth. Sativa is felt more in the body, making you want to go out and do stuff or to just be more physically active. If I choose to take a hit of weed at my 4:20 p.m., I'll opt for a mid-potency sativa with about an even proportion of CBD to THC. This will help facilitate my mind flip without getting me so stoned that I can't be productive and perfectly capable of doing whatever it is I decide to do or anything that might turn up. It will also give me the sort of energized feeling in my body and mind that I want to use as a launchpad into the fun and very active hours I squeeze between finishing my work and sitting down to dinner. After dinner, I'm usually ready for a hit of indica with a higher THC content. Evenings after dinner are a good time to play piano or guitar or maybe paint a bit, maybe take Daisy for a leisurely stroll. Active but mellow active. Eventually, I peter out and it's time to veg out for a while, maybe watch the tube a bit as I hazily descend into sleep. It's optional, but a tiny little bit of the ol' high-THC-content indica often hits the spot right about then. It helps keeps my thought process away from the anxious depressive ruminations about tomorrow that cause insomnia and sleep deprivation and puts me on the right track, a winding road descending peacefully down to dreamland. Maybe, as a friend suggested, I should change my name to William Indica?

Now, some people say that the difference between the indica and sativa strains aren't real and that the whole phenomenon persists as a meme via the power of suggestion—that is, a placebo effect. I'm quite certain that the energizing effect of my 4:20 sativa hit is turbocharged by my concurrent third and final cup of coffee for the day, but I also believe in the indica-sativa distinction, be it chemistry or myth. If it's a placebo effect, so be it. The placebo effect, after all, has always been and will always remain the most consistent and universal effect in all pharmacology and the primary active effect in the vast majority of substances prescribed or taken for anxious depression. In other words, *mind over matter.*

If You're Smoking to Disengage from the World, You're Smoking Weed Wrong

> *The basic thing nobody asks is why do people take drugs of any sort? Why do we have these accessories to normal living to live? I mean, is there something wrong with society that's making us so pressurized, that we cannot live without guarding ourselves against it?*
>
> —John Lennon

We all need to disengage at one point of the day, to step back, "depressurize," stop stressing about time as duration, stop self-commoditizing, to stop "doing" for a moment and just "be." That's an important moment, and we must respect that moment. I respect that moment by ingesting an herb that certain cultures have worshipped as a sacrament for thousands of years as an "entheogen."[7] Disengagement must and should occur, but that's just step one. Step two (vastly more important) is *reengagement*.

Reengagement in the world is accomplished either by switching from one medium (likely to be linguistic and/or mathematical) to another or by flipping one's mode of engagement (such as receptive) to another (such as expressive). Flipping from writing emails to reading a novel, for instance, is a mode flip from expressive to receptive. Disengagement from email writing is a step in a process, not a process in and of itself. If you don't complete the process via reengagement (picking up the novel), then you're missing the entire point, and you're definitely smoking weed wrong. **"Drink deep, or taste not the Pierian spring!"**

You may be under the wrong impression that the function of weed is to mellow you out so you can disengage, veg out, and do nothing when the real function of weed is to energize you so you can reengage in something fun and creative, or at least something that's satisfying or recreative. Part of the problem may be when you smoke. Admittedly, 4:20 p.m. is a down time, a time of low energy, a time when both saturation nausea and saturation fatigue are at their peaks. We need a break, and we naturally think that a "break" entails prolonged disengagement. Wrong again. A "break" entails momentary disengagement, followed soon after by active reengagement. Because we're tired and burned out, we use 4:20 p.m. as an excuse to veg out and do nothing the rest of the day and the night, in which case, you're definitely smoking weed wrong. Four twenty is the time to redirect your energies, not to quash them. Be mindful of your saturation nausea and saturation fatigue at 4:20 p.m., and balance your engagement by switching your media environment. Don't just turn off your computer and smoke weed. Turn off your computer, grab a snack or maybe a cup of tea or small coffee to help reenergize yourself for the next part of your daily adventure, go outside if possible, take a deep breath of fresh air, set up your next medium of engagement, and then smoke weed as a deliberate means of launching off into your next escapade. You'll be surprised at how much energy you have after 4:20 p.m. once you change your media environment, and you'll be surprised at how much your mood changes as a result of changing your behaviors within that environment (and not just as a result of smoking weed). *Change your behaviors, and your thoughts will follow.* Smoking weed can be the catalyst for change, but it does not constitute change in and of itself. If you think it does, then you're definitely smoking weed wrong.

"Temporal distortion," the feeling that time is being stretched out or distended, is a common side effect of marijuana, and I believe it's a crucial aspect of its appeal. In our extremely myopic perspective, any sense of time not governed by the construct of time as duration is perceived as "distorted." This is a bias that does us undeniable harm. Weed can help. "High time" is different from "time as duration." "4:20" has become a symbol for marijuana use, which is unfortunate because embedded within the symbol itself is a direct reference to time as duration, one of the anxiety-inducing constructs that marijuana is supposed to help us overcome. By fostering a focus on the present moment rather than the future, smoking weed reduces my chronic impatience, which is just another form of time anxiety. If used properly, marijuana can help break the chains that lock our minds in the temporal prison cell of time as duration.

I find it interesting that when my mind is locked into the left hemispheric work mode of maximum efficiency, I experience time as duration as a sense of time compaction, a constant feeling of dread that time is running out. However, when I flip to the right hemispheric recreational mode facilitated by marijuana, my sense of time expands and extends, giving me the feeling that time is stretching out. My guess is that "temporal distortion" is not purely the effect of marijuana, but rather, it's the effect of the stark **contrast in our perception of time** from the left hemispheric mode in which our sense of time as duration is artificially condensed to the right hemispheric mode in which our sense of time is untethered from the construct of duration and therefore felt more fully and more freely than before. Hence the "temporal distortion" attributed to the marijuana high is merely the feeling of **temporal freedom,** attained once our sense of time is liberated from the construct of duration.

If You're Smoking because You're Bored, You're Smoking Weed Wrong

Marijuana mindfulness is about being aware of how the drug affects your body, brain, and mind. Even more important, it's about being aware of how the drug interacts with your media environment. Marijuana's anxiolytic and antidepressant effects are well known. If you're smoking weed to reduce your anxious depression, that's fine, but that's just the first step. Reducing or masking the symptoms of anxious depression is the drug's **"negative effect,"** the thing it takes away from your mind and behavior. The negative effect is real but temporary. Your anxious depression will return once your mind recovers from the curveball it was pitched by the ingestion of a psychoactive substance. That's because your anxious depression comes from your media environment, not your mind, and certainly not from the substances that alter your mind. If you smoke weed and stay stuck in your toxic media environment, you'll just be high and anxious at the same time, concurrently stoned and depressed. The high takes the edge off anxious depression for sure, but is that all you want, an edgeless anxious depression? That's why the second step is 1,000 times more important than the first. In fact—and this is the gospel truth—*you must not take the first step unless you are already prepared to take the second step.*

The first step is dangerous because it offers the illusion of anxiety and depression relief, but it's really just taking the edge off. People get stuck in that first step, complacent with feeling high and stoned and therefore only vaguely anxiously depressed rather than acutely anxiously depressed. Satisfied with just the negative effect, they never bother with invoking the positive effect—the thing the substance *adds* to your mind and behavior—possibly because they're unaware of the existence of both a negative and positive effect in the first place (they are, after all, just metaphors). Many if not most people self-diagnose their anxious depression as "boredom," and then they self-medicate with marijuana, fooling themselves into thinking that the marijuana relieves their boredom when, in fact, it just takes the edge off. The only way to cure "boredom" or "anxious depression" is to change your media environment and engage your body and mind in activities that disengage your mind from the hyperconscious rumination that generates anxious depressive thought. *Change your behaviors, and your thoughts will follow.* That's where the "positive effect" of marijuana comes in.

The marijuana mind flip opens wide the "doors of perception" and of cognition as well. It can and has been used as a launchpad into more intuitive, imaginative, and creative media of engagement. Take advantage of the creative juices that marijuana can help make flow, and plan out the ways you will channel the positive effects of the marijuana flip *before* you smoke weed. By taking advantage of both the negative and positive effects of marijuana, you realize the maximized benefits of the drug as it affects you, and more important, you realize the full potential of your Self as it is affected by the drug and beyond.

One reason why marijuana is often misused as a cure for boredom is because it helps turn a mindless task into a mindful one. Walking the dog, doing the dishes, mowing the lawn—these are tasks we avoid because they seem stupid, boring, and mindless; therefore we pay someone else to do them, or we pawn the chores off on others because each moment of our time as duration is too precious to waste on such mindless and meaningless chores. Smoking weed helps release us from the prison cell of anxious depressive thought in which each minute is calculated in terms of a profit or loss, and there's not a second to spare for anything that doesn't earn a dollar. Walking the dog becomes a walking meditation on life, washing the dishes becomes a standing meditation on the Self, and mowing the lawn becomes a moving meditation on Nature. The positive effects of marijuana naturally lead our mind in the right direction, which is away from itself, away from the bottomless dark pond of narcissistic self-reflection that it loves to wallow in. The positive effects of marijuana, when acknowledged and properly employed, help to redirect our behaviors away from narcissistic or anxiety-driven pursuits, and I think you may remember what follows when we change our behaviors.

It's also quite likely that you may be getting *too high*. When a substance is illegal, users tend to use the substance in ways that are less than ideal. They're limited to whatever they can get, which is likely to be too potent, and because supply may be irregular, there's a tendency to binge when you have some and abstain when you don't have any. For marijuana, that's a bad pattern because cannabinoids have very high lipid solubility, so they are absorbed in the fat molecules in our body and persist there for long periods. A common occurrence is for people to not get high the first few times they smoke. That's because it takes a while for the cannabinoid lipids to reach a high enough concentration in the body for the high to be felt. However, once that concentration is reached and surpassed, the body actually needs much less cannabinoids to feel the effect. In practice, that means the more often you smoke, the less you need to smoke to get high. So if you smoke weed almost every day, you really don't need to smoke very much at all. As they used to say, *"a dab'll do ya."*[8] In short, if you smoke every day and you also smoke a lot, you're most probably smoking too much weed. Personally, I find two to three hits of a quarter teaspoon of vaporized ground flower per day is just fine (one at my personal 4:20 p.m. for that day, the other after dinner, and the last, maybe, as a nightcap). Needless to say, somedays I don't smoke at all, especially if I'm not engaging in work that requires a mind flip.

It's also true that the older you get, the less you need to smoke to get high because of the changes in the body that increase the relative potency of most substances as we age. So if you're an old fart like me, but you still smoke like you're in your 20s, you're probably smoking too much weed. Another fact is that there are strains sold in dispensaries that are much more potent than the strains available in previous decades, so you may be smoking very little but still getting too high. You may be smoking too frequently as a nervous habit. You need to be mindful of what you're doing and not just smoke because it's there or because you can't think of anything better to do. *How high do you need to be, for Pete's sake?* You may be smoking the wrong strain in general. If you're feeling like a couch potato, try switching to a sativa strain or to a strain with less THC. You may be smoking the wrong strain at the wrong time. I prefer sativa in the afternoon because it energizes and indica in the evening because it sedates, so you may want to be more mindful of which strains you're smoking and when—something that would've been very difficult to do when marijuana was illegal. Sometimes being high in and of itself leads to getting too high. Here are some tips for that:

1. If you can't remember if you smoked weed or not, you smoked weed.
2. If you can't tell if you're high enough, you're high enough.
3. If you're smoking from a bong any bigger than an old-fashioned glass bottle of Coca-Cola, you're using a sledgehammer when a rubber mallet will do. Do you really need to smoke out of that three-foot bong, or could something smaller, cleaner, and healthier suffice, like a vaporizer for ground homegrown flower?

One final and excessively important rule about the 4:20 rule is that the rule is a prohibition, not a commandment. **"Thou shalt *not* smoke weed before your own personal 4:20"** is a prohibition that shalt be obeyed. "Thou shalt smoke weed at 4:20," however, is not a real command, and should never be obeyed. Don't smoke weed just because you think it's "time to smoke weed." Don't smoke weed just because you're accustomed to doing so at 4:20 p.m. or at any other time. If you do so, you're falling into the habit of the stoner—smoking out of habit—rather than mindfully smoking for the purpose of balance. If you don't want to smoke, don't do it. How do you know when it's *not* time to smoke, even if it's your personal 4:20 p.m.? Trust your intuition. If the thought of getting high evokes even the tiniest hint of nausea or fatigue, immediately interpret that as saturation nausea or saturation fatigue, and refrain from smoking weed. I promise you, not only will you not regret that choice, but you'll appreciate the fact that you personally decided you didn't want to get high just because it was 4:20 p.m. In other words, the master of the environment was not the medium of the marijuana high or the medium of time as duration embedded in the 4:20 symbol. The master of the environment was you, not the media that envelopes you. By mindfully deciding what sense of balance you need in that moment, you establish yourself as the undisputed master of your environment, your behaviors, your mind, and your Self.[9]

Short-Term Memory Loss

> *Blessed are the forgetful, for they get the better even of their blunders.*
>
> —*Nietzsche*

Short-term memory loss is an observable side effect of the marijuana high. Side effects are bad, right? Not necessarily. The side effect of the antihistamine diphenhydramine is drowsiness. Pharmaceutical companies have made billions by marketing the negative side effect of the drug (inability to stay awake) as a primary positive effect of the same drug (increased ability to fall asleep). Lemonade out of lemons. A negative effect can be a positive effect if viewed through the proper lens.

In general, when neurologists speak of "deficit," it's presumed to be a bad thing. However, the disruption of short-term memory facilitated by marijuana may be the key feature of how the drug works to redirect the focus of consciousness from future to present. I've often had the experience of being worried about something, then after smoking marijuana, I soon realize that I'd forgotten what I was worried about. It's not that I completely forgot about it—the concern was still in my long-term memory where it should be—but in terms of my short-term memory, which is basically the gas tank for my working memory or consciousness, both the concern and the anxiety associated with it are gone. When short-term memory is delayed so that thoughts in working memory fade more quickly, it makes room in our consciousness for new thoughts to come in. At the same time, it helps us escape the vicious circle of ruminative thoughts that we perseverate on even though that perseveration does nothing to "solve the problem"; it just keeps our minds spinning in circles, hovering perpetually over a perceived problem that doesn't necessarily exist in reality and therefore doesn't actually have a solution. The marijuana high and its forgetfulness effect releases us from the repetitive loop of perseverative ruminative thought. The "absent-minded" marijuana user does, quite literally, forget her troubles, at least for a while, and that's OK.

The "absent-mindedness" of the marijuana high must not be conflated with mindlessness. It's no coincidence that the cultural acceptance and usage of marijuana over the past half century has increased in perfect tandem with the advances in digital media technology that drive the information age. Marijuana is the drug of choice in the information age because it helps our brain deal with the daily problem of information overload and hyperconscious rumination. In an age of information overload, we crave mindlessness as an escape, but it's the opposite of mindlessness—*mindfulness*—that will enable us to recognize the patterns of experience that will relieve our overburdened and overloaded minds. Through mindfulness and media balancing, we can get our minds and our brains in sync, working together on the same page. That's when you'll see the true long-term benefits of marijuana mindfulness. We as a species have voted to legalize marijuana across the country and increasingly around the world because we as a species—struggling to survive within the maelstrom of total information overload—recognize its utility as an aid to mindfully reducing symptoms of the anxious depression evoked by our toxic media environments. Mindful marijuana users (ironically) don't smoke as much weed as other users because the cognitive effects of the drug are fostered and sustained by the users' purposeful and reflective experience of those effects.

YoDEM to ODEM

My YoDEM was a behavioral thought experiment on the effect of balancing my media engagement. In that year, I gave up being a full-time specialist who functioned primarily in linguistic and logical-mathematical media in favor of being a generalist who spread his functionality quite deliberately across the eight media of thought in Gardner's model. Admittedly, I found mixed success. My plumbing work as a whole was mediocre at best (except, of course, for the kitchen sink). I made a ton of mistakes, but I learned from them and stumbled upon some interesting paradoxes and ironies that only experience can teach you, though I'm doing my best to relay them to you in this book.

The psychological results were an unmitigated success, with one reservation. I was definitely happier and in better physical, psychological, and emotional condition than I had been for a very long time, perhaps ever. I enjoyed each day to the fullest, and the balancing of my media inspired me to write this book in the hope that it might inspire you. My reservation about the experiment is in its applicability to the average person in an average year. Even in the midst of my YoDEM, I knew it couldn't last. I didn't even call it a "YoDEM" until 18 months had passed and the pandemic was still happening—nothing that I or anyone else would've predicted. How many times in your life are you tied to your home for many months at a time with some work to do but not much and all of it online. Rarely does anyone have that much "free time," and I was painfully aware of that and tried to maximize its use. Not knowing how long it was going to last kept a bit of a fire burning beneath my rump too, which helped. Also, I can't assume that the average reader will have access to all the "things" I had access to, with "things" being inclusive of anything the reader can imagine. As always, the best I can do is provide a metaphor that you may be able to relate to. I'm hoping that YoDEM as a symbol of media mindfulness and balance may resonate with you and that you can interpret that symbol into your life as you see fit.

A year is a long time, especially when there's no pandemic or quarantine to keep you stuck at home all the time. I suggest starting with a

DoDEM—a day of doing everything myself. If that works out, try stretching it to a week (WoDEM), and then a month (MoDEM), and maybe then you go can for the full YoDEM. If, after a YoDEM or two, you're still doing everything yourself, you may consider yourself a full-blown ODEM—one who does everything myself. If you're at that level of self-determination and you're also doing the marijuana mind flip, then you must integrate this one final bit of advice, from one gardener to the next: *Grow your own.*

CHAPTER EIGHT

Visual-Spatial Media
Addiction and Counterbalance

Make no mistake: we are dependent on image-technology; and the better the tech, the harder we're hooked.
—David Foster Wallace[1]

I was a "latchkey kid," and I got hooked on TV early in life. Television was my babysitter, my companion, my good friend, my safety zone, my security blanket, and my primary "window" to the world. (I was unaware then that all media are mirrors, not windows.) It took me about 10 years to realize I had a problem with TV, and it took me about 45 years to realize that my problem was related to the window/mirror illusion embedded in all media. In its day, TV was the biggest mirror the world had ever seen, though it's now merely one of the prime elements within the entire gamut of entertainment media that's being subsumed by digitality, along with film, music, news, and so forth. When I read David Foster Wallace's insightful essay about his own TV addiction, "E Unibus Pluram: Television and U.S. Fiction" (1993), I immediately felt a kindred spirit, who was able to express both the allure and the shame of being a TV addict.

A novelist by trade, Wallace was, indeed, a media psychologist. The combined fascination and terror of the insidious effects of the media of words and broadcast images on the psyche of the average American was a leitmotif in his work. I feel that Wallace understood TV far better than McLuhan, who, after all, grew up many years before television was even a thing. McLuhan's dichotomization of media into "hot" and "cool" categories never resonated with me, and I don't even really agree with his labeling of TV as a "cool medium." Even though I do "get it," I feel that McLuhan was an outsider looking in when it came to TV, an excessively literate theorist peering through the living room window of society at the kids huddled around the glowing blue box and commenting as if he were an anthropologist observing an exotic and primitive tribe with whom he could not personally relate. Wallace, however, was like me. He grew up on TV, just like me. He grew emotionally dependent on TV at an early age, just like me. TV sucked him in and he became a part of it, and TV became a part of him, just like me. So now I will lean on Wallace's words to project an insider's account of TV addiction, coming to you straight from inside the box, *right after this important message from our sponsors.... Stay tuned!*

The Window/Mirror Illusion

> *Television, from the surface on down, is about desire.*
> —David Foster Wallace

Wallace gets to the heart of the issue when he boils down the allure of TV to "desire." We're all searching for something: love, company, security, distraction, engagement, or even a friend. TV sucks that desire into itself and, in the process, sucks in the viewer. We consume TV because we have an appetite for other people. TV consumes us for exactly the same reason. The more we sate our appetites for other people by gorging on the people in the box, the more TV consumes our time and attention, providing us with the illusion of what we desire but not with the real thing that will actually sate our desire. The process then becomes a positive feedback loop. We crawl into the box because we want company. Inside the box, we feel accompanied, but our companionship and our companions themselves are an illusion. The more we stay in the box, the more connected we get to the illusion, the more dependent on it we become, and the more disconnected we become from the real people and places outside of the box. The more truly disconnected we become, the more we rely on TV to feel connected. Although TV does not provide what we truly desire, it emits a glow of hope that we can attain it because we see the reflections of people inside the box who do have love, company, friends, and all that would make us happy. Our desire is to crawl into that box and snuggle up closely with our TV friends and lovers with whom we share "**parasocial relationships**" that are in no way real. At the same time, those parasocial relationships seem more real than our real relationships with real people, who are often unavailable, undependable, unaccepting, and unpresent. TV is always there, though. Always accepting, always available, always reliable in the illusion it projects. No matter what time of the day or night, you can crawl into that box and find a "friend."

> *Whether I'm "passive" or "active" as a viewer ... my real dependency here is not on a single show or a few networks any more than the hophead's is on the Turkish florist or the Marseilles refiner. My real dependence is on the fantasies and the*

images that enable them, and thus on any technology that can make images ... fantastic. Make no mistake: we are dependent on image-technology; and the better the tech, the harder we're hooked.

Once again, Wallace breaks it down to the core element. The images media engage us in are fantasies. The appeal is that the fantasies are not the fantasies of the TV show producers or of the TV show characters; they are *our* fantasies—sucked in by the tube and projected back to us in images that are uncannily familiar in the way that Narcissus's reflection seemed uncannily familiar to him. It's the uncanniness of seeing our own fantasies reflected and projected back to us that keeps us not just engaged but entranced, mesmerized by what is both us and not us. Numbed and hypnotized by our own reflections, we sit glued to the screen. We are fixed in place by the box which is also a "fix," the "*narcissus narcosis*" (to borrow McLuhan's term) of oblivious self-addiction.

Television, in Wallace's view, is not just addictive; it's "*malignantly addictive*" because "*it offers itself as relief from the very problems it causes.*" Like a cancer, it grows, feeding on its host as its host feeds on it. "*The cycle,*" as Wallace explained, "*is self-nourishing.*" Like Ouroboros, the serpent swallowing its own tail, the consumer continually consumes himself. His hunger is staid but never sated. As the "*substitute for something nourishing and needed,*" TV provides us with an illusory meal, a "naked lunch" of our own reflected desires, so that the "*original hunger,*" never satisfied yet never unattended, "*subsides to a strange objectless unease.*" Like Erysichthon of old, punished with eternal hunger by the goddess Demeter, we continue to feed blindly and mindlessly on ourselves until we're entirely consumed. The television binge doesn't end until the entire series is over, leaving us in a pit of our own shameful self-indulgence, a "show-hole" of our own wasted time and energies. The hole itself represents the bottomless pit of emotional need we're addressing in watching the show and the glaring evidence that despite the countless hours of watching, to our shame, we're no closer to true connection than we were before. The show-hole is a shameful recognition of our own dashed hopes, the fisherman rowing home empty-handed because there was no worm on his hook to begin with.

As a "cool medium," TV does not require interaction because "*it engages without demanding.*" Because we can watch for eternity, with nothing expected in return but our blank blind gaze, we fall victim to our own passivity, our own petty desire for satisfaction without effort.

My personal TV addiction ended in early adolescence. The process was fairly simple. At a certain point, I got sick of TV. It was merely the saturation principle at play. It's fortunate for us that saturation does exist, though it may be harder for people nowadays to reach a point of saturation in any one medium since digital media has subsumed all other media, providing not only infinite content but a wide variety of media in which content can be delivered. In my case, I just got disgusted with TV (saturation nausea), finding it, at last, to be stupid and insipid and boring. I'm very glad that I intuitively interpreted my feeling of saturation correctly and that I responded to it correctly as well. In response to my long stage of dormancy in passive television watching, I was craving media that was more expressive, active, and engaging. That's when I began writing, a medium that requires reading just as a car requires fuel, so I became a reader as well. I also became obsessively interested in music, beginning with a period of intense listening that eventually flipped into a compulsion to learn how to play music myself. In short, my TV addiction culminated in saturation, at which point, I switched over to other more expressive media—media that had been displaced by my TV addiction—but were now the lifeline that I used to pull myself out of the magical box of fantastic illusions. I returned to TV later in life, as an adult who was not only able to put limits on his TV watching but who was also well acquainted with the siren call emanating from within the box. Having been a total TV junkie, I now know that TV has nothing to offer me beyond the reflections of my own dreams, and I know better than to seek something real in a box that projects illusion.

Flipping Visual-Spatial Media

> Many video games involve multiple lines of action, increasing speed, and increasing rate of increasing speed. These aspects are all foreign to the one-thing-at-a-time, one-thing-after-another, and take-time-to-think world of reading.
> —Joshua Meyrowitz[2]

For many of us, our visual-spatial media engagement is the least balanced, as we tend to watch TV and movies, play games, and surf the internet for images and clips but rarely create our own visuals. We perseverate in the receptive mode and neglect the expressive mode. It would be wise and beneficial to balance each hour of passive/receptive visual-spatial media consumption with an hour of active/expressive production. Paint a watercolor, create a collage, arrange some flowers from your garden. Not only is it fun and liberating to create one's own visual media; it feels good to use physical materials for a change—paint, paper, brushes, canvas—instead of interacting with virtual images on digital screens, as most of us do most of the time. Obviously, if you could integrate some create expressive visual art in your work, you'd be increasing both your efficiency and productivity, while making work more fun.

When I started teaching as a professor, for example, I was completely "old school." Blackboard and chalk, handwritten notes on the lectern, the occasional transparency slide. A traditional lecture is an overwhelmingly linguistic and/or logical-mathematical affair. Professor speaks and writes on the blackboard; students listen and take notes. And then, if the professor is any good at their job, students speak, and professor and other students listen. When visual aids are offered, they're typically in the form of written words or logical symbols etched or projected onto a sheet, board, or screen. As the medium of teaching moved toward digital slideshows, I found myself obliged to update my approach. I also found that the slideshow presentations provided by my textbook publishers were too dull because they were simply words copied from the book and pasted into slides. The enhancement provided by a digital slideshow is the ability to provide visual aids that complement the words of the lecture. A visual aid that merely displays the same words is redundant and no enhancement whatsoever. Words on a slide accompanying a lecture can hardly even be considered a "visual aid" because nothing is being visualized. The words printed on the slide provide no aid to understanding the same words being spoken by the lecturer; they merely accentuate specific words graphically so students know to write them down in their notes. (Clever students now know to ask their professors to post their slides on the class web page, so they don't even need to take notes, and they probably don't need to attend class either, as all the words they need to know for the tests will most likely be on those slides.)

It was clear to me, at least, that the enhancement provided by a digital slideshow is that ideas could be presented nonlinguistically using images and videos as examples or demonstrations. When an idea being presented linguistically in a lecture is also presented visually using an image (rather than a word), associations are created in the student's mind that are much stronger than if they'd been made in one medium of engagement alone because the brain is now processing that idea in a lot more locations, fostering more neurological connections, resulting in better learning. Put more simply, "a picture tells a thousand words." So I began creating my own slideshows, and that process made a world of difference. I gradually transformed each of my very boring handwritten lectures into slideshows that, by design, had as few words as possible. My slides are image-based. When lecturing, I try to evoke the feeling of a narrated film in which the words I speak are expressed visually in the images on the slides, though unlike a movie, I include prompts for questions to engage students in discussion. As a result, the very boring and monotonous linguistic task of updating my lecture notes has become a fun and interesting visual-spatial task. It's quite fun finding new and interesting images to represent my lecture words visually in ways that are naturally more colorful and creative than words alone and then arranging them nicely on the slides. It's the art of the montage and collage within an intellectual frame. Now I enjoy working on my lectures rather than hating it; I enjoy delivering my lectures rather than dreading them. And my students ... well, let's just say I didn't know how bad a professor I was until I actually became a pretty good one. What changed wasn't me; it was my media and my understanding of how to use them.

Similarly, video games, when used correctly, can provide the perfect balance to purely linguistic media engagement. In terms of neurological balancing, linguistic and mathematical media are so overwhelmingly left hemispheric dominant that extended engagement in a right hemispheric task following school would fulfill the function of a necessary counterbalance.

> Just as the left hemisphere of the brain has, over the course of evolution, been selected as the pre-eminent site for linguistic processing, the right hemisphere of the brain, and in particular the posterior portion of the right hemisphere, proves to be the site most crucial for spatial (and visual-spatial) processing.[3]

A child who spends all day reading, writing, and listening to lessons in school will naturally want to engage herself in an activity that's nonliterate, nonlinguistic, nonlogical-mathematical, interactive rather than passive, expressive rather than receptive, and fast-paced rather than slow and methodical. Denying a child video games after school is denying her the counterbalance to school studies that her mind and brain desperately need. Obviously, a game of real football with real other kids in the real outdoors is also a perfectly good counterbalance, probably much better than video games, but my point is that video games can have a positive balancing effect for both children and adults who spend so much of their days focusing on words and words alone.

The "Rearview Mirror"

> We look at the present through a rear-view mirror. We march backwards into the future.
> —Marshall McLuhan

We tend to devalue anything that's not directly related to productivity. Our Puritan/capitalist work ethic urges us to use every moment to either make money or to learn how to make money. When we see a child reading books and doing homework, we say, "*Now, there's a kid who's going to get ahead in the world.*" When we see a child playing video games, we think to ourselves, "*There's a kid who's going nowhere.*" This type of thinking is doubly myopic. First, we know that the brain is not a machine that can function in one medium indefinitely without the need for balancing media of engagement. If a child is focusing on linguistic and mathematical media all day long at school and all night long at home, her productivity is likely to be rather poor because most of her mental energy is spent fighting saturation fatigue. The productivity paradox tells us that the more balanced her intellectual processes as a whole, the more productive she will be because she'll be maximizing her mental energies rather than draining them. We win more battles when we stop fighting ourselves, but we don't know that we're actually fighting ourselves until we cut it out.

For example, everybody knows that if you have a big exam in the morning that you absolutely must ace, you should stay up all night cramming, right? In fact, empirical studies have demonstrated clearly that students who review the materials once and then get a good night's sleep do exponentially better on the exams than students who stay up all night reviewing the materials again and again and again. The notion that we learn by repetition is a falsehood that we learned at school because the falsity, ironically, was drilled into us again and again and again. Ironically, we learned by repetition that we learn by repetition, but the lesson is wrong. If anything, *we learn by doing*, which is antithetical to the way that most learning takes place in schools. We also learn by observation, if we give those observations the time and space to sink in, even if that time and space is in our sleep. We also learn better when the stimulus being observed is inherently interesting and engaging—like a video game—as opposed to inert little black ink marks on a white page.

The second reason why we devalue video games while overvaluing homework and schoolwork is because "*we look at the present through a rear-view mirror.*" As parents, we learned that the skills that will get you ahead in the world lay in the linguistic and logical-mathematical fields of study. That was true for us and for our parents and for our parents' parents, but it's unlikely to be true for our kids. A "rearview mirror," as McLuhan pointed out, is completely useless when traveling at the speed of light. We live in a digital world now, a world in which information travels at the speed of light, and the skills required for a digital world are different than the ones required for a postindustrial world. The skills required for the worker of tomorrow rely heavily on quick response time, hand-eye coordination, and pattern recognition. The worker of tomorrow will need to be able to connect lots of different information together from lots of different media sources in all forms of media content, and because the digital world functions at the speed of digital information—the speed of light—they need to do it all incredibly quickly, so quickly in fact that they will rely more on their intuition and pattern recognition faculties rather than on highly analytical, theoretical, and incredibly slow methods of information processing that are learned in school. In short, kids today are preparing for the work of tomorrow by playing video games. Time in school is largely misspent. When playing a video game like the interactive online team game *Fortnite*, a child is mastering cutting-edge technology while also mastering the process of collaborating with partners remotely while focused intently on a group project that is being completed in real time. What useful skill, other than literacy, does the child actually learn to master in school?

Mindful Gaming

> What mindfulness disrupts is mindlessness—that is, being mindlessly involved without realizing that that is what one is doing. It is only in this sense that the observation changes what is being observed.
> —Varela, Thompson, & Rosch[4]

Games reel us in because they're fun and entertaining and extremely engaging—so engaging, in fact, that we become immersed, finding it difficult to recognize the telltale signs of saturation nausea and/or saturation fatigue, our brain's way of telling us that we need to switch or flip our media. Children are at most risk for becoming "addicted" to digital media in general and video games in particular because they have very little if any personal experience with saturation. They don't know what saturation feels like, they don't know what it is, and they don't know what to do about it. Rather than telling our kids to stop playing video games and finish their homework, we should speak with them about the issues of saturation and media displacement and help them learn how to mindfully balance their own media. Taking control over their media by pulling the plug does them a disservice because the primary challenge of their generation will be media self-management, so they need to learn it for themselves as early as possible. That single subject is exponentially more important than anything our kids can learn at school. In fact, the subject of media self-management should be taught in school as a practicum for a necessary skill rather than overloading them with content (facts and figures) that they will immediately forget after the exams. Kids need video games as a counterbalance to the toxic media environment of school that they're imprisoned in during the day. Video games, for most kids, are an escape hatch from the linguistic and mathematical media they're overdosed with at school, as well as a connection to their friends and, most important, as a means of experiencing something as a master—an opportunity to be completely in charge of their minds and their media. This is something precious that they rarely get but sorely need, and we shouldn't take it away from them.

If you could teach your kids the basic principles of media saturation and displacement and how to mindfully apply the basic tenets of media balancing to their lives on their own, you will be giving them the wonderful gift of media mastery, which they will need and depend on for the rest of their lives. I've reached the point of media mindfulness where I'm extremely sensitive to how any given medium is making me feel so that the instant I feel frustrated or tense while doing something that should be fun and relaxing, I immediately stop. I'll stop playing in the middle of a game, even if I'm doing well (though usually, it's when I'm losing) because if a game is no longer being experienced as fun, it's perfectly appropriate to stop playing. The impetus to keep going just to finish the round or to get to a certain score or level reveals the tendency for us to get stuck in activities simply because we've been ingrained with certain rules, such as "Finish what you started," or "Don't be a quitter," or "High scores are for winners; low scores are for losers." We pretend while we're playing that the game is important because it's more fun that way, but then we get wrapped up in the fantasy and continue playing even beyond the point of saturation just because our anxious depressive mind is perseverating on a certain number such as your score or your completion time or your ranking. We forget that all of that stuff is meaningless.

It's like going to a casino and playing with chips. While you're in the casino, the chips are all important because they measure how well you're playing the games, and on a basic existential level—for a person gambling in a casino—the chips tell you whether, at that moment, you're a winner or a loser. We invest a lot of mental energy into those chips as well as a lot of time and money. (*That's how they get you.*) However, even if you do well and manage to have some chips left when you're finally done gambling, if you leave the casino and try to buy a sandwich with a chip, you're out of luck because guess what? Those chips are meaningless when you're not playing the game. And so too, all those high scores and rankings seem beyond important when playing the game, but they're truly meaningless the moment you stop. If children could learn to understand that, and if they could learn to turn off their games immediately as soon as it feels a little bit not fun anymore, and if they can shut off the game in the middle of playing regardless of their score or position in the game, they will be displaying a level of media mindfulness and balancing that most adults couldn't even comprehend (presuming they didn't read this book).

A lot of the time "wasted" on video games is the time that we're forcing ourselves to play when we're no longer having fun anymore. Because video games are so engaging, you can't tell that you're getting full until you're already stuffed. Each time that I recognize how I'm feeling in relation to the medium I'm engaged in and each time I mindfully disengage, I immediately feel a sense of freedom and empowerment. In my decisiveness, I declare to myself that my mind is free of bondage to any medium. I will never be addicted to or enslaved by any medium, be it a game or a show or even a book, because my awareness of the principles of media engagement and my mindfulness of the effect of the medium on my thoughts and feelings is enough to disentangle me from the knots that many media form in my attention. **Mindfulness alone disentangles me.** There's no physical or mental effort involved. The moment that I'm mindful of a feeling of medium saturation, my mind has dealt with the problem. The subsequent physical movement away from the medium is merely the inevitable windup of the process, the inconsequential tossing of the coin into the fountain once your wish has already been made. Logic shows this to be true because if I'm mindfully aware that a medium is reducing rather than enhancing my pleasure, it would be truly illogical to persist in it. The fact that most people behave illogically most of the time in relation to their media engagement does not free us from the obligation to apply logic to our own media engagement once that logic is revealed to us.

Awareness of physical imbalance while walking will naturally lead to a corrective posture of physical balancing. This is not a conscious process. Similarly, simple awareness of the mentally unbalancing effect of a medium will naturally lead to a corrective movement away from the medium. This process could be conscious, or it could be unconscious. In my experience, media mindfulness requires conscious self-observation and self-implementation at first, but once it becomes a habit, it carries on more or less unconsciously. This is similar to driving. At first, driving is quite hard because it's a new task that requires a specific form of coordination and awareness. However, once you've been driving for a while, most driving becomes a relatively automatic unconscious process that we hardly think about at all.

So too with media balancing. Media mindfulness is a simple process of self-observation. Once an imbalance is observed, the corrective balancing movement will automatically occur by itself, a situation in which the observer is changed as a function of her observation. *The mindful observation changes the mindless observer.* This construct is known as "**psychological causality.**" In practice, it's closer to the true meaning of the Buddhist concept of **karma** than the typical way that karma is understood in the West (as a synonym for "*fate*" or "*predestination*").[5] Karma is neither predestination nor fate because those are things that happen *to* someone, while the word "karma" refers to the antecedents and consequences of one's *own* behavior. The Buddhist principle of karma is simply the notion that every action has both a cause and an effect. Karma only becomes mystical when the very different constructs of reincarnation and multiple lives are added to it because then, we must assume that every action has a cause and an effect, but the cause could be coming from a previous life, and the effect could be imposed on a future life. But that doesn't concern us here. Simple karma is the cause and effect of thought and action, or in the case of media mindfulness, the cause and effect of observation and correction. Habitual media mindfulness will lead directly, by law of cause and effect, to habitual media balancing. We may think of the process as a sort of "**instant karma.**"[6]

Mindfulness in the Buddhist tradition is aimed at subduing the feeling of desire or craving, as all misery ultimately stems from desire. If you can stop wanting things, you free yourself of the constant need to attain and possess things. The only truly free person is a person without desire because that person has "*cut the chain of conditioned origination at the craving link.*"[7] Media mindfulness is absolutely not about Buddhist austerity or self-denial. However, being mindful of the media we crave, why we crave it, how the craving affects our behavior, and what we can do to control our craving and postcraving behavior is at the heart of media mindfulness. Mindless media engagement results from an ignorance of psychological causation, a passive engagement in which unconscious craving leads directly to "*automatic grasping*" of the craved media without reflection.[8] Mindful media engagement, however, begins with a conscious and deliberate awareness of psychological causation, creating a cognitive gap between unconscious craving and automatic grasping, a precious moment of reflection that can interrupt the automatic craving/grasping process, thus allowing ourselves to free our minds and bodies from mindless automatic enslavement to media craving and media bingeing. The "middle way" of mindfulness is to neither grab nor reject but to reflect—to be aware of both the cause and the effect of both potential behaviors in any given situation and then to prefer one over the other for one's own personal reasons, depending on the situation.[9] In all situations requiring choice, **freedom is attained through decision**. By making the decision to switch, flip, sustain, or turn off your medium of engagement, you take control of your media environment, rather than letting it take control of you. By mindfully deciding how to engage in media in a balanced way, you free yourself of even the possibility of media addiction prior to your actual engagement.

The Peril of Infinite Content

Digital media provides a particularly challenging situation for media mindfulness because of the bottomless feedbag of infinite content. If we're bingeing on TV, the feeling of saturation nausea and/or saturation fatigue will prompt us to switch or flip our medium. Rather than doing that, the user who is uninitiated in the realm of media mindfulness will simply switch to new content—a different show—rather than switching to a different medium or flipping into an expressive mode of engagement. Rather than changing her media environment, she simply changes the "channel" to new content. She's unaware of the cardinal aphorism of media mindfulness—*the medium is the message*—so she fails to see that changing the content of her medium, rather than the medium itself, is entirely inconsequential. Media addiction is fostered by an inability to detect saturation nausea or fatigue in oneself because the perpetually new content fools us into thinking that we're engaging in something new, while we've actually been bingeing on the same medium forever. Infinite content is therefore infinitely dangerous, and because of this, we must be exceptionally mindful when engaging in any digital medium. If possible, I suggest avoiding them whenever you can in favor of nondigital media. Read a book made of paper instead of a digital one, play an actual board game with friends or family rather than a digital game, play real football rather than video-game football. By deliberately and consistently choosing reality over digitality, we simplify our media engagement and avoid the invisible peril of infinite content.

The Game Metaphor

> *Life is what happens to us while we are making other plans.*
> —Allen Saunders[10]

Games reel us in and keep us locked into the present moment, focusing our attention on the next immediate move in the game. As such, games are good practice for living in the moment in real life and focusing on the here and now at all times. We may even say that games reduce our stress by channeling our normal future-oriented anxiety into a focus on the present moment. Future-oriented fears perseverate over events that cannot be controlled because they don't yet exist, while gaming locks us into a task that's completely within our control, a task that's immediately executable with immediate outcomes. Since so much of our life and our anxious depression stems from our rumination on the uncontrollable and unknowable, the totally controllable and knowable media environment of the video game is a useful and necessary counterbalance.

In a game like baseball, tense moments arise, such as the pitch to a batter in the bottom of the ninth inning with two strikes, two outs, the bases loaded, and the score tied. That single pitch is likely to determine the outcome of the entire game. The fans are anxious, the coaches and players are anxious—everyone is stressing out about the pitch—except for one person. Can you guess who's experiencing the least anxiety at that moment? You're right. It's the pitcher. Everybody in the stadium is experiencing "**spectator anxiety**," the stress you feel when something very important is about to happen, but you have no personal control over it. There is no greater anxiety than spectator anxiety. The pitcher is not a spectator; she has control, which means that she can channel her anxiety directly into action, while the spectators have no such channel. They can release some of their anxiety through cheering or booing, but a partial release is not the same as a full release. The spectators will remain anxious until the situation itself is resolved.

We spend most of our lives as anxious spectators in the game of life. Real games give us the real and rare opportunity to be dynamic actors rather than passive spectators. We can learn a lot from the game experience. First of all, we know from gaming that freedom comes from decision. While playing a video game, we need to instantly decide what to do. There's no time for deliberation, no time to think about it; we must immediately react. "*If you think long, you think wrong.*" This forced decisiveness that is directly channeled into action is liberating as a counterbalance to our everyday existence full of future-oriented anxiety about things we cannot directly control or even act on. One of the things I enjoy about a good game of Tetris is that the more I proceed in the game, the less time I have to think about my moves until it reaches a point of zero-time response—instant reaction—no planning, no thinking, no strategizing, just pure in-the-moment playing. At that level of play, the **inner spectator**—our voice of consciousness—simply cannot persevere in its anxious depression rumination. It must focus on the present because there's so much to focus on. For me, at that level of play, my inner spectator transfigures into an inner broadcaster, watching the game and making play-by-play announcements and comments: "*This kid's really got something going on here.... Cinderella story.... Came from nothing but now at the top of his game.... He just may break the record.*" The game fantasy, when experienced in the moment, gets both hemispheres of the brain and both poles of the mind (consciousness and unconsciousness) playing together and on the same playing field—for once.

Finding Your "Flow Zone"

Lev Vygotsky, the Russian theorist whose ideas made a lasting impact on the fields of developmental psychology and education, introduced the construct of a **"zone of proximal development"**—the range of tasks that a child cannot accomplish alone but can accomplish with the help of a teacher, adult, or peer. Teachers employ Vygotsky's "zone" when they employ "scaffolding" techniques in their lesson plans.

When a brick building is being built, the level of scaffolding is always just above the top. If the scaffolding is too low, the bricklayer can't reach the top to lay down new bricks. If it's too high, the scaffolding itself will be unsteady and it will collapse. Similarly, when a lesson is too remedial, students will get bored because the bar is set too low. Boredom leads to disengagement. When a lesson is too advanced, students get frustrated because they don't understand. Frustration also leads to disengagement. By adjusting the amount of instruction based on the student's current level of understanding, the student can master more on her own, while relying less on the teacher's instructions, all the while staying engaged in the task. In short, the scaffold of the teacher's lesson must always be neither too low nor too high for the student for that student to grasp the lesson. The same basic principle is also known as the **"Goldilocks effect."** When engaged in a medium, the content could either be overstimulating, understimulating, or "just right." When we have control over the medium, like in a video game, we can adjust it to our preferences and make it just right. When we have no control over the medium, our choices are limited to disengagement or continued but reluctant engagement.

Mihaly Csikszentmihalyi's famous construct of **"flow"** piggybacks on Vygotsky's construct of the "zone." Csikszentmihalyi's model has two dimensions: the level of challenge in a task and the perceived degree of skill that the subject has in that particular task. For instance, when I play Tetris, the level of challenge is always too easy at first because the "tetrominoes" fall quite slowly, and my perception of my own skill level is high. When challenge is low and skill is high, the appropriate response is **boredom**. I'm too good to be completely engaged because the tetrominoes are too slow. As the game continues, however, the tetrominoes fall quicker and quicker, and I soon find myself **"in the zone"**—or to use Csikszentmihalyi's term, I'm experiencing **"flow."** This is the point where the challenge is high, just like my skill level. When I'm "flowing," I'm completely engaged in the task to the point of immersion. This is when I feel like I'm part of the game, connected to it, inside of it because all of my attention is focused intently. I don't think because I don't have time to think. I react. Eventually, the tetrominoes are simply falling too fast for me, and I experience **"anxiety"** because the challenge level is beyond my skill. Usually, the game ends soon after the "anxiety" kicks in. Sometimes I play to the end, and sometimes I just quit. The point of the game is not to feel anxiety about losing, and it's certainly not to get a high score or even to increase my skills. ***The point is to have fun, so the moment I'm not having fun anymore, I quit.*** That's probably the most important mindfulness tip for playing video games, unless you're playing with others, in which case, it would be rude to just abruptly quit, but you can certainly give your friends a heads-up that you'll be quitting soon. The feeling of "anxiety" in the flow zone is a sign of saturation, and it may feel like nausea or fatigue or maybe a bit of irritation or frustration. However it feels for you, recognize it and react immediately by quitting the game and then switching media or flipping modes.

Csikszentmihalyi's "flow" demonstrates how you can attain a state of pure and complete cognitive behavioral engagement when you find the correct media environment and adjust the content of that medium to yourself. We must note that sometimes we are in a media environment where the level of challenge is low and your perceived level of skill is also low, resulting in a state of **"apathy"** or indifference. It's hard to stay engaged in a task that's too easy, especially if you don't care about the task, don't perceive yourself as skillful at it, and don't really care about becoming more skillful. Sadly, I think the majority of kids in the traditional classroom feel exactly that way about school. (I know I did.) The challenge for the teacher is to find a way to make education as stimulating as a video game so that kids would actually want to pay attention and be engaged. The challenge for the media consumer is to become your own teacher and your own student. Find your **personal zone of proximal development** within your own media environments. Locate the places where you feel both skillful and challenged. By courting that special place, you set yourself up for **an experience of flow**, when you feel happily immersed in an experience that engages all of your attention. The "flow zone" challenges you to transcend yourself—to do better than your peak performance—to truly maximize your developmental potential. Think about which media environments bring you into your own personal flow zone. For me, it's playing with my kids, playing music, trail biking, being in the ocean, writing, dreaming, and on occasion, a nice game of Tetris.[11]

Csikszentmihalyi's model is summarized in the chart below.

	Perception of one's own skill level	
Level of challenge	Low	High
Low	**Apathy**	**Boredom**
High	**Anxiety**	**Flow**

Jung's Construct of the Self

> *We become what we behold.*
> —William Blake

Carl Jung, a disciple of Freud who went on to become the master of his own approach to psychoanalysis, encouraged his patients to explore the symbols they saw in their dreams. As part of that process, Jung had them draw **mandalas** in which they placed the symbols from their dreams. "Mandala" is the Sanskrit word for "circle," an ancient symbol for the "Self." When drawing and interpreting the mandala, Jung's patients were able to objectify their internal needs and issues, visualizing them symbolically and then projecting them onto paper. The modern term for the same practice is "**art therapy**." By allowing us to imagine the different parts of ourselves as symbols that exist in relation to each other within the mandala, we could imagine arranging the different parts of ourselves in ways that evoke a sense of balance, simplicity, or peace. Unlike a person who's always in the process of seeking balance, a mandala, when completed, is a static image that can remain fixed in a state of balance. The personal mandala thereby becomes a frame of orientation, a symbolic image to meditate on, a mirror to view oneself as a work in progress, with "balance" as the guiding ideal. Mandala making could be considered a mindful practice of balancing all of the different sides of the Self—yoga for the introspective mind—expressed through the visual-spatial medium.

"**Individuation**" in Jungian psychology is the process of becoming one's true Self by recognizing and integrating the various aspects of one's personality into one whole. The Tibetan Buddhist mandala tradition uses the medium of colored sand. Initiates spend weeks, months, even years making beautiful and intricate mandalas of sand that are ultimately blown away by the wind. No paintings or photos of the mandalas are allowed. So, too, each one of us, like our mandala, fades into the wind. The mandala is transitory because we are transitory, physically and psychologically. We're always changing, developing, growing as people, and that's why the mandalas that represent us are also always changing and developing. Like a person, a mandala is a process, not a goal, an ambition, a finished product, or an object. The creation of a mandala is a mindful, expressive, creative, and reflective practice in the visual-spatial and intrapersonal modes of thought. It is a meditation on the Self. Modern media environments (social media most particularly) fragment our identities into the bits and pieces we want to project to the outside world and the bits and pieces we want to hide. The ancient media environment of the mandala is engaged in

unifying the Self. When we make the mandala, we behold the image that we've become. When we meditate on the mandala, *"we become what we behold."*

Structure for the mandala exercise/practice is optional. Your specific medium is up to you as long as you're in the visual spatial realm. You can draw, paint, color, sculpt, shape, collage, montage, whatever you'd like, though I suggest working in a real physical medium rather than a digital medium (but that's just a suggestion). The circle structure is optional. The contents of your mandala are completely up to you, but keep in mind that this is a visual-spatial task and the notion is to reflect on symbols that represent your Self, so words and numbers should be represented symbolically.[12] I hesitate before offering too much structure because when I do this exercise in a psychology class, providing too much structure is likely to work against the goal of each student conjuring and providing their own structure for the mandala and their own symbols to fill it. However, this is a book, not a class, and you're a reader, not a student; so I must offer a baseline of structure just so you can get what I'm talking about, and I must rely on you, the reader, to understand that the process is personal, introspective, and reflective. Most likely, you'll adopt the structure provided in this book initially, but then as you continue the process of mandala making as a means of meditating on your Self, the structure and symbols will gradually be coming directly and only from you. Also, if you continue the process, it will gradually become internal rather than external. That is, your mandala will eventually be in your mind rather than on paper or canvas or clay, and you'll be able to envision it, manipulate it, and change it just by thinking about it. In that sense, your mandala is an internal image of your inner Self that is, at a certain level of cognition, always present, always accessible, and always developing.

Jungian Dichotomies

> *The meaning and design of a problem seem not to lie in its solution, but in our working at it incessantly.*
> —Carl Jung[13]

Jung's psychoanalytic philosophy was very much inspired by Eastern spiritualism in which nothing exists as a singularity but only as a part of a larger whole, in relation to something else. There is no black (absence of color) without white light (all colors combined). There is no good without evil, no masculine without feminine, no high without low.

The symbol of the yin and yang is a mandala that we're all somewhat familiar with, and it's an excellent example of a very simple yet very elegant mandala, that is purely symbolic, so that the contents of the "sacred circle" can mean something different to everyone. Notice that there are two sides to the yin-yang mandala, representing the two sides of any dichotomy, whether its masculine/feminine, old/young, good/evil, and so forth. The mandala as a whole represents unity within dichotomy, the notion that we are all a combination or a balance of opposing pairs, all contained within the sacred

The Yin and Yang—a Quaternal Mandala.

circle of the Self. There is no space for singularity in the human soul, as we are all infinite. Notice also that within each side is a core of the opposing element (the white core in the black side and the black core in the white side). This is another reminder that absolutely nothing within us is singular, not even a particular side of us. The mandala represents a process, and that process is life. A process is always changing, and so are we. A process is interactive, and so are the sides of our Self. Only by relating to each part of our Self can we become engaged in the process of mindfulness, and only by understanding how each part of our Self exists only in relation to other parts of our Self can we become engaged in the processing of balancing all of the different parts of our Selves.

The yin and the yang is a "quaternity," a pair of dichotomies comprised of four elements (the two sides and the cores of each side). Jung believed that quaternities represent

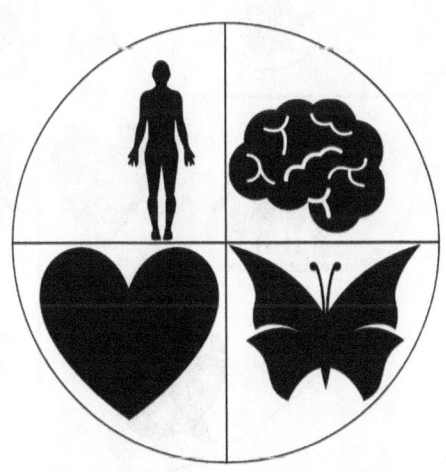

Mind, Body, Heart, & Soul—a Quaternal Mandala.

174 **Media Mindfulness**

wholeness, completeness, or a balancing of opposing pairs. Obviously, your mandala does not need to be a quaternity, but it may be a good first step. For example, I have a simple mandala that I reflect on, which is a quaternity representing the paired dichotomies of mind and heart, body and soul. (In Jungian psychology, those dichotomies would represent the dichotomy of thinking and feeling [mind and heart] and the dichotomy of physical and metaphysical existence [body and soul]). In the quaternity mandala provided on the previous page heart is represented by the heart symbol, mind by the brain symbol, body by a body, and soul by the butterfly, which is an ancient symbol of the soul.[14]

In this book, I propose a model of the Self in eight parts, calling for a mandala in the form of an "octernity." Without too much fuss, I was able to expand my fairly generic Jungian quaternity above into the Gardnerian octernity provided below. In that mandala, the body quadrant is divided into the bodily kinesthetic medium (yoga symbol) and the naturalistic

Gardner's Eight Ways of Knowing—an Octernal Mandala.

medium (nature/gardening symbol). That division made sense to me because the body and nature are both physical forms that are experienced on a physical level, and they both ground us in the physical world of real people, places, and things.

The soul quadrant is divided into the musical medium (music symbol) and the intrapersonal medium (inner-eye symbol). This made sense for me because the intrapersonal deals specifically with spiritual and existential introspection (matters of the soul), while music, in my own personal philosophy, is the "medium of the soul."

The mind quadrant contains the linguistic medium (book symbol) and the logical-mathematical medium (time/money symbol), representing the two media of thought that tend to dominate our conscious minds.

The heart quadrant is divided into the interpersonal medium (family/home symbol) and the visual-spatial medium (visual arts symbol). Once again, this division makes sense to me because the core of my interpersonal existence is centered on family (though friends and colleagues are integral too), while my obsessive love for film (and healthy love for TV) represent personal passions that I also share with loved ones (I usually watch TV and movies with my kids).

My mandalas aren't perfect, and of course that's not even close to the point.[15] The mandalas I created are personal to me and are probably not applicable to you in a lot of ways, and that's OK. I'm providing them for demonstration purposes only. I cannot create a completely generic mandala that would apply to everyone because such a thing could not possibly exist and would be, in fact, completely antithetical to the process of individual personal introspection that I'm suggesting. Your mandala will represent your Self. My mandalas are provided as an example of a structure that you could apply. Although your mandalas may look like mine at first, if you continue the process, they will change and become more personally representative of you as a unique individual. The mandalas I provided made sense to me as I was making them as I wrote this chapter, but they too are fleeting glimpses of my reflected Self as I continue to grow and develop. The more I introspect, the more the images of those mandalas in my head will change and develop. The same will be true for you.

Chapter Nine

Interpersonal Media

The Paradoxes, Illusions, and Delusions of Social Media

> *By continuously embracing technologies, we relate ourselves to them as servo-mechanisms. That is why we must, to use them at all, serve these objects, these extensions of ourselves, as gods or minor religions.*
>
> —Marshall McLuhan[1]

Jaron Lanier is my favorite living author on the topic of digitality.[2] A founding father of virtual reality, he's a true Renaissance man in the manner espoused in this book and beyond. His books *You Are Not a Gadget* (2010), *Who Owns the Future?* (2013), and *Dawn of the New Everything* (2017) were formational in my own thinking about media. Lanier's intimate knowledge of digital technology and his intuitive psychological theories are invaluable to me, as I lack the insider knowledge that a coder, designer, and computer engineer like Lanier knows implicitly. Unlike myself, Lanier can not only see mathematical landscapes composed of algorithms and binary code, but he can also paint a portrait of those virtual landscapes in words so clear and elegant that even I can understand the inner mechanizations of the incredibly sophisticated technology at play. Lanier's most recent book, *Ten Arguments for Deleting Your Social Media Accounts Right Now* (2018), will be referenced often in my discussion of interpersonal media, which will be preoccupied with the problem of digital social media.

In my case, Lanier was preaching to the choir when he wrote his book. I have minimal social media presence. I only use it when I truly must. My desire to be completely off social media, like Lanier himself, points to the mild overstatement in his title (which he acknowledges in his introduction). Like many of us, I truly wish I could delete all of my social media accounts right now, but I can't, primarily because of professional obligations. If I was incredibly wealthy and successful (like *some* people), I would certainly delete them right now, so the fact that I can't and that many or most people can't points to both the iniquity of the technophilic economic system that digital media technology has established and the stranglehold that the same technology has on the denizens of the digital world (except for the vastly wealthy ones who created it). All of us mere mortals who don't live in Silicon Valley are locked in and enslaved by the technology that descends on us from the valley. Although the gods of digitality reap unimaginable fortunes by stealing our personal information and selling it back to us in the form of ads, they are not our masters. **We are the "servo-mechanisms" of our own technology!**

Social media is the most psychologically toxic media environment ever created by humanity because it's orchestrated and managed exclusively by algorithms that are designed to deconstruct and dehumanize humanity. The environment established by the algorithms is purely nihilistic, plain and simple. The algorithms have no emotion, no taste, no sense of feeling or conscience. They know neither right nor wrong. Their only function is to methodically deconstruct the life of the user into data that are deliberately used against the user to monopolize their attention and commoditize their anxieties, fears, desires, and most base instincts, all for the profit of a handful of trillionaires who control all of the information in the world.

When my name is searched in Google, a profile with my name, picture, and personal information appears. I did not create that profile, nor did I give permission for that profile to be created, nor do I know from where the information was obtained (though I know some or most of it was from my Amazon.com author page). The lesson learned is that doing anything on any social media site (like making an Amazon author page to promote my work or making a Facebook page to post pictures of the kids for family) will result in all of my personal and professional information being captured and mashed up by Google and then reposted as a profile of me that I never consented to. That's a hard lesson to learn about social media, especially because I didn't know that once my information was posted, it was public and therefore no longer my own, and I was unaware that the media corporations could then take ownership of my information and do whatever the hell they want with it. I also didn't know that my mistake was irreversible. My Google profile is filled with incorrect information, out-of-date information, and personal information that I don't want the world to see. I've tried to get access to "my profile" for deleting or at least for editing or correcting—filling out online request forms at least a dozen times—but to no avail. I honestly tried really hard repeatedly, but I always get this response from Google: "*We're unable to approve your verification request. Specifically, we did not see sufficient evidence that you manage the existing social platforms or web profiles related to 'William Indick.'"* No matter how hard I try (following all of their directions to the letter), I just can't get permission from Google to own my own name and my own identity. As a result, the first things that people see about me are wrong, and there's absolutely nothing I can do about it. ***I do not own my name or my identity; Google does.*** If that's not omniscience, omnipresence, and omnipotence, then what is? Google and similar supernaturally powerful media corporations have managed to take possession of all of our information—including our own identities—by harvesting data from our social media accounts and then refusing us access to that same information. In response, I would love to delete all of my social media accounts right now, but I can't because Google and similar supernaturally powerful media corporations have created a global media environment that demands participation at the threat of personal and professional exile. Believe it or not, these are the *least* evil aspects of the social media environment.

The algorithms that run the social media environment reward narcissism and deter honesty, genuineness, humility, modesty, courtesy, kindness, and integrity. They do it not because it's right or wrong, but because they're tweaked by their programmers to exploit the most easily exploitable aspect of the human psyche—our *self-consciousness.*

Although, like Lanier, I advocate avoidance of social media up to and including the point of total withdrawal, I also note that I personally cannot completely avoid social media, and I presume that the average reader and I are in the same boat. It's quite well known that the vastly wealthy and powerful aristocracy of Silicon Valley restrict their own use of social media and severely restrict or forbid the use of social media in their own children, sending them to elite private preparatory schools and boarding schools like the Waldorf schools, where digital devices are not allowed.[3] They avoid the same technology they designed because they know perfectly well how insidious and harmful it is. When people ask me why I don't personally use social media unless my arm is twisted, my response is similar: *Because I'm aware of the insidious nature of the medium and the real harm it inflicts.* The fact that many or most of us cannot simply delete their accounts is evidence enough of its insidiousness, while the horrendous effects that social media has on our mental health, political discourse, and manner of social engagement is fairly clear and evident for everyone to see and is also backed up by a wide and growing body of research literature.[4] Our world of mere people cannot disentangle ourselves from the vast net of addictive technology that the digital gods have slung on us from valley high. If, like in the movie *War Games* (1983), *"the only winning move* is not to play," then the "commodores of attention" have made losers of us all by creating a system in which everybody is obliged to play, but nobody can win (except the commodores themselves). Our only recourse is mindfulness and a process of balancing.

I recommended Lanier's book to my teenage daughter and gave her my copy. She said she'd read it, but that she didn't need a book to tell her that social media was "bad."

"If you know it's bad," I replied, *"then maybe you need a book to tell you why you shouldn't use something that you know is bad."*

"I could use something that's bad for me a little bit just for fun," she patiently explained. Despite my wariness at the thought of my daughter doing something bad for fun, there was also the sense that having grown up immersed in digital media, her relationship with that media, and social media in particular, is much more natural and intuitive than my own. Like McLuhan in the 1960s, peeking through the living room window at David Foster Wallace and me and the rest of our TV-addicted tribe, huddled around the blue glow of the screen, I peek through my own living room window at the digital tribe of my own children, each one peering intently into their own little blue screen—but at whom? *"If it's bad,"* I persisted, *"why do you use it at all?"*

"Mostly to chat with new people."

"Strangers?"

"Yes, Dad [rolling her eyes], but it's safe because they can't see my real name and number."

The irony is clear. Her intuitive understanding of social media is so grounded in her existence within it that I cannot even conceive of the level of confidence and dexterity with which she hops and skips through that virtual world that's so native to her and so alien to me. While I write abstractly of the construct of "media saturation," she's experienced it many many times, intuitively learned from her experiences, and applies them without thinking to her behaviors. I'm personally afraid of the existential danger lurking in social media, so I avoid it. She seems to be intuitively aware of the same dangers in social media, but she accepts them as an entrance fee to the realm of enhanced connectivity that she experiences with new people in a virtual world that has, as its greatest asset, the virtue and preliminary safety of not being physically real. As a final query, I ask, *"Do you know about the research on social media—the anxiety and depression and body dysmorphia from social comparison?"*

"Yes, I know, Dad. I know social media is bad because I get sick of it really quick. Now I basically just look at it for fun. I don't look at anything that doesn't make me laugh."

I was glad to see that she recognized her own saturation nausea and that she made a pretty good behavioral adjustment in response to it. Her current viewing policy for social media is also, I must admit, better than anything I could've thought of myself, outside of total avoidance. The native child will always be more fluent than the alien adult. Although I can see the world descending into chaos, a victim of our generation's Tower of Babel, there's still hope because the next generation of native children will be better adapted to the algorithms of deconstruction than my generation could ever become. As a blind man in the land of reflected shadows, I can only offer tepid suggestions for mindful balancing. If a true solution to the social media conundrum does arise, it will doubtlessly find its source among the native children of the digital tribe. *"And a little child shall lead them..."* (Isaiah 11:6).

The Window/Mirror Illusion (Revisited)

> *The version of the world that you are seeing is invisible to the people who misunderstand you, and vice versa.*
> —Jaron Lanier[5]

The primary illusion that engenders social media is that of connectivity. It's a "window to the world," enhancing our ability to connect with virtually anyone in the world, anywhere in the world instantly. This is true, but it's also an illusion. While enhancing our ability to connect with complete strangers on the other side of the world instantaneously, the medium obsolesces the media that we used previously to connect with actual family and friends. Now the medium that connects us to limitless strangers whom we don't know and will, with very rare exception, never *really* know, has become the same medium that we use to communicate with our mothers and fathers, sons and daughters, sisters and brothers, and our closest friends. Rather than making us "friends" with everyone (a logical impossibility), it degrades our real friendships and relationships by dragging them down to the same level of interaction that we have with total strangers. We have cast our pearls among swine, all for convenience. We have put our mother on the same playing field as a complete stranger, an anonymous bot, or a Russian hacker. We've drastically reduced our actual communication in real time and real space with the people we love in favor of virtual exchanges with strangers in virtual time and virtual space. We have allowed Facebook to co-opt the cherished word "friend" and degrade it to the level of a contact point with a total stranger who was "friended" because Facebook told us to do so. What kind of a real "friend" can be "unfriended" in an instant?

While social media promises connection, its algorithms run by "*corralling people*" into "*filter bubbles*" based on their online preferences, profiles, and purchase histories.[6] This filtering process ensures that the information you get and the connections that are suggested will always be based on your own preferences. The algorithms are designed to absorb your personal data and then reflect back to you in bits and pieces the parts of you that you want to engage in or purchase. The people the media encourage you to connect with are the people who are filtered into the same bubble—they are just like you. In other words, **social media is a mirror**, reflecting you back to yourself as a fragmented collection of purchase and connection suggestions that the algorithms predict will increase your purchasing and engagement behavior. The irony is that the sales pitch for social media has always been that of opening us up to more connection, but the media is mathematically designed to close us down to any connection that is not a mirror reflection of ourselves. Social media is obsolescing our real and meaningful connections with real people by placing these real connections on the same playing field as the fake and meaningless connections that are made within a fake media environment. The outcome is unsurprising. I'll spare you a comprehensive literature review of the current research on the psychological effects of social media on mental health, but I invite the curious reader to see the articles cited in the endnotes and in the bibliography. Lanier sums it up precisely: "*Science reveals the truth. Research shows a world that is not more connected, but instead suffers from a heightened sense of isolation.*"[7]

The Mind-Reading Delusion and the Narcissus Carousel

> *The word Narcissus ... is from the Greek word* narcosis, *or numbness. The youth Narcissus mistook his own reflection in the water for another person. This extension of himself by mirror numbed his perceptions until he became the servo-mechanism of his own extended or repeated image. The nymph Echo tried to win his love with fragments of his own speech, but in vain. He was numb. He had adapted to his extension of himself and had become a closed system.*
> —Marshall McLuhan[8]

You may recall the lesson I learned from Daisy, my dog, in the Nature chapter. Just as it's impossible for me to know my dog's mind because her dominant sense is smell, I'm equally incapable of truly knowing your mind because your mind is locked away in your own private kingdom that is completely inaccessible to anyone accept you. Nobody will ever gain access to your private kingdom of mind, just as you will never gain access to mine. The most I could do is toss paper airplanes with messages written on them from the tower window. Those are my words. You can do the same. If you think the missives that I lob out from my kingdom in the form of oral and written words represent my mind in any real way, you're deluded. The words themselves are extremely poor representations of my actual thoughts, but they're all I've got. I cannot express any thought to you unless it's squeezed through one of the word-shaped cookie cutters in my mind. The words that come out are re-representations of thought, not thought itself. You can eat the cookies, and the cookies came from my mind, but the cookies don't accurately represent me in any real way, just as eating an actual cookie tells you extremely little about the actual baker who baked it.

Consider how much time and mental energy you spend thinking about what other people may be thinking about you. You may be having an issue with your mother, and you're thinking, *"Mom is upset because I haven't visited her in a long time. She's disappointed in me."* Is this what your mother is truly thinking? It's impossible to tell. That's what *you're* thinking, and you're projecting that thought about yourself onto her. Unless your mother actually said those words to you, she's most likely not thinking that thought at all. It's just you thinking your own thoughts about yourself through the reflection of your mother. This is something we do all the time. We presume we know what other people are thinking about, and we specifically presume that we know what they're thinking about in reference to our favorite subject—*ourselves*—because that's the one subject we perseverate on day and night. I call this the **"narcissus carousel**,**"** as it's a mind game we play on ourselves that never ends because we're lost in a delusion.

We spend so much time thinking and believing we know what people are thinking about us, but it's just pure narcissism because we have no way of knowing what other people are truly thinking. It's almost certain that the people on whom you're attributing thoughts about yourself are not thinking about you at all. *How do I know?* Because human nature tells me that the other person is most likely on the same carousel, deluding herself into believing that she knows what you or some other person is thinking about her and perseverating on those thoughts. She's not thinking about you at all, but she's likely to be thinking about what someone else is thinking about her, just like you are. You may think you know what someone else is really thinking about you. You may even hear the words you think they're thinking about you in your own head. I'm sorry to burst your bubble, but you're deluding yourself. **The words you think you hear are just the echoes of your own narcissism.**

The social media environment is one big narcissus carousel. We cannot read other people's minds, and the fact that we do truly believe that we know what others are thinking about us is merely a testament to our own deluded narcissism. All we know about others' minds is what floats down to us from the towers of their private kingdoms, as it's posted in their social media account. Those re-representations tell us very little. The magic mirror of social media has a shrinking effect on communication because of the curtness required of social media messages—the extremely brief posts, comments, tweets, or simple likes and dislikes of the digital response, which communicates almost nothing in terms of actual thought. Nevertheless, by reeling us into a world of mirrors that appear to us like windows into other people's minds, we're easily deluded, like Narcissus, into believing that we're not only gazing at others, but we're gazing at the minds of others when we're merely gazing at our own reflections. The promise of social media is that of an open system that connects us with limitless others, but what's actually delivered is a closed system of extremely limited interactions with an extremely filtered set of others. In response, our mind animates those limited interactions by filling in the blanks with our own thoughts about ourselves and then projecting those thoughts onto the personas of other people. By promising so much but providing so little in terms of real connection, social media lures us into the narcissus role of terminal self-reflection in which we're completely oblivious to the worshipping of our own personas.

The Static Thought Fallacy

What are you thinking about right now? Please take a moment to write that thought down. OK, did you do it? All right, now tell me, what are you thinking about right now, a second or two after the first time I asked you that question? Is your thought right now exactly the same as your thought from a few seconds ago? I didn't think so. Why not? Because thought is not a product; it's a process. My thoughts are constantly changing from one moment to the next, and so are yours. The water that runs through a stream changes every moment, just like the stream of thought that runs through your mind is constantly changing. The stream of consciousness itself has continuity, but the content of that stream of thought is constantly changing as it flows. This is a basic truth that we intuitively understand about our own minds but rarely attribute to the minds of others. I know that my thoughts are always changing, and you know that your thoughts are always changing, but when we think of someone else's thinking, we forget to make that same attribution. That's the left hemisphere of the brain at work, focusing on a process as if it were a product by nailing it down in the mind so it can be static, held still while we analyze and deconstruct it.

One of the primary dangers of social media is that it reduces people from the incredibly complex processes that they are into the extremely simple and trite products that we see in a profile. The profile is neither a person nor a process; it is a product representing a personal process. When we engage with others on social media, we delude ourselves into believing that we're engaging with others, but all we really have access to are these scanty profiles. We see the profile and we immediately fill in the blanks by imagining what this other person is thinking, as if their thought process was actually as static and superficial as the content in their profiles.

The Imaginary Audience Delusion

> *Through me you pass into the city of woe: Through me you pass into eternal pain.... Abandon all hope, ye who enter here.*
> —Dante, "Inferno," *The Divine Comedy*

Upon entering the virtual realm of social media, we're immediately pulled down by the immeasurable gravity of our own self-consciousness into the black hole of narcissism from whose grasp nothing can escape. On the registration page for each social media app, the following warning should be displayed: *"Abandon all hope, ye who enter here."*

How many "followers" do you have on social media? If you know the answer, you're likely to be locked into the delusion that there's an audience of real people out there in the ether who follow everything you do and are constantly consumed with you and your life. *How do I know?* Human nature. People are inherently narcissistic. We're always thinking about ourselves, leaving precious time for anyone to be thinking about you. Even when your followers are looking at your posts and streams, they're really just thinking about themselves through your imaginary perspective. Your followers will never really know you nor you them, and their interest in you was merely a momentary click evoked by the social media algorithms. Their interest in you exists only because you are a good mirror for them to look into because your profile displays similar interests, achievements, or ambitions. Nobody follows anyone who is completely unlike themselves because somebody unlike themselves is not a good mirror. Your audience of followers is an "**imaginary audience**" seated in the theater of your own mind, and the static thoughts you attribute to them are just the echoes of your own narcissism. A human identity is an ever-changing and therefore infinitely complex process. The belief that you can *"communicate an identity"* within the ethereal space of a social media profile *"requires some degree of self-delusion."*[9]

The Narcissus Paradox and the United State of Narcissism

> [T]he wisdom of the Narcissus myth does not convey any idea that Narcissus fell in love with anything he regarded as himself.
> —Marshall McLuhan[10]

The essence of narcissism is *not* conceited self-obsession. It is **obliviousness** to one's own conceited self-obsession. A narcissist who is completely aware of his own narcissism is therefore, ironically, not a true narcissist. This is because awareness of an issue necessarily evokes a response to that issue, even if it's just a psychological response (i.e., "psychological causality"). Awareness of being narcissistic would necessarily cause someone to reflect on that self-truth which has been made self-evident, and as a process of reflection, the image of that reflection would change. This process of observation leading to reflection leading to personal change is hardwired within a real social system in which real people interact with other real people in real time and real space so that real reactions to one's real self could be observed and reflected on. This process is completely derailed when we digitally transfer social interaction into a virtual social system in which fake re-representations of people interact with other fake re-representations of people in virtual time and virtual space. *"Fake readers, fake commenters, fake referrals."*[11] In this virtual hall of mirrors, there's no way to really know which people are real and which aren't because to a very large degree, it's all so completely fake.

What happens when real people must fake their own identities to compete in a fake arena against other fakers for the goal of earning fake popularity? You guessed it. The fakers who are the best at faking identity will win the fake game, though the prizes—revenue for being an "influencer" or for selling the fake product of the fake self—is *actual* money or politico-economic success. In the toxic arena of inverted values, narcissism is the only way to establish identity because it's the only possible way to escalate one's individual online platform to stand above the quintillion other platforms. In a world where only narcissism matters, the greatest narcissist will naturally rise above all and maybe even become the king of this Kingdom of Fake—the president of our united state of narcissism.

The "Social" Media Paradox and the "Asshole" Machine

> *It's as if we've been placed on a lookout that oversees the entire world and given a pair of binoculars that makes everything look like our own reflection. Through social media, many people have quickly come to view all new information as a sort of direct commentary on who they are.*
> —Jia Tolentino[12]

The word "social" in the term "social media" presupposes that the media enhance our social relations, social skills, and social values. In fact, the evidence is quite clear that using social media on a societal level has made us more **"asocial,"** more **"unsocial,"** as well as more **"antisocial."** Social media makes us more asocial by allowing us to replace real social interactions with real people in real time with the fake interactions found online. Every time we choose to interact with somebody through the virtual technology of social media rather than a normal one-to-one correspondence or actual social meeting or gathering, we choose the convenience of **asocial isolation** over the realness of actual socialization. The research on this subject is quite clear. *Social media use is not just related to social isolation; it is a primary cause of it.*[13] Rather than engendering connection, social media fosters disconnection, replacing it with an invasive and insidious form of delusional narcissism in which the other is replaced by the self, without the self even being aware of it. At best, social media encourages us to be more **asocial** with the people who really matter in our lives, but it gets much worse.

"*What might once have been called advertising must now be understood as continuous behavior modification on a titanic scale.*"[14] Unlike clinical "behavior modification" designed to improve ourselves, the behavior modification applied by social media algorithms are designed only to extract the maximum amount of attention (measured in time) and the maximum amount of purchase revenue (measured in dollars) out of each of us. The insides of our minds have become gold mines for the commodores of attention from which we profit nothing but lose everything, including our loved ones, our attention, our sense of self, and our minds themselves. By feeding us only the content that's filtered specifically for us, social media entrenches us in our predetermined sociopolitical positions rather than opening us up to new ideas from people unlike ourselves. In the "God's eye view" of the algorithms, we're all just a collection of preferences that must be grouped together for marketing purposes. Rather than enhancing our ability to socialize with people in a way that broadens our horizons and opens up our identities to new ideas and new possibilities, social media is specifically designed to narrow our horizons to package our "identities" as products for the marketplace. Hence, social media is a deliberately "**unsocial**" medium because it closes us to the possibility of actually socializing with genuine people, resigning us to the narcissus role of relating to only mirror reflections of ourselves. The social media environment reels us in, addicts us, and locks us in a cage of our own self-consciousness from which we can never escape because it's a *"cage that goes everywhere with you."*[15]

The algorithms at play in social media favor negative over positive feedback loops because human attention is naturally drawn to the baser emotions of fear, anger, envy, hate, desire, and sexual prurience. The lowest common denominator will always be more profitable than the higher, and social media is a business run by corporations to profit off your lowest and most base impulses. *"The prime directive to be engaging reinforces itself, and no one even notices that negative emotions are being amplified more than positive ones."*[16] We've known about this human tendency forever. We're not interested in hearing news about people unless it's bad news so we can feel a bit better about ourselves in comparison. We don't want to hear gossip unless it will make others look bad, making ourselves look better in reflection. We secretly crave the downfall of others so we can feel slightly uplifted by contrast. The ugly side of human nature is nothing new, but never has it been capitalized on so greedily and so insidiously by robot algorithms that never cease in their determination to suck every nickel's worth of attention from our brain for the profit of their masters in the valley. The algorithms capitalize on human vulnerability by turning our worst natures against us and turning us into **antisocial "assholes."** *"With nothing else to seek but attention, ordinary people tend to become assholes because the biggest assholes get the most attention."*[17] Although assholes come in all shapes and sizes, the specific type of asshole that social media engenders is the narcissistic asshole because the implicit rewards for narcissism rigged into the social media system have a purposeful and *"inherent bias towards assholedom."*[18]

It was once said that one should never discuss politics or religion in polite company because one never knows whom one might offend. Guess what the most popular topics on social media are? Social media rewards narcissism but negates any sense of courtesy or personal accountability by allowing for total anonymity. *This is a total reversal of social values.* When we care about the people we're with, we're careful not to offend them, not just because we fear retribution and the censure of others but because we actually care about the other person's feelings. On social media, *the goal is to offend people* because that provokes reaction and response, which fuels the algorithms. Each response or reaction to our own stimulates what the social media engineers and executives call a "*dopamine hit*" in the brain, a self-perpetuating neurological reward system that they refer to as a "*social validation feedback loop*."[19] The algorithms don't care about the content of the responses; they just amplify the noise that comes out of it. Since negative noise is the loudest and most upsetting, the negative feedback loop will always prevail and dominate within that environment. And since it's hard to actually care about people who aren't really real, we don't care if we hurt their feelings. The system, in fact, rewards us for hurting people's feelings by feeding us more attention.

On the flip side, people love to go onto social media for the specific purpose of being offended. They seek out the specific forums that they know will offend them. Why? Because *taking offense is merely a pretense for going on the offense*. Our polite upbringing tells us to never cast the first stone, so we don't. We merely situate ourselves in a forum where stones are being thrown and wait to be hit. Once hit, we can throw as many stones as we want at whomever we want at whatever velocity we want, safely behind the screens of our sanctimoniousness and anonymity. Another strategy for deliberately taking offense is "**hypersensitivity**" to any perceived offense regardless of the intention to give offense. The art of "taking offense" when nobody is "giving offense" is creative in the sense that the person is concocting a reason to be offended out of thin air. This is called "**virtue signaling**." It's a sign to others of how virtuous you are because the only way to be holier than thou in an environment grounded in negative feedback is to react negatively to someone else—that is, to be offended. Being offended shows everyone how virtuous you are even though you've done nothing other than complain. Social media is a toxic cycle of deliberate offense-taking in the form of sanctimonious hypersensitivity, followed by deliberate offense-giving in the form of hateful and mean-spirited "shitposts." The common thread is that somehow—quite miraculously—*everyone* is a victim.

By constructing a culture based on intentional offensiveness facilitated by self-perceived "*victimhood*," social media has turned us against each other in a way that no other medium could have ever done. Social media is a decidedly **antisocial medium.** It has degraded political discourse by promoting "**negative partisanship**" in which communication is not about what you want or the rights you want to protect but only about negating what other people want and the rights they want to protect. True political discourse is drowned out by the ceaseless loop of negative feedback in which people scream "no" to abortion rights, "no" to gay marriage rights, "no" to citizenship rights for immigrants, and so forth while never actually having to support their claims or make a positive statement about anything. Negative partisanship turns every political issue into a personal issue in which the basic measure for policy is not truth, fairness, or justice but one's personal feelings and what may or may not personally offend you. Social media has turned politics into just another venue for narcissism in which the biggest narcissists—the biggest assholes—have not only the tallest platform but also the longest pole for vaulting into elected office. At the same time, social media's negative feedback loop turns us against each other in a much more vitriolic and hateful manner than ever before because of the way it deliberately rewards offensiveness, evoking hatred and retributive vitriol. The hyperpartisanship that has destroyed political discourse in America and around the world is a direct product of the most toxic media environment ever constructed. It is truly **antisocial media**.

The Human Product—Objectification and Fragmentation

> *In the beginning is the relation—as the category of being, as readiness, as a form that reaches out to be filled, as a model of the soul; the a priori of relation; the innate You.*
> —Martin Buber[20]

The algorithms of social media cannot perceive you as another person because they are not people. They can only perceive your engagement and measure it in terms of attention time and market value. They don't see you as a person but only as a series of digits. This digitalization process fragments your Self, not just in the God's eye view of the algorithms but in your own self-perception as well. Your social media identity is your profile and nothing else. No matter how many selfies and favorite shows you pack into your profile, it will always be a fragmented image of your Self because you are so much more than your profile. Hence, the "persona," the mask that we construct and wear for others to see, is all important on social media, as it's the only thing about you that's seen. As such, it reduces you to something much more fragmented and much more diminutive than you really are, while simultaneously validating your flimsy persona to the point of superficial surrealism. The end result is a complete reversal of personal values. The only thing that matters is how you appear. How you are on the inside, your true personality, your true identity, anything about you that can't be encapsulated in a selfie or a tweet is not only devalued, but it simply does not exist.

The idea of taking a selfie at sunset to post on social media embodies the notion of **the persona extracted from the Self**. Actually enjoying the sunset, seeing it with your own eyes, experiencing it in real time and real space has no personal meaning because those experiences can't be posted on social media. The only thing that matters is the image, the fragment of yourself that you can capture and post for everyone on social media to see. Without that image posted on social media, the sunset and your experience of it are not only worthless, but they simply did not exist, as if they never happened.

Humans in the social media environment are not people—they are not even users, consumers, or providers; they are products, objects on sale for profit. The algorithms are designed to break people down into marketable products. The media corporations sell the product—our personal data and attention—to companies for ad revenue. The media corporations are the service providers, the companies buying ads are the consumers, and your identity and attention are the product. Social media turns you into an object and uses you like a slave to constantly make money off you as its owned and manufactured product. The objectification of humanity that social media is built on creates an environment of objects relating to other objects rather than people relating to other people. Martin Buber's classic, century-old distinction between the "I-Thou" and "I-it" relationships is incredibly relevant and applicable today.

When I'm communicating—*truly communicating*—with another person, I accept her as another person like me. That means I listen to what she says without preconceiving her message. My goal is to understand her and for her to understand me, not to agree or disagree, to judge or be judged. Social media interactions negate the true I-Thou relationship to such a degree that it makes it impossible to truly communicate with another person. Since we interact with profiles rather than people and profiles are products, there's no way I can attempt to understand you without first perceiving you as a set of predetermined values and preferences on your profile. I cannot *not* preconceive your message. Even though I may think I'm interacting with a person, I'm actually interacting with a profile, a product, an object, an "it." The "I-it" relationship does not carry the same weight as the "I-Thou," because an "it" isn't a real human; therefore, I cannot learn anything from "it" and I can't respect "its" opinions or consider "its" opinions in any way other than how well "it" reflects my own. The fact that social media is filled with "bots" who mimic real profiles and users and that *"there is now an industry that sells counterfeit humans"*[21] in the forms of bots and fake profiles makes it even less possible to interact with a real human on social media because we can no longer tell the difference between humans and bots. In response, the "its" that you interact with on social media regard you as an "it" as well because the algorithms and the environments they construct can only sustain its. Real humanity cannot breathe in the ether. Instead, we allow ourselves to be fragmented and objectified into a community of its, all interacting in *a virtual kingdom of its* without a "Thou" in sight.

"Cancel culture" is a prime example of "it" relations. If a celebrity or politician (whose livelihood depends entirely on popularity) has offended her public, she can now be "canceled," just like a show or a magazine subscription can be canceled. The only problem is a person isn't an object like a show or a subscription. A person cannot be "canceled" because a person exists on a metaphysical plane that transcends the dimension of pure objects and its. The fact that people on social media can no longer perceive even the most elemental difference between a human and an object is a testament to the profound degradation of humanity that social media engenders. What's more, the fact that cancel culture is blind to its own hypocrisy—punishing the objectification of women and other groups by objectifying offenders as if they were cancelable objects—shows how blind social media makes us to our own inability to perceive how we objectify others even in the name of anti-objectification. The fact that "Fakebook" refers to the hundreds or even thousands of virtual strangers connected to our profiles as "friends" shows how tragically lost we've become in our perception of human relation. To call a stranger a "friend" and to then raise that stranger/friend to the same level of interaction as your mother and child is sacrilege, a desecration of everything precious and revered that's associated with the word "friend," which Fakebook has now defiled. The ability to "unfriend" someone with the press of a button shows how meaningless relationships are on social media because they are merely objects. The ability for you to press the Delete button on your social media accounts is really the only way that you, as a person, can assert your autonomy and reassert your identity as a human being and not just another "it" in the vast virtual kingdom of "its."

Adrift in a hall of mirrors populated by virtual personas posing as identities, we lose our sense of self. We begin to perceive ourselves as virtual representations of our own identities. We project our fake identities into the ether as objects of desire, adulation, spectacle, or scorn. Should we be surprised when our children begin to view their own bodies as alien objects and when they treat these unhuman objects callously by mutilating, starving, exposing, exploiting, and otherwise objectifying their own bodies? If a person is just an "it," then why not treat it like an "it"? ***Self-objectification is not a risk of social media; it's a requirement of***

social media. If you cannot objectify your identity as a profile and accept the fact that while on social media, you're being judged and measured and objectified just as you judge and measure and objectify others, then you cannot exist on social media. If you use social media and you don't believe that you're engaging in self-objectification, then you're deluding yourself. Self-objectification is an a priori prerequisite for entry into the virtual realm. Once you enter, the algorithms filter you into bubbles that foster group identities rather than personal individual identities. You are ***depersonalized*** because you are treated as part of a group rather than a person, and you are ***deindividualized*** because the only way to exist is to conform to the groupthink of the bubble you're filtered into. Within that bubble, the only way to be heard is to be the loudest asshole, requiring ***anonymity*** on your part, which is the self-abnegation of your own individual identity for the purpose of fitting into the bubble. There is no easier and more direct way to negate your own self-worth as a person than to go on social media. "*By putting yourself out there, you are erasing yourself.*"[22]

Self-Commoditization and Self-Exploitation

> *An unfortunate combination of biology and math favors degradation of the human world.*
> —Jaron Lanier[23]

My philosophy about the perils of social media are completely impersonal. I totally understand that, when I write copy about myself on Fakebook for the purpose of publicizing a book, that I'm commoditizing my persona for money; that I'm turning my personal life and my identity into objects that I can manipulate for the purpose of making my name, as both a brand and identity, more profitable; and that the entire process of propping myself up on a "platform" as high as I can in the glare of a million mirrors is the very essence of narcissism, the narcotic of the soul. My awareness of my narcissistic activity on social media is the one thing that spares me from being a complete narcissist. The fact that I do it to support my family is my only excuse. I know the devil that I lie down with, so I get out of that bed as soon as I can, and while in it, I use protection. My real concern is for the generations of people who have been forced to become copywriters to market the only brand they can market—themselves. The current and future generations of entrepreneurs have no option but to objectify and commoditize their own identities as a prerequisite to following their professional dreams. This is becoming increasingly true for everyone in every profession. We're all being forced into the narcissus role of oblivious self-reflection. Required to put ourselves out there as information processes rather than living people, we use technology for our own purposes while remaining oblivious to the fact that the technology, in turn, is using *us* for its own purposes. As we self-commoditize and exploit our personal identities for market share, the media we use to do so is commoditizing and exploiting us.

Context Collapse and the Forest of Mirrors

> *We have given up our connection to context. Social media mashes up meaning.*
> —Jaron Lanier[24]

Social media is virtual, which means it has no physical context. As such, everything on social media is decontextualized content, posted by users, bots, hackers, and companies to capture our attention. Social media makes up for its total lack of context by providing a surfeit of content. In a real environment, like a store, we see the content laid out in front of us in aisles and bins. Whereas the products in the store provide the figures for our attention to focus on, the store itself is the ground of our experience, the physical context that cradles not only the store's products but also the people engaged in the store's products. That's why we feel sad when a local brick-and-mortar store we used to patronize closes down. The reason it closed is because you and everybody else now buys the products that they used to buy at the store from Amazon. You don't need the store anymore because you now get the content delivered to your doorstep, but you miss the physical context of the store itself, the physical place you used to inhabit. The closing of the physical store is just another reminder of context collapse in the virtual environment—how everything is going online—so that the physical place and the actual people who inhabited those places are quickly vanishing, replaced by limitless content with zero context. To quote Gertrude Stein, "**There's no there, there.**" In social media, we enter a world of a trillion figures but absolutely no ground. Whereas Lanier can visualize this groundless landscape mathematically, the only way I can envision it is in the image of a vast *forest of mirrors*, where we can't see the forest for the trees, and the trees themselves are just reflections.

As a contextless environment, social media has no boundaries and thus can invade every aspect of our lives. Social media erases the line between personal and professional personae, especially on networking sites such as Facebook that encourage the incestuous intermingling of personal and professional interests. When someone is trying to get ahead professionally, they need to "package" themselves to appear appealing to potential employers or clients. The space for personal expression—real family, real friends, and fake "friends" we communicate with—are just as easily exploited for professional purposes, when the space itself has no real context. We've all been turned into desperate salespeople, frantically trying to sell a product that has been obsolesced by technology and that nobody seems to want or care about anymore. That product is the human self.

Social Anxious Depression and the Loser Machine

> *Since negative emotions can be utilized more readily, of course such a system is going to tend to find a way to make you feel bad.*
> —Jaron Lanier[25]

The driving force behind social media is "FOMO"—the fear of missing out. Although the acronym is fairly new, the fear is not. FOMO is just envy without specific content. We all want something, even if we're unaware of what exactly that thing is. Social media provides a continuous answer to that never-ending question. It showers us with infinite profiles of infinite people who indeed have what we want. FOMO is a desire that can never be sated because there will always be something that we'll be missing out on. Social media captures this desire by making us afraid that we're missing out, then it lures us into an environment with limitless things we desire, and usually no way to attain even a tiny fraction of them. What's more, by associating those unattainable desires with profiles of others who did attain them (supposedly), we're forced into a state of **negative social comparison**, the no-win game of comparing our lives with the lives of others. We can never win this game because there will always be a profile of someone richer, younger, prettier, thinner, happier, more successful, and just plain better than you. The *"magic mirror on the wall"* will always find someone fairer than thou; the system itself predetermines it. Never mind that many of the profiles are fake people or bots and that you're comparing your real self to fake, phony, or robotic selves. In the value-reversed social media environment, appearance is all that matters, so fake profiles are the only things that are real. The negative social comparison on social media, driven by envy, desire, and fear, sets every user up in a no-win situation. *This unwinnable contest is, in essence, a loser-making machine that profits on your sense of ego loss.*

The Digital Media Paradox

The more advanced and sophisticated our media environments become, the more our behaviors in those environments regress. That is the paradox of digital media, and here are some examples.

Social media is a forum for narcissism. When narcissism is "wounded," the narcissist strikes back with the desperate fury of his emptied soul. If image and attention are all that matter, an insult is no small thing; it is a dagger to the heart. The vicious and spiteful trolls and lurkers who hate themselves so much that they can't even bear an identity remain anonymous to hide their shame. Anonymity protects their fragile egos from any backlash that might arise from their vicious and spiteful posts and comments. It is this vicious circle of **wounded narcissism** and **anonymous vitriol** that keeps the wheels of social media lubricated with the liquidated spirits of its users, while keeping the steady stream of revenue flowing out of our wasted attentions. The ironically **antisocial** nature of social media is in large part due to this hateful cycle. The emergence of violence sites, hate sites, sites that encourage self-harm, suicide, terrorism, mass shootings, and other acts of nihilism are a clear sign of the poison that social media injects into our society. The dramatic increase in hate crimes and senseless violent crimes such as school shootings are a testament to how social media encourages narcissism, wounds that narcissism, and then provides a forum in which narcissism is encouraged, validated, and reinforced through acts of senseless violence that destroy innocent lives as well as the life of the wounded and heavily armed narcissist, whose only meaning in life could be found in the attention he garnered online for being a violent hateful narcissist.

Social media enslaves us by capturing our desire, so we shouldn't be surprised when social media caters to our most basic desires in the most blatant ways. "Chaturbate" and similar streaming pornographic social media sites invite users to video chat as they masturbate. Sounds wholesome enough, but it's just a ruse. All the "cammers" are there to make a buck off the penny tips they receive from their viewers. It's a peep show but with no real context, so anyone can play with no threat of discovery. The viewers tip for what they want to see, and the cammers—mostly kids in their teens and 20s with no other way to make a living in the modern technocratic oligarchy we provided them—have no choice but to give the viewers what they want. The levels of self-degradation and self-exploitation on these sites are too dark for me to describe. The cammers don't think they're exploiting themselves because they're getting paid, but who ever said that self-exploitation was negated by a paycheck? In fact, self-exploitation is generally reinforced by a paycheck. The most troubling issue is that the notion of "*self-exploitation*" in and of itself seems to be an obsolete construct for the cammer generation. In a world in which everyone must always be commoditizing, objectifying, and exploiting their own identities online all the time, "self-exploitation" as a thing is not a problem; it's a solution. Whereas "selling out" used to be perceived as a corruption of the true self, selling out is now an ambition, an aspiration, with the ultimate goal of becoming completely "sold out," like a product that has reached its maximum market value as a brand. If my tone is alarmist, it's because this total reversal of cultural and personal values has occurred so suddenly—not just in my lifetime—but in my adulthood, before my very eyes. The reversals are clearly and directly attributable to social media. The values of privacy, prudence, humility, modesty, and restraint have become not just obsolete but nonexistent like the other prime derelicts of the social media age, such as patience, forbearance, integrity, and mercy.

The Global Village Idiot

> *The global village is at once as wide as the planet and as small as the little town where everybody is maliciously engaged in poking his nose in everybody else's business.*
> —Marshall McLuhan

McLuhan foretold of the "global village" over 60 years ago. The idea that we would all be interconnected across the planet through media technology was perceived by some as a future Eden of world peace, but that's not what McLuhan meant at all. The global village is a return to *preliterate tribalism*, a state of constant contention—limitless never-ending arguments with countless sides, all vying to be heard above the din. When discourse devolves into a shouting match, the loudest voice (the biggest asshole) always wins. The loudest voice becomes the loudest by getting as many voices as possible to chime in behind him. Thus, the global village is a place of "**retribalism**," a place where sophisticated technology serves only to regress us to our most base and primitive state. The village's tribal chief will always be the biggest asshole.

The "global village" is the interconnection via social media of all the villages in the world, and every village has an "idiot." Since social media algorithms filter users into bubbles, social media creates bubbles specifically inviting to the village idiots from every village around the world. All these village idiots can now band together via social media into one unified voice—***the global village idiot***—who, by the power of their own loudness, legitimize and validate idiocy itself. They then establish their own idiot platforms; espouse their own idiot policies, conspiracy theories, and hateful beliefs; and vote together to elect their own idiot leaders. *Sound familiar?* This political idiocracy, however, is only feasible in a cultural technocracy. These two systems feed and regenerate each other in a way reminiscent of a mama bird vomiting predigested content directly down her chick's throat.

Super-stupid politicians could only be elected if there's a means of mass discourse that encourages and legitimizes idiocy. In turn, super-wealthy social media tycoons can protect their insane untaxed incomes and corporate freedom by using their power, influence, money, and media control to make sure that the idiots in power are *their* idiots. Hence, an idiocracy is merely a front for an oligarchy in which the people with ultimate economic, political, societal, and cultural power are the handful of people who own and control the dominant media of political discourse, which has become social media.[26] The tyrants of today are not the politicians but the people who control the media and the money that the politicians rely on for their very existence. The tyrants of today are the puppet masters holding the strings of the idiots in "power." They are the commodores of attention.

The Commoditization of Friendship and the Double Bind

> *The dopamine-driven feedback loops [are] ... eroding the core foundation of how people behave by and between each other, and I don't have a good solution. My solution is I just don't use these tools anymore. I haven't in years.*
> —Chamath Palihapitiya, former vice president of user growth at Facebook[27]

As an author, I get to do the very occasional book signing, and the same thing has happened to me twice. Prior to the signing, I'm asked by my publisher to bring around 50 of my "friends" to the event. The number took me aback both times. *"Fifty?"* Do I even have 50 friends? I counted the contact numbers on my phone of people whom I considered real "friends"—people not in my family whom I regularly spend time with socially—and I didn't get close to 50. I immediately felt like a loser both times. *"Maybe he was talking about my friends and family,"* I reasoned. I was also being instructed to post everything on social media, but of course it was then (both times) that I realized he wasn't talking about my "real" friends; he was talking about my social media friends. I was supposed to be using them as "followers," as if I was some sort of "influencer" and the people I love and care about are the customers for my "brand." The first experience led immediately to saturation nausea. The second led directly to saturation exhaustion. The worst part was, I still had to do it, though simply posting an event on Facebook is not quite as sinister as shilling for rubes. This relatively common situation is a "**double bind**," a construct developed in the 1950s by the brilliant anthropologist Gregory Bateson, who was one of the founders of cybernetics.[28]

A double bind is a situation that drives someone crazy, either literally in the sense of psychosis or more broadly in the sense of anxious depression or any other mental health issue. The first condition of the double bind is that the subject is "locked in" somehow so that there's really no viable escape. A child living at home is the perfect example. An employee at work is another. Marriage yet another. A prisoner is also a good example. When someone is not free to leave a situation, they will be obliged to do things that they don't want to do, which often leads to a double bind. The first bind is the aspect of being locked in. In my example, I couldn't refuse to publicize my book because I agreed to do just that in my contract. I had to go onto Fakebook and at least do what was required of me. I was bound and locked in to the "everywhere cage."

The second bind comes in the form of a contradiction.[29] For instance, a mother tells her child to dress up nice for dinner. When the child sighs, she berates him: *"Like it's such an ordeal! You should want to look nice for your family!"* She knows he doesn't want to dress up, but she's ordering him to not only do something he doesn't want to do, but he must also *want* to do what he doesn't want to do. The boy is being forced to act in a way that contradicts himself, and ***forced self-contradiction*** is the essence of the double-bind scenario.

The classic adult example is when Partner One wants to have sex, and Partner Two has a "headache." If Partner One complains, Partner Two may concede and say, *"OK, go ahead, but please be quick about it because I'm tired."* Partner One is then likely to respond, *"I don't want to do it to you; I want to do it with you."* For Partner Two, the request is not just to do something they don't want to do but to also *want* to do what they don't want to do. *Self-contradiction!* Bateson's theory was that living in an environment of mind games driven by contradictory psychological loops breeds a Kafkaesque form of psychosis in which reality makes no sense, so fantasy becomes more real than reality.[30] Although his theory was only marginally relevant to schizophrenia, it appears to me to be almost *too relevant* for social media.

The toxic social media environment gives us the implicit injunctions, "Be genuine!" "Be authentic!" "This is *your* space to be *your* self!"

"My space," you say? If this space is for me, why do I need to fill it up with all of my personal BS? I'm the only person in the world who is

completely familiar with all of my weird movie preferences, and I know how I look fairly well, so I certainly don't need to see the pictures of myself. Obviously, I'm creating the space for *you* to look at, not for me because I already know what I look like and what my favorite movies are. How is this "my space" if I'm designing it for your eyes? How can I be "myself" when everything I post *"is being fed into a judgment machine?"*[31] How can I be "genuine" if the most disingenuous act imaginable is creating a profile for "yourself" on Fakebook?

Social media engages us so insidiously because it's constantly double binding us. If you don't get on an app because someone wants you to, you're being "asocial." If you do it halfheartedly, you're "lame." If you put lots of effort into it, you've become exactly what you didn't want to become in the first place. Self-contradictions!

Someone tells you to take a "selfie." A selfie is supposed to be a candid snapshot. How can I take a candid snapshot of myself by myself? That would require planned spontaneity. Contradiction!

Other paradoxes, delusions, illusions, and contradictions of social media engagement have been explained above. The window/mirror illusion reels us into social media with the promise of connection to others, but it provides only a mirror that reflects our own narcissism. Social media locks us up in never-ending loops of deluded thinking—the delusion that we can know what other people/profiles are thinking about us, the delusion that other people's thoughts are static products that could be analyzed rather than ongoing processes that constantly change, the delusion of the imaginary audience. Social media forces us to be fake and narcissistic as an entrance fee to its toxicity, contradicting our own better natures and setting us on a road to "assholedom." "Social" media contradicts itself by being a forum that engenders asocial, unsocial, and antisocial behaviors. By creating profiles to be digitized by algorithms for the marketplace, we contradict our own identities, erasing our true selves by turning them into marketable products. Most troubling of all, we willingly contradict ourselves by voluntarily engaging in a medium that we know is both addictive and harmful. By constantly double binding us within the toxic media environment, social media forces us to become someone we don't want to become. All too often, that someone is an "asshole."

The Addiction Machine and the Power of Off

> *Deleting has become reputable.... The evidence that deleting is good for you continues to grow.*
> —Jaron Lanier[32]

Social media algorithms feed my profile the content that corresponds to tiny fragments of my identity—the cough drops I buy, the music I listen to, the shows I watch—the commoditizable aspects of my Self. The common thread between all of those fragments is *desire* because that's the only fragment of me the algorithms can detect—**an environment that automatically detects and caters to your every desire in an addiction machine**. The fact that heavy social media users experience *anhedonia* (the diminished ability to experience pleasure) whenever they're not on social media[33] points to both the powerfully addictive quality of social media and the power that it has to cause anxious depression. So what's the solution to a scenario that seems to recall the classic dystopian science fiction stories involving antihuman artificial intelligence? Well, what's the quintessential ending to any of those sci-fi stories? Some clever person invariably figures out a way to "pull the plug," the irony being that for all of its omniscience, omnipresence, and seeming omnipotence, artificial intelligence is still invariably defeated by the manual disconnection of the machine from its fuel. In other words, humans are still vastly more powerful than the incredibly intelligent devices that rule our lives. We need only invoke that power to demonstrate our superior intelligence. If we revoke the "*power of off*"—the power of individual human decision—we deny our own human intelligence in favor of artificial intelligence, thus enslaving ourselves to the machine.

In a previous chapter, I suggested that we can all learn a lot from dogs. In a similar vein, Lanier suggests that we can all learn a lot from cats. In particular, cats, while domesticated, are still relatively autonomous. Although they live with us and depend on us and cooperate with us, we are not their masters because cats remain "*in charge*" of their own behavior.[34] In reference to social media use, the best lesson to learn from cats is that of autonomy. You can free yourself of social media addiction or enslavement simply by invoking "the power of off." Start with a "SMOD"—a "social media off day"—then extend the "off" to a SMOD2 and a SMOD3. If you enjoy the freedom of an "off" existence outside of the "everywhere cage," keep going. Extend the off for a week (SMOW), a month (SMOM), or even a year (SMOY). If you get that far, you've probably unburdened yourself of the social media habit for good, making yourself a "SMOFER"—someone who is "social media off forever." Get out of that "everywhere cage" and stay out.

If you're still not convinced to drop out of social media or avoid it as much as possible, then do what Jaron Lanier and I have done. Write down as many arguments as you can think of for how social media may cause you to contradict or devalue your own identity, degrade or regress your behavior, depress you, stress you out, or in any way make you feel bad, sad, or mad. If we can't convince you, maybe you can convince your Self?

Chapter Nine. Interpersonal Media

How will you replace social media? If you're on social media to stay abreast of current events, you're in the wrong place. Social media is a distributor of **misinformation** (aka "fake news"), which should be avoided at all costs. If you must stay current, select a news medium that's more reliable and valid, perhaps one with actual journalists. If you're using social media to remind you of things that are happening in your life, you can just download a simple calendar app that will keep track of all your events and remind you about them without you having to stick your personal business into the ether for the algorithms to do with as they please.

If you're using social media to stay connected with families and friends, I suggest you **replace the many-to-many correspondence of social media with a one-to-one correspondence** such as a phone call, email, text message, letter, or card. In a many-to-many correspondence (as in all social media), posts—even personal ones—are generally seen by everyone. Your personal birthday wish to your mother is read by all, and her response is also read by all, making the exchange less meaningful to the one person you want it to be meaningful to—your mother. **Personal relationships are meaningful because of their exclusivity**, which is the thing that makes each relationship special. I have one mother, one daughter, one son, one wife, one brother, one sister. These are exclusive relationships that would remain exclusive even if I had several brothers or sisters. The exclusivity resides in the fact that each human is an individual, so my personal relationship to you is entirely exclusive because that specific relationship between two entirely unique individuals can only exist as a single irreducible and irreplaceable relation. To recall Buber's I-Thou distinction, when I'm relating to Thou, I'm an individual relating exclusively to another individual, accepting my individuality and Thou's individuality as a precondition of the relation. When I disrupt the exclusivity of the one-to-one correspondence by posting it on social media for the world to see, I contradict my own individuality, Thou's individuality, and the individuality of the relationship itself. When I'm not speaking directly and exclusively with you, my attention is not exclusively on you, so whatever may be special or unique about my relation to you is lost by the inherent unexclusivity of the medium itself.

Replacing that generic "happy birthday" post on social media with a simple one-to-one correspondence such as a text message tells that other person that you think they're special, so special that they deserve an individual message rather than a general "shout-out," and that you respect the individuality of the relationship and the individuality of the person as well. Rather than being just another one of dozens of social media birthday greetings (most of them mechanistically sent by bots or fake profiles), your greeting stands out because you acknowledged that the true implicit content of a genuine birthday greeting is the simple message—"*I care about You*"—a message sent by an individual to another individual. The same message would be meaningless if it were sent in a nonexclusive medium ("the medium is the message").

I have a simple birthday reminder app on my phone that notifies me of each loved one's birthday (or anniversary) so I can reach out to each one individually on their birthday or special day. I've found that they appreciate the exclusive message much more than the social media shout-out. And what about the dozens or even hundreds of social media "friends" whose phone numbers you don't have? How do you wish all those "friends" happy birthday? Simple. You don't. Exclusivity is meaningful because it's exclusive. The fact that I only send individualized personal birthday messages to people that I love and that everyone else gets exactly nothing makes my love more exclusive and therefore more meaningful and valuable both to me and the people I love. Social media, by "spreading the love," makes love nonexclusive, and nonexclusive love is meaningless love; in fact, it's in no way comparable to real love at all.

One recurring question in this book is, *"How can I find the time to balance eight ways of engaging in my life when I barely have time for two or three?"* Well, are you aware that the average social media user spends up to three hours per day on social media? That's over 20 hours per week, 120 hours per month, well over 1,000 hours a year.[35] Drop social media or severely cut back to just the absolutely necessary level of engagement, and you will have a windfall of time at your disposal. Use that time to actively engage in a medium that values your individuality and your relationships and allows you to be you rather than coercing you into becoming a narcissistic asshole.

Chapter Ten

Intrapersonal Media

The Spiritual Dream in the Temple of Sleep

> *If the doors of perception were cleansed, every thing would appear to man as it is, infinite. For man has closed himself up, till he sees all things through narrow chinks of his cavern.*
>
> —William Blake[1]

Sleep takes precedence over everything. This is something we all know from experience but often fail to apply to our daily lives. We've all been sleep deprived for one reason or another. Maybe it was a very late night of fun followed by work or school early in the morning, or maybe it was "jet lag," or even just a restless night of tossing and turning. We've all been there. When we don't have enough sleep, we cannot function at all. Our brain and body feel like they're floating on sacks of lead, our mind is a black cloud, our emotions are dead until something frustrates us, and then we simply explode. We have no emotional resources to fall back on, no patience, no way of focusing on anything other than getting through the next moment. That's just from missing less than one night of sleep. Imagine if you were perpetually sleep deprived. Well, you probably are.

In his eye-opening book *Why We Sleep* (2017), neuroscientist and premier sleep researcher Matthew Walker argues that if you're regularly getting less than eight to nine hours of restful sleep per night, you're in a state of chronic sleep deprivation. You just don't feel the deprivation because it may be a low level and because you're used to it. If you're like I used to be, you probably got into the bad habit of staying up past midnight every night, then getting up before 8:00 a.m. each weekday for work, and then sleeping in on weekends through the morning to compensate. In my case, by only getting around six hours of sleep on Sunday through Thursday nights, I was functioning at a low level of sleep deprivation most of the week, which I countered with caffeine stimulants (mostly coffee). By the end of the workweek, I owed myself a sleep debt of about 10 hours, so I made up for that by sleeping through the mornings on weekends (if I could), getting as much as 20 hours of sleep over the weekend. If you're doing the math, you noticed that the sleep debt is never fully repaid. If I slept only about 6 hours each weeknight ($5 \times 6 = 30$), plus up to 11 hours on weekend nights ($2 \times 10 = 20$), then my total for the average week was only 50 hours, while the total amount I actually needed was significantly more ($7 \times 8 = **56**$). I, like most people in our society, was functioning at a low level of chronic sleep deprivation (perpetually at least four hours, or half night, behind on sleep). I denied and counteracted my sleep deprivation by doping myself with coffee and binge sleeping on weekends.

I decided to change my ways about five years ago, following what I considered to be a professional failure. I flew out to the West Coast for a conference, which included a couple of research talks led by me, a couple of job interviews, a discussion with a publisher about a book proposal, a few events I wanted to attend, and a few people I knew whom I wanted to hang out with while I was there. It was a busy three days, and I scheduled only two hotel nights, figuring I'd sleep on the plane on the way there and back. Well, I couldn't sleep on the plane, which was a red-eye flight from New York to Seattle. I spent the first day of the conference in a haze of sleep deprivation (aka "jet lag"). My two research talks did not go well because I couldn't concentrate and I was easily flustered. Rather than just focusing on sleep, I focused on forcing myself to stay awake until bedtime so I could "reset" my sleep schedule and be rested for the next two days. However, even though I was dead tired my first night, I couldn't fall asleep because of the stimulating effect of being in a strange place and because of all the caffeine in my system. The next day, I was still horribly sleep deprived. I sleepwalked through my job interviews and book proposal discussion. I honestly can't even remember them; they were so hazy, and they didn't go well, I presume, because no job offers or book contracts were forthcoming as a result. By the end of the second day, I was so grumpy and sleepy that I blew off my remaining events and dinner plans with friends and just collapsed in my hotel room. I finally did get some good sleep but only after I either underperformed, blew off, or completely failed at all of the things I really wanted to accomplish on that trip. My last day was the only day I could focus at all, but it was too late to redeem myself. On the sleepless flight home, I reflected on how my failure was due 100 percent to my stupid mistake of not prioritizing sleep over everything else. The simple truth is that when sleep is not given precedence over *everything*, you will not be able to perform well at *anything*.

At the time (2017–2018), I was working on a book about the effects of media on spirituality, and I was developing a novel theory that placed dreaming at the center of spiritual experience. Struck by how completely devastated I was physically, emotionally, and psychologically by just a short period of sleep deprivation, I began a period of deep research into the psychology of sleep and dreaming using Dr. Walker's excellent book as a launchpad. By tweaking my daily schedule slightly, I was able to increase my average weeknight's sleep to at least eight hours per night. In turn, my weekend binges of 11–12 hours per night reduced themselves to about 9 hours per night with no effort on my part. My brain and body, when generally well rested, don't need more than nine hours of sleep at most, so I found myself getting out of bed on Saturday and Sunday mornings at around 9:00 a.m., rather than at the crack of noon, simply because I wasn't tired—an entirely new experience for me. I then found that I was much more focused and engaged in my daily workweek activities because I wasn't constantly fighting the uphill battle of chronic sleep deprivation, and it was also a joy to have weekend mornings to enjoy consciously, instead of just sleeping those mornings away every week.

The real test came when I attended the same conference a year later. I had a similar number of commitments and plans, but I decided to prioritize sleep above all else. I booked a daytime rather than nighttime flight, and I scheduled my talks and interviews for the afternoons rather than the mornings. There were a few things I did want to attend in the mornings, and I had some invitations to join people for breakfast or coffee, but I declined them all in the name of prioritizing sleep, and it was the best possible decision I could've made. When I got off the plane, I went directly to the hotel, checked into my room, got some food, and then went straight to bed. Although I'm not a huge fan of sleep aids, I took some diphenhydramine[2] that first night to help me fall asleep, and it did help. I was in a nice hotel in an exciting city with people I knew who wanted to socialize that evening, so I spent the entire night alone, in bed, with no regrets.

The next day, I was well rested and performed exceedingly well at all my events. I went out for dinner with friends and stayed out late, knowing I had no commitments the next morning. I slept well that night, slept in a bit, and had a very successful second day at the conference and another nice evening out as well. My third day was equally successful, and as I flew home, I marveled at how huge a difference prioritizing my sleep had made on the whole trip. Rather than perceiving it as a failure, I perceived it as a great success. I was much more productive, performed at a much higher level, and actually enjoyed myself the whole time. I didn't plan as much activity as I did the last time, but because I didn't have to blow anything off due to sleep deprivation, I actually accomplished a lot more and engaged in more activities as a whole. I learned from that experience and from the year of research and discovery that preceded it that getting enough sleep on a daily basis is by far the most important thing you can do for your emotional, mental, and physical health. I had also developed a model for why sleep and dreaming is the most important thing you can do for your spiritual and intrapersonal well-being. It's fortunate for you that I'm dealing with the matter of sleep and dreams in the last chapter because we often remember the last thing told to us the best of all. So here it is, once again. The most important thing that I or anyone else is ever likely to tell you about finding peace and balance in your life and in your Self: **Sleep takes precedence over everything!**

The Productivity Paradox (Revisited) and the Consciousness Bias

> *Sleep is the single most effective thing we can do to reset our brain and body health each day—Mother Nature's best effort yet at contra-death.*
> —Matthew Walker[3]

By pulling back from overengaging in the one or two media of thought that you must focus on to be productive, you balance your mind in such a way that you'll actually be more productive in all of your mental engagement, including the ones associated with productivity. In short, a well-balanced mind is a more productive mind, even though that means spending less time and energy on being productive. This is the "productivity paradox." Nowhere is that paradox more paradoxical than in the domain of sleep; and within the domain of sleep itself, no paradox is more paradoxical than the phenomenon of "paradoxical sleep,"[4] aka "dreaming." By focusing on getting enough sleep at night rather than on being productive each day, you increase your productivity during the day. Furthermore, by increasing your time spent dreaming each night, you increase your ability to fulfill your dreams during the day because dreaming enhances learning, memory, and creativity along with a host of other cognitive benefits. Meanwhile, increasing your time spent sleeping and dreaming will decrease your anxiety and depression, increase your physical energy and mental stamina, enhance your ability to remember and learn, lower your risk for cancer, dementia, and strokes, while keeping you slimmer and more resistant to illness.[5]

In a previous book,[6] I coined the term **"*consciousness bias*"** to refer to the way that we humans are inherently biased against any experience that's not conscious. This is one of those human tendencies that's so obvious it's invisible, so we fail to notice it even when it's killing us. At the moment, your body and brain are quite aware of many things, such as the presence of oxygen in the room, the presence of light, the presence or absence of other people, background noise, silence or the lack of ambient noise. These are things that fall under the category of your **subliminal awareness**. While your conscious mind is focusing on the words in this sentence, you're not thinking about the light or oxygen in the room— you're not consciously aware of them—but the moment either of them change significantly or cease to exist, your conscious attention will attend to them, raising them into your conscious awareness. In short, we're not really aware of anything we're not "*conscious*" of. This is also referred to as "*inattentional blindness*," our blindness to anything we're not aware of because of the laser focus of left hemispheric attending, which spotlights the details but leaves the rest of our field of attention in the shadows.

In its monomaniacal conceit, consciousness denies the significance and often even the existence of any cognitive process other than itself. Since sleep is by definition an "unconscious" process, we remain blind to its incredible daily importance and deny our total dependence on it. "*I can get away with just five or six hours a night,*" we lie to ourselves and others, as this is an empirically proven biological untruth.[7] "*There's time enough to sleep in the grave,*" we drolly say, even as our sleep deprivation hastens the grave. Sleep is the time when we deliberately focus on not focusing, when we allow conscious awareness to drift into another mode of attending that is described as "unconscious," though it really is just another form of consciousness, another invisible media environment. To balance our media engagement across the spectrum of all forms of consciousness, we must illuminate this media environment so we can see it, and we must be aware of our conscious tendency to ignore, deny, and repress our need for sleep and dreams so we can overcome those fatally ignorant tendencies.

The Dream Environment as "Overnight Therapy"

> *Faced with information overload, we have no alternative but pattern-recognition.*
> —Marshall McLuhan

After thousands of years of pondering why we dream, we're finally able to analyze the neurological processes at play during sleep and dreaming and deduce what's happening and why it's so important.[8] Sleep can be broken down into a variety of stages, but the primary distinction is between REM (rapid eye movement) sleep, when we dream, and NREM sleep, also known as "deep sleep," when we're not dreaming. During deep sleep, our brain waves are much longer and slower. The brain is combing through its short-term memory, weeding out things that we don't need to remember and restoring the things we do need to remember in long-term memory. NREM sleep is absolutely vital to the processes of memory and learning, so much so that it's not an overstatement to say that while we *acquire* information during the day, our brains actually *learn* and *remember* information at night while we sleep.

During dreams, our brain waves look much like they do when we're awake and actively engaged. Dreaming is, of course, a form of consciousness, but it's a consciousness that we're unconscious of, a somewhat confusing distinction that requires us to admit that consciousness is not in any way a singular experience, but rather, there are many states of consciousness. In dream consciousness, our perceptual faculties are turned on once again (hence REM), but our eyes are still closed, as the perceptions originate from within our own mind. Dreams are, in fact, autobiographical stories filled with the sensory and psychosocial information we received during the day. Dreams are a creative and integrative process. They do not "replay" our memories in any way.[9] Walker sums it up by saying that waking consciousness is a state of information *"reception,"* NREM a state of *"reflection"* in which information is processed and stored, while REM is a state of *"integration"* in which information is connected with past experiences and also projected into future hypothetical scenarios. Recalling McLuhan, dreams collate the ***"information overload"*** of our daily existence via a process of ***"pattern recognition,"*** weaving myriad threads of meaningless data into meaningful ongoing narratives about ourselves and our interactions with the world—*the story of our lives*.

Of the three things we do with information—receive, reflect, and integrate—the third is the most crucial because without it, there would be no meaning in our minds or in our lives. Dreaming is by far the most creative thing we do because it literally creates meaning out of inherently meaningless patches of data. The fact that when deprived of dreams (but not sleep), we soon lose our grip on reality and experience not only intense anxious depression but also utter psychosis proves the point that dreams are absolutely essential for our sanity because they make sense out of our insane world. The intrapersonal dream environment of constructed meaning is the only anti-environment we have to counteract the waking environment in which we're constantly bombarded with random information that confuses us and makes us anxious and overwhelmed. By fashioning order out of chaos, meaning out of emptiness, dreams give us the hope to carry on in a hopeless situation. Walker refers to dreaming as a form of "**overnight therapy**" because "*it takes the painful sting out of difficult, even traumatic, emotional episodes you have experienced during the day, offering emotional resolution when you awake the next morning.*"[10] If, following Victor Frankl, "*despair*" is defined as "*suffering without meaning,*"[11] then dreams relieve us of despair by reimagining our suffering within the frame of a meaningful narrative. Dreams transform despair into hope. If dreams "*did not perform this operation,*" Walker asserts, "*we'd all be left with a state of chronic anxiety in our autobiographical memory network.*"[12]

On a broad level, we can say that the left hemispheric mode of attending that dominates waking consciousness is adept at studying the "*trees*" in our environment, while it is the right hemispheric mode of attending, which dominates dream consciousness, that not only perceives the "*forest*" of trees but also actually creates the frame of meaning that is the "forest." Without the meaningful frame of the forest, without this crucial metaphor, the trees would merely be an existential wasteland of groundless figures. Dreams provide the invisible ground to our conscious existence. We ignore that invisible ground at our own peril. The bias that denies the importance of anything beyond our conscious awareness leaves us all sleep deprived and bereft of the dreams that we need to bear conscious existence itself. To admit that consciousness is not "*the master of its own house,*"[13] to let go of conscious control and simply "rest assured" that our minds will detoxify themselves in the integrating media environment of the dream, is anathema to our conscious mind, which is narcissistically blind to anything other than itself. In dreams, we transcend our mundane consciousness of daily worries and aggravations, entering the Eden of pure creative imagination, where we re-create the world in our own image as we integrate in narrative form the one figure that needs grounding most of all—our true Self.

A Brief Interpretation of the History of Dream Interpretation

> ...[W]e lose the power of a dream and other unconscious experience when we reduce them to rationalized words, for they then become "signs" rather than "symbols."
> —Rollo May[14]

The history of dream interpretation could be summed up in four models. In the first model, constructed many thousands of years ago by the first consciously aware hominids, people believed that their dreams were messages from the gods or the spirit world, providing insight and direction for their lives. This "primary model" is by far the most common interpretation of the function of dreams, both historically and cross-culturally. A more rational interpretation was provided by Aristotle a couple of thousands of years ago, who believed that dreams were just a continuation of the perceptual processes of the senses, persisting even after the eyes close and external stimulation is shut down. In other words, dreams are like the TV show that keeps playing even after we fall asleep. The only reason the TV show is on is because we forgot to shut the TV off, and there's no deeper reason or meaning to the show beyond that oversight. Aristotle's explanation made sense, but not many people believed it. He was also almost completely wrong, with his only correct insight being that dreams originate internally rather than externally.

In his book *The Interpretation of Dreams* (1899), Freud argued that dreams were products of the "unconscious mind" and that by interpreting them, we could understand ourselves better. By inventing an ill-defined construct called the "unconscious"—something that's defined exclusively by the absence of something else—and then labeling that nebulous thing the generator and repository of our dreams, Freud was making an assertion very similar to the pre–Aristotelians—dreams are meaningful messages to us—coming from a source that's exponentially older and wiser than we are. By attributing dreams to an internal source (the unconscious mind) rather than an external source (the gods), Freud effectively assimilated Aristotle's key insight into his own (dreams come from within). Beyond that, his theory was limited by a lack of insight into the neurological processes going on while we sleep. That insight is the strength behind Walker's first book, *Why We Sleep* (2017), which demonstrates through a review of empirical research that dreams are personally meaningful to us and that they serve incredibly important functions related to memory, learning, creativity, and emotional self-regulation. In other words, *dreams are important and personally meaningful*—the same basic theory we came up with thousands and thousands of years ago. Nice work, human mind. Just running us around in circles, like you always do.

Aristotle's rational interpretation of dreams as meaningless sensory information was not only wrong, but it also devalued a process that's inherently more valuable and important than anything our mind does consciously. Nice work, Aristotle.

Freud's interpretation was less incorrect, but it also gave us the false hope that we could cure our own neuroses by psychoanalyzing our dreams and other "unconscious" issues. After over 120 years of this folly, we now know that psychoanalysis, while fascinating, doesn't cure anything. The mind is too stupid to figure itself out and too arrogant to admit that it can't. Freudian dream interpretation is certainly no cure for neurosis. In fact, the process itself is a form of neurosis—driven by the delusion that our anxious depressive thoughts ("neuroses") are puzzles that could be solved if we could only find the missing pieces, buried deep down in the fictional oubliette of an unknown kingdom defined only by what it is not. Nice work, Freud.

The most recent interpretation, championed by Dr. Walker, has the benefit of being backed up by real science. Even though I relish the correct interpretation—dreams are self-originating and incredibly important for our mental health—I'm wary of the inference—that by studying and possibly meddling with our dreams, we can understand ourselves better and, maybe even by tinkering around a bit, help ourselves. Although I have no problem with studying dreams, I stop short at the notion of tinkering with them, as the notion itself reeks of the same hubris found in Aristotelean and Freudian theory. We don't understand dreams. Studying them is fine, but please, let's not mess around with something we don't really understand. In fact, if we look at the pure utility of the dream interpretation process—the usefulness of acknowledging our dreams in any way at all—we see the clearest irony. Of the four interpretations of the origin and function of dreams that humans have constructed, the first interpretation was by far the most useful. If we truly believe that our dreams come from the gods, we would not only respect the importance of dreams and the need to get the right amount of sleep to support them, but we would respect the process itself and not fiddle too much with the workings of the gods, who know much more than we can ever know. Similarly, if we admit that dreams come from the brain rather than the ill-defined "unconscious" mind, we should also admit that the brain (like the gods) is much older and wiser than us, that it knows what it's doing far more than we do, and that (like with the gods) we should primarily have faith in the wisdom of the process itself.

The plain fact is, the more we think and theorize about gods and the meaning of dreams—the tighter we grip these metaphorical constructs—the more, like grains of sand, they slip from our grasp. Gods played (and play) an incredibly important role in the human psyche, providing the very necessary illusion of meaning, safety, security, and control in an otherwise random, chaotic, and meaningless existence. As we thought more and more about gods and the universe, the more rational and scientific our minds became. The more rational our minds became, the tighter our grip on the construct of gods became in a frantic attempt to hold on to the illusion we so desperately need. At a certain point, for many of us, the bottom of the construct fell out completely, emptying the metaphors of all their inherent meaning. In short, many of us have lost the ability to believe in gods—the one thing that used to provide inherent and universal meaning to all of us—simply because we let our conscious minds think ourselves out of it. Nice work, human mind. But it's not done.

The mind is still zeroing in on our dreams, configuring them as yet another problem that needs solving. Will we begin overthinking and possibly even physically tinkering with our dreams? If so, I'll give you one guess about the probable outcome. The mind's greatest falling is its hubristic conceit. Its greatest mistake is overthinking everything, especially itself. If it thinks it can understand the dreaming process better than our brain, it's sorely mistaken, and it will lead us into yet even more folly. Dreams used to be our only direct means of communication and communion with the "gods"—*the medium of spiritual perception*—and the wellspring of intuitive wisdom and inspiration. Now they are patterns of neural processing that reflect personally relevant thought patterns, but that's all. The mind has taken away so much of what is intuitive, innate, and inherently meaningful. For many of us, it has taken away God itself. Please, don't let it rob us of our dreams as well.

"Temporal Lobe Personality" and the "Sacred Disease"

> Could it be that human beings have actually evolved specialized neural circuitry for the sole purpose of mediating religious experience?
>
> —V.S. Ramachandran[15]

Herodotus labeled epilepsy the "sacred disease" because seizures were occasionally accompanied by divine inspiration. These theophanies[16] are common in a specific form of epilepsy that afflicts the temporal lobes of the brain. (I refer to theophanies and any experience in which a spiritual presence is seen, heard, felt, or in any way sensed as "**spiritual perception**."[17]) Unlike grand mal seizures that affect the entire brain, temporal lobe seizures are localized within a small region of the brain so that the effects are temporary and the epileptic does not lose consciousness or control of their bodily functions. The term "temporal lobe personality" has been applied to temporal lobe epileptics who experienced a drastic change in their worldview subsequent to experiences of spiritual perception resulting from seizures. The temporal lobe personality is obsessed with spiritual matters, oftentimes in direct contrast to their personality prior to their spiritual perceptions. They often come off like a self-proclaimed prophet who has "seen the light."[18]

Following the trail of clues left by epilepsy, neurologists have found that the temporal lobes seem to be integral in the human experience of spirituality, giving rise to the new field of "neurotheology." The neurotheological premise is that just as the human brain is hardwired for certain evolutionarily advantageous behaviors such as language acquisition and social engagement, the brain may also be hardwired for spiritual experiences (or for experiences that we humans tend to interpret as "spiritual"). Spirituality as a phenomenon is clearly advantageous for survival because it provides a meaningful frame for existence, answering troubling questions such as "*What happens to 'me' when I die?*" "*Will I ever see my recently deceased loved one again?*" "*What is the purpose of my existence?*" and "*What is the meaning of life?*" All of these troubling and essentially unanswerable questions are answered in comforting ways when posed in reference to a spiritual dimension of existence. The belief in this spiritual dimension itself reduces anxious depressive thoughts about death and suffering, while a shared "belief system" becomes an incredibly strong cementing bond within social groups. Neurotheologists have also found that by stimulating the temporal lobes using transcranial magnetic waves, spiritual perceptions could be evoked in many people.

The notion that humans are hardwired for spirituality is supported by the fact that belief in spirituality is one of the relatively few universals in human psychology. Every culture and society that has ever existed has had some form of spiritual belief system or religion. The vast majority of people on this planet believe in God or some form of spiritual dimension despite the clear lack of objective proof. Evidently, there's something about the human condition that demands or even requires a spiritual component. Perhaps it's the advent of consciousness itself that requires a counterbalance in spirituality. If the mind creates a part of itself that is constantly asking the question "Why?" of its own existence, would it not make sense for the mind to also conjure a countering part of itself that regularly *answers* the question "Why?" Perhaps it has become the job of the left hemisphere to ask "why?" during the day, while it has become the job of the right hemisphere to answer "why?" during the night. These "two ways of attending" to our existential concerns would seem complementary, as they fall into the well-established roles of the left hemisphere as problem/solution seeker and the right hemisphere as merging integrator.

The premise I've been working up to is encapsulated in my construct of the "***spiritual dream***." It's a well-built construct because the building blocks are so sound that most of them can be considered "facts." First, we know from dream research that we all dream multiple times every night and that dreams are absolutely essential for our mental health because they integrate our daily intake of information into meaningful patterns of knowledge. Second, we know that spirituality is a historically and cross-culturally universal phenomenon and that spirituality as a belief and practice is associated with decreased rates of anxiety and depression as well as increased levels of happiness, life satisfaction, and psychosocial integration and adjustment.[19] Third, in the modern age of rational skepticism, many of us have abandoned the "lies" of traditional organized religion but not necessarily the "hope" that there may be an underlying spiritual dimension to our existence. Finally, there is significant overlap between the spiritual experience and the dream experience, so much so that the *spiritual dream* could not only be considered a normative human experience but an absolutely *necessary* and *essential* normative human experience.

Spiritual Perception and the Spiritual Dream

> *In the long pre-Freudian centuries, before the mystery of the dream was reduced to all too human terms, when men still listened for the voice of God in the still of the night, dreams played a greater rôle in shaping ideas and actions and careers than it is easy for us today to believe.*
> —Joshua Trachtenberg

I met with my father a few months ago, though he died nearly 20 years ago. I met him in a dream. Was this an experience of spiritual perception, or was it "just a dream"? The answer, truly, is a matter of subjective interpretation. If I believe that I met with my father's spirit, then the dream would be my own subjective experience of spiritual perception. However, if I believe that a dream is just a mélange of memory, hallucination, and imagination, then it would not be spiritual perception. In the end, it's *belief* that gives form and being to any potentially spiritual experience. *We see what we believe and not the other way around.* Nowhere is that fact truer than in the subjective intrapersonal media environment of the dream, where perception is created rather than received.

Spiritual perception is when we interpret a perception as having a spiritual origin, making belief in the existence of spirituality a prerequisite to the phenomenon of spiritual perception. *If you don't believe in it, you cannot experience it.* It is this ontological concern—the inability to take a "leap of faith" and believe in spirituality—that afflicts many agnostics who want to believe but cannot consciously allow themselves to believe. Thus, the inability to believe becomes a wall to both spirituality and religion but only during the conscious state. No such wall exists in the dream environment because dreams are not beholden to consciousness, nor are they beholden to logic or reason. As the environment of pure imagination, anything can exist in dreams, including God, gods, angels, spirits, demons, and even one's own soul. If a spiritual dimension does exist, humanity's primary access to it (while living) could only be through the inner portal of dreams. *Where else?* Whereas the fortunate faithful can still experience spiritual perception through prayer, ritual, and other forms of devotion and worship, the unfortunate unfaithful (like me) have no media environment to experience spiritual perception because all of our windows to that world have been nailed shut by logic, reason, and rational consciousness. All of our windows save one—the inner window of dreams.

William James's book *The Varieties of Religious Experience* (1902) is still considered the classic text on the psychology of spirituality. In the book, James refers to spiritual perception as a *"mystical state of consciousness"* that's fundamentally different from our normal experience of consciousness.

> Our normal waking consciousness, rational consciousness as we call it, is but one special type of consciousness, whilst all about it, parted from it by the filmiest of screens, there lie potential forms of consciousness entirely different. We may go through life without suspecting their existence; but apply the requisite stimulus, and at a touch they are there in all their completeness, definite types of mentality which probably somewhere have their field of application and adaptation.[20]

James observed and documented hundreds of experiences of spiritual perception, summarizing his observations by delineating four essential qualities of the mystical state of consciousness. First, the experience is *"ineffable"* in that it cannot be expressed rationally in words, but rather, it's a direct perceptual experience of spirituality that transcends rational thought or logical analysis. Second, it's a *"noetic"* experience in that it imparts a sense of truth, wisdom, or higher meaning. Third, it's a *"transient"* experience. And fourth, it's *"passive."*[21]

All four of James's observations regarding the mystical state of consciousness are directly applicable to my construct of the spiritual dream. The ineffability of the experience is a key feature because the linguistic medium of conscious attention—language-based consciousness—acts as a cognitive inhibitor to spiritual thoughts. Waking consciousness, dominated by the left hemisphere, is circumscribed by the rules of logic and noncontradiction that cannot rationally accept the paradoxical existence of a spiritual dimension to life. When we sleep, however, language-based consciousness is inhibited or turned off, allowing all of our repressed and denied irrational beliefs to come out and play. Hence, for those of us afflicted with FDD (faith deficit disorder),[22] all spiritual perception is ineffable by default, as the lack of analytic language is a precondition for the occurrence of the experience itself. This doesn't mean that the experience is always completely bereft of words, as Abraham Maslow explains:

The word "ineffable" means "not communicable by words that are analytic, abstract, linear, rational, exact, etc." Poetic and metaphorical language, physiognomic and synesthetic language, primary process language of the kind found in **dreams**, reveries, free associations and fantasies ... are more efficacious in communicating certain aspects of the ineffable.[23]

In his book *The Forgotten Language* (1951), Erich Fromm argued that dreams bypass the logical restraints of conscious language by speaking to us in a primordial dialect of pictorial symbols. "*...[T]he language of the universal symbol is the one common tongue developed by the human race, a language which it forgot before it succeeded in developing a universal conventional language.*"[24] The universal symbols (aka Jungian archetypes) that run through our collective and personal consciousness and pervade our myths, literature, art, religions, and culture compose the "*picture language of the soul,*" which is the same language that speaks to us in our dreams.

> *The dreams of ancient and modern man are written in the same language as the myths whose authors lived in the dawn of history. Symbolic language is a language in which inner experiences, feelings and thoughts are expressed as if they were sensory experiences, events in the outer world.... It is the one universal language the human race has ever developed, the same for all cultures and throughout history.*[25]

James, Maslow, Jung, Fromm, Frankl, and essentially any other psychologist who admits to the possibility of a spiritual dimension in humanity (even if it exists entirely on a psychological level) noted that the vast majority of spiritual perceptions are experienced as dreams and that dreams have always been the primary entryway to spirituality, the "royal road"[26] to our inner kingdom.

The "noetic" quality of the mystical experience is the revelatory aspect, the feeling that wisdom or a deeper knowledge of the Self is being imparted. Dream perception is prefiltered perception, as it comes from within the mind rather than from without, so it purveys a sense of wisdom that can only come from someone who knows us better than we know ourselves. This uncanny level of self-knowledge, when encountered as a figure other than ourselves in our dreams, makes us believe that the wisdom is coming from a spiritual force outside of us—because who else but God could know ourselves better than we do? Dream images often appear to us with "super lucidity" because they are perceived directly from the internal dream factory of imagination rather than being filtered through the physical senses. When a noetic message of uncanny personal significance is delivered in the form of a super-lucid symbol that has both personal and collective spiritual associations for the dreamer, how could the message not be interpreted as a form of spiritual perception?

The "transient" and "passive" aspects of James's mystical state are inherently true of the dream state as well. All dreams are transient, often ending all too soon. Dreams are also passive experiences in the sense that we're physically asleep when we have them and also, while in the dream, we tend to fall into the role of passive observer, the sole audience member within the theater of the mind. To James's four aspects I will add a logical fifth, which is *"solitary."* As a general rule, spiritual perception is experienced alone, a single person encountering a spiritual presence. This single observation is the main reason why the conscious mind cannot accept the premise of spirituality—the total lack of any empirical validation of spiritual presences by objective witnesses or recording instruments. All we have is the word of the one person who claims to have experienced a spiritual presence while all alone, usually within a dream, thus negating any chance at objective validation. Nevertheless, it is the solitary spiritual perception that has given humanity its primary glimpses of existential meaning: *"The intrinsic core, the essence, the universal nucleus of every known high religion, has been the private, lonely, personal illumination, revelation, or ecstasy of some acutely sensitive prophet or seer."*[27]

Like Freud, Carl Jung believed that dreams are the *"royal road to the unconscious,"* yet unlike the master, Jung was not an atheist but an intensely spiritual seeker. For Jung, dreams were not just the manifestations of unresolved issues and unfulfilled desires emanating from the *"personal unconscious."* Jung believed that dreams performed a *"transcendent function"* for the dreamer, allowing them to transcend the personal issues of their individual egos by encountering and integrating the symbols in their dreams that have collective or shared meaning. The *"archetypes"* are symbols from the *"collective unconscious,"* the psychological realm of collective associations that connects all humanity. It's impossible to discuss these terms without embracing the spiritual because Jungian language itself is so inherently spiritual and Jung so firmly believed that humans have a *"spiritual drive."* What exactly is the "collective unconscious" if not the shared spiritual connection through symbols that pervades all religious and spiritual experience? What exactly is an "archetype" if not a collective belief in a shared symbol that transcends the individual human experience, making the archetype universal and immortal? Are the universal and immortal symbols for mother, father, and the self—represented in archetypal form as God, goddess, and semi-divine hero—not direct representations of our desire to connect spiritually with those aspects of humanity that proffer meaning to life? Jung asserted that *"the unconscious mind is capable at times of assuming an intelligence and purposiveness which are superior to actual conscious insight.... [This] is a basic religious phenomenon.... The voice [is] a product of the most complete personality to which the dreamer's conscious self belongs."*[28]

Jungian psychology is, indeed, mystical spiritualism written in the guise of psychoanalysis. And that's OK. In Jung's words: "*It is the role of religion*[29] *to give a meaning to the life of man.*"[30]

Dream Time versus Waking Time

> *Man becomes aware of the sacred because it manifests itself, shows itself, as something wholly different from the profane.*
> —Mircea Eliade

We all know that time works differently in dreams. Our circadian rhythms give us an instinctual sense of time that we often battle during waking hours, using alarms, caffeine, sleep aids, and a thousand clocks to keep us constantly locked into our hyperawareness of measured time. Time as duration gives us the dreadful sense of time compaction—that time is forever growing shorter and running out—like the sand in an hourglass. Sleep is the only state of existence that frees us completely from our chronic focus on time as duration (at least until the alarm goes off). No doubt, one of the prime benefits of sleep is the experience of "atemporality,"[31] the very necessary respite sleep gives us from worrying about time all the time. Atemporality is another key aspect of spiritual perception that William James did not focus on discretely but noted in his observations. When encountering a spiritual or divine presence, "**time stands still**" as if it does not even exist in the spiritual dimension. Since most spiritual perception occurs during the spiritual dream, it wasn't necessary for James to note the experience of atemporality because that's a precondition of the sleep/dream state. However, since my model specifically inculpates our waking perception of time as a primary curse of consciousness, atemporality arises as a rather major benefit of sleep and especially of dreams.

Walker refers to the "*temporal distortion*" experienced in dreams as "*time dilation*"—the elongation or stretching out of our sense of time.[32] In part, the sense of time dilation might be a relic of the sense of time compaction we feel when conscious. If, while awake, we always have a superficial sense of time shortening and thus running out, then while asleep, the simple lack of time compaction would feel to us, in relation to our waking state, as a sense of time being released from its compacted state—time expanding, dilating, elongating, and rolling out ahead of us like an infinite red carpet. That may be why, when we dream, we feel like we've been experiencing the dream state for hours or even days, though it may have only been minutes. Walker notes that there is a "*dramatic deceleration of neural time*" during dreams. When lab rats are awake and learning a maze, their neurological recall process moves quickly, but when the rats are asleep and dreaming about the same maze, their recall process moves much more slowly—as slow as a quarter of the speed than when they were awake. Like in a slow-motion film, time stretches out as the individual frames pass by at a slower rate. The lab rat research demonstrates the process of time dilation (how it occurs) but not the raison d'être (why it occurs).[33]

My theory is that sleep in general and dreams in particular, and the spiritual dream especially, owe much of their psychological benefits to their inherent atemporality. Mircea Eliade's famous distinction between "*sacred time*" and "*profane time*" provides the appropriate metaphor. Eliade's interpretation of preliterate ritual and myth establishes a world consisting of two parallel dimensions of existence that share the same physical space but different experiences of time. "Profane time" is the time of ordinary mundane conscious existence. It's "profane" only in the sense that there's nothing sacred about it and it's ruled by the normal passing of time. One can transcend the limits of profane time by entering the dimension of "sacred time"—the magical time before the beginning—when gods and goddesses walked the face of the earth and created everything, including humans and their profane sense of time. Since time, in preliterate cultures, is always cyclical, sacred time is always present, always repeating itself, and therefore always accessible. The gods in sacred time are still present, still creating the world, still directly in contact with their mortal children, as sacred time never begins or ends but, like Nature herself, is always "eternally recurring." We transcend into sacred time via one of two portals: the communal spiritual ritual or the personal spiritual dream. In both cases, it is the experience of being *inside* sacred time that heals the spiritual wound. All beings are restored to their pristine state of creation once they return to the sacred time of creation. Sleep, in both Eliade's classical model and Walker's scientific model, is a restorative process. It restores our bodies and brains to their natural resting states; and in the spiritual dream, sleep restores our "soul" to its natural state of existence even if (or especially if) you don't believe in the constructs of "spirituality" or the "soul." Overcoming our conscious resistance to the irrational aspects of existence that nonetheless offer experiences that transcend ration and reason is perhaps the greatest gift that dreams have to offer us.

Transcending the Paradox of Faith

> *The evolutionary biologist Edward O. Wilson has decreed that you cannot tread the path of spirituality and the path of reason; you must choose between them.*
> —John Horgan

All dreams are not necessarily spiritual, just as all spiritual experiences are not necessarily dreams. Nevertheless, the overlap of the experience of dreaming and the experience of spiritual perception is great enough for me to build a model around it. Despite many years of trying to commune with God via fruitless prayer and ill-fated rabbinical guidance, I personally have never experienced anything close to real spiritual perception outside of the intrapsychic dimension of dreams. My model of the spiritual dream is not necessarily true for everyone, but it is *potentially universal*. If I told two people about my dream in which I encountered my deceased father, it's likely that one person would consider it "just a dream," while the other would consider it a "spiritual encounter." Who's right and who's wrong? The interpretation is up to me, making my dream—and all dreams like it—*potentially* spiritual depending on personal interpretation. Since any dream involving a supernatural encounter is potentially spiritual and since supernatural encounters are universal in dreams, the "spiritual dream" as a construct is potentially universal. That's the best I can do for you, but it works for me. **To benefit from the spiritual dream process, you just need to believe in your own innate human potential for spiritual experience; you don't have to actually believe in a spiritual dimension.**

The main reason the spiritual dream model works for me is because of its exclusivity. The only experience I ever had or have that I can point to as "spiritual perception" is the occasional spiritual dream. It's all I've got. My options are (1) reject all spirituality just as I've rejected all religion or (2) accept the possibility of a spiritual dimension that exists, at the very least as a psychological phenomenon within myself that I experience while dreaming. Because the first option offers me nothing, I'll choose the second option because at least it's something, and something is better than nothing. The choice is similar to Pascal's famous "wager,"[34] only I'm not betting on the existence of God, just on the possible existence of a spiritual potentiality within myself, which is a wager I'm willing to make. The choice is also a direct contradiction of Horgan's interpretation of E. O. Wilson, "*You cannot tread the path of spirituality and the path of reason.*" **Don't tell me where I cannot tread.** Why can't I tread the path of reason by day and the path of spirituality by night? My brain seems predisposed toward those diverging paths, so why fight myself? Although I may see only "*through narrow chinks of my cavern*" by day, may I not see the "*infinite*" when I close my eyes at night? Is it entirely irrational to be spiritual? "*Do I contradict myself? Very well, then, I contradict myself! (I am large; I contain multitudes.)*"[35]

Spiritual belief is hamstrung by the "*paradox of faith,*" the inability of a mind dominated by logical thought and reason to believe in the existence of an invisible entity with absolutely no objective evidence to support it. If there is God or gods, then let me speak with them, hear them, see them, or feel them. If I can't, then ipso facto, there is none. This deduction is based on sense perception and pure logic, a *"path of reason."* Anything that cannot be objectively measured or sensed with our senses is "non-sense" and therefore nonexistent. How can I logically accept an illogicality?

The paradox of faith is ancient. Theologians have been battling it for millennia, as rationalists chose their path and believers chose their own. However, the paradox only exists in the cold light of day when the left hemispheric problem finder is at work, scouring its environment for paradoxes and contradictions in need of resolution. When day turns to night and the right hemisphere takes over, all paradoxes and contradictions are resolved, as all figures of thought blend into the ground of the larger picture in which paradoxes may coexist as diverging but complementary worldviews. In Walker's words, the *"dreaming brain"* is free of the *"logic guards"* on duty during the day, opening us up to a process of *"transformational creativity"* that's impossible to experience consciously when *"we take a myopic, hyperfocused, and narrow view that cannot capture the full informational cosmos on offer in the cerebrum."*[36]

Ludwig Feuerbach argued, *"In the perception of the senses, consciousness of the object is distinguishable from consciousness of self; but in religion, consciousness of the object and self-consciousness coincide."*[37] Waking consciousness attends to the world by discriminating and distinguishing between the real and the unreal, the logical and the illogical, the natural and the supernatural, the metaphysical subject and the physical object. Asserting that a metaphysical subject like God has a real physical presence like a human body is paradoxical and is therefore rejected by the logical mind. In the spiritual dream, however, the objective self encounters the subjective self, and in that moment, the subjective self is perceived as being objectively real. Aldous Huxley put it this way: *"The mystical experience ... [is] the experience in which the subject-object relationship is transcended, in which there is a sense of complete solidarity of the subject with other human beings and with the universe in general."*[38] This is the process of self-transcendence, rising above the personal ego that's bound by logic and objectivity and integrating a sense of self that is egoless, unbound by logic, accepting of the possibility of all things, and open to new ways of experiencing the self and the world. In the dream, the objective self who is ruled by logic and the subjective self that yearns to transcend logic and perceive the infinite are merged into one complete Self, who transcends all of the paradoxes and contradictions posed by the lesser selves.

The ultimate function of every religious ritual and spiritual practice is to evoke this transcendence from the personal isolated ego, locked away in his solitary kingdom of mind, to the collective communal spirit, a paradoxical kingdom of merged opposites, accessible to some via the outward portal of communal ritual and to all via the inward portal of the spiritual dream. Of the two routes, the first requires a toll in the form of faith, while the latter is a free temple that's "open to people of all faiths," including the unfortunately unfaithful.

The Sleep/Wake Flip

> *Considering how biologically damaging the state of wakefulness can often be ... we can pose a very different theory: sleep was the first state of life on this planet, and it was from sleep that wakefulness emerged.*
> —Matthew Walker[39]

So where does Daisy the dog stand on the issue of spirituality? It's hard to say. If she regarded me as a god, she would probably be more obedient, so perhaps she's agnostic like me. She does dream, though, quite a lot actually, which brings me to yet another lesson that I learned from her. **Sleep is the natural state of the body and dream consciousness the natural expressive state of the brain.** Daisy sleeps most of the time—I would say at least 15 hours a day. She'll walk into a room, look around for something that interests her, and if nothing catches her fancy, she'll just plop down somewhere and go to sleep—*instantaneously,* just like that. She just closes her eyes and goes to sleep. That extraordinary ability, which we mere humans have lost in a poor exchange for consciousness, is yet another reason why our dogs are so much smarter than we are. Daisy's sleep is not at the mercy of a mercurial and hyperactive mind. When asleep, she seems the most comfortable and the most at ease, as do most if not all creatures. If she's asleep more than awake and if she's more peaceful and satisfied while asleep, then it would make sense to consider sleep her natural state and wakingness her contrived state in which she's temporarily obliged to leave her natural state for a while to take care of business related to survival, such as eating, drinking, and elimination of waste. The same observation could be made about most nonhuman mammals, who, on average, are asleep more than they're awake. As sleep is so much better for the body and brain than being awake, I suggest (following Walker) that sleep be considered our "default mode" of physical and mental activity rather than the waking state of anxious depressive rumination that we now consider the default mode. If we think of sleep rather than waking consciousness as our natural state of being rather than the other way around, then our priorities flip, as the primary objective each day is to take care of all of our business related to survival so we can exit the toxic media environment of daily consciousness (the "primary environment") and return to our natural state of being, the far more healthy and mentally restorative condition of sleep (the "prime environment").

Dreaming is the natural expressive state of the mind and brain (as opposed to waking consciousness) because it's entirely intuitive, instinctive, and creative with no limits, filters, or "logic guards" narrowing our thought process. The brain is allowing the mind to be as creative as it could possibly be, and the mind is taking the ball and running with it with no conscious interference, nothing holding back creative expression by insisting that its creations make sense in any way. Pure unfettered free association is like free jazz for a musician, or free play for a child, or an errorless field of play for the imagination.

Your balancing experiment for intrapersonal media is to flip your wake/sleep priorities for a week. Rather than thinking of sleep as a process that supports your daily functioning, think of your daily functioning as a process that merely takes care of your personal and professional business so you can get back to the far more important business of sleep and dreaming. This flip is quite different from just letting yourself sleep as much as you want for a week. I've done that before, and you probably have too and you probably had the same experience. On the first day, you sleep in until the crack of noon. Then when midnight comes around, you're not tired at all, so you watch late-night TV until you pass out. Now you're on a wacky vampire schedule of staying up all night and sleeping into the afternoon until vacation is over and you have to go back to work. So you revert to the sleep-deprived schedule you were on beforehand. That's not an experiment; that's just a free-for-all. An experiment, by definition, is a controlled condition. The sleep/wake flip is an experiment, so you must administer controls.

Start off by estimating how much time you think you'd sleep at night if you didn't have an alarm waking you up each morning. If you have no idea, use 10 hours as a rough estimate, as that's probably much more sleep than you usually get each night, while it's also a generous but realistic approximation of how much sleep you actually need each night. If you go with 10 hours of sleep, that means you also need to plan out your 14 hours of wakefulness.[40] Since the focus is on sleep, you'll need to schedule activities during the day that will foster good sleep at night, which means lots of physical activity outdoors, as much as possible. You'll also need to avoid things during the day and evening that might negatively affect your sleep. No coffee, caffeine, or other stimulants within eight hours of your experimental bedtime. That means you cannot have a cup of coffee after dinner, or even if you like a coffee when you take a 4:20 flip at 4:20 p.m., you'll have to ditch the coffee if your bedtime is midnight or earlier. Avoid being totally passive and receptive in the evening (i.e., vegging out on the couch watching TV all night). That's relaxing, but you're not engaging in the active expressive behavior that tires you out and makes you ready for sleep. Instead, we can just veg out on the couch indefinitely, feeling lazy and tired but not sleepy enough to actually fall asleep. I like to play music in the evenings until I'm literally too tired to play one more song on the piano or guitar, and then I veg out for a bit before going to bed. It's so obvious—do things that make you tired at night so you can fall asleep and stay asleep—but we humans seem to always ignore the obvious. The point of the flip experiment is not just to invoke a temporary drastic change in your sleep habits but for you to critically observe your own sleep habits—to observe how it actually feels to get the right amount of sleep and to feel adequately rested—and then to make permanent adjustments to your sleep habits based on those observations.

Spiritual Dream Mindfulness

> *Very old are we men;*
> *Our dreams are tales*
> *Told in dim Eden*
> *By Eve's nightingales.*
> —Walter de la Mare[41]

During your sleep/wake flip, you may also want to take a peek at what's going on in your dream world. I'm not suggesting that you analyze or interpret your dreams. (My position on that was made quite clear earlier in this chapter.) I'm just suggesting a quick peek at your dreams so you can have an inkling of what's going on up there and apply that to your understanding of how critical dreaming is for your mental, emotional, and spiritual health. Freud and Jung had their patients keep **dream journals** at their bedsides so they could note the symbols and themes in their dreams as soon as they wake up for later psychoanalysis. Rather than an actual journal, I suggest a **dream note**—just one of those little sticky memo notes stuck to your nightstand—so you can quickly jot down a word or two or possibly a visual symbol and then immediately return to the dream. The dream note is not enough material for an interpretation or an analysis; it's just a little peek into your dream self.

In actual Freudian/Jungian dream analysis, the dreamer writes down as much as she can about what she saw in her dream. This is called the "**manifest content**." A journal is necessary because, as you may have noticed, the dreamer upon awakening almost immediately forgets the entire content of her dream. *Why so?* My guess is that it's because dream consciousness is so incredibly different from waking consciousness. Dream consciousness functions by process of free association in which one memory or idea leads to another in ways that are entirely peculiar to the dreamer. Waking consciousness, which is generally dominated by verbal consciousness, proceeds according to the linear logic of language in which each thought logically proceeds from one point to the next in a way that makes sense to a logical person, like the words in this sentence. Dreams, on the other hand, are notoriously illogical. When we awake from the dream, we recall what we've just seen, but when we try to nail down the content of the dream, it slips away like sand in our grasp because there's no logical core binding the dream content together, no way to logically trace how one part of the dream succeeded from the previous part and proceeded to the next part. To the logical conscious mind, it all seems like "nonsense"—and logical minds are notoriously bad at remembering nonsense. Hence, Freud and Jung required dream journals so that later on, when the dreamer and analyst psychoanalyzed the dream, there was as much "manifest content" as possible available to deconstruct. The interpretation itself proceeds by process of association to reveal the "**latent content**," the hidden "true" meaning of the dream. Freud and Jung had one part right—dream content functions according to the process of association.

Classic psychoanalytic dream interpretation is an interesting process to be sure, but I argue against it. My primary criticisms of psychoanalytic dream analysis is that it presumes that the dream is a message from the unconscious mind to the conscious mind, it presumes that the message is disguised or hidden in some way that requires conscious interpretation, and it presumes that we can reveal this hidden message by exploring our associations with each symbol, figure, and theme in the dream. All of those presumptions have no basis in reality; it's just a very neat and interesting analytic process, much like "free association" or projective measures such as Rorschach tests that elicit subjective associations from exposure to ambiguous random stimuli such as ink blots. Dream analysis is essentially the same thing, with the dream content replacing the inkblots as the ambiguous stimuli. In reality, we have no reason to presume that dreams are "messages" of any sort, we have even less reason to believe that our "unconscious mind" is trying to communicate with our "conscious mind" in any way, and we have no reason to believe that one part of our mind is trying to hide or disguise something from another part of our mind. All of those presumptions only make sense when perceived through the lens of Freudian psychology and the **consciousness bias**, which presumes that nothing is important until it's consciously interpreted and that consciousness itself is somehow smarter than our brain so that we can take over the instinctual dream process and somehow, miraculously, do something smarter with it than our brains.

Personally, I believe that the dream "message" fallacy is a relic of our most ancient dream interpretation—the primordial belief that dreams are messages from the gods or spirits from the spiritual dimension. Freud just took that juicy little nugget and clothed it in the jargon of psychoanalysis, which is, in its own way, a religion in and of itself, with the almighty and unknowable "unconscious" as the omniscient god of the psyche. Once we're disabused of the fallacy that a dream is some sort of "message in a bottle," thrown out by our lonely inner selves into a sea of undifferentiated consciousness, the entire premise of dream interpretation collapses. If there's no message, then there's nothing to interpret, and that's that. And that's exactly why I discourage attempts at analysis, even as I encourage you to take a quick peek, just out of curiosity, to see what's going on. A quick dream note may be elucidating, followed by an immediate return to the dream because the dream is the important part, not the journal or the interpretation. Writing a dream journal requires that you consciously focus on the dream upon awakening, consciously trying to remember and write down as much content as you can. This process will awaken your mind completely into consciousness and bring you further away from the dream itself, defeating the entire purpose. A quick one-word note, however, won't necessarily carry you too far away from your dream so that you cannot return. I was going through a similar process a couple of years ago when I woke up one morning to find a single word written on a piece of paper on my nightstand. I had no memory of waking up that night or of writing down the word, but when I saw it, I immediately remembered the figure from my dream and its personal spiritual significance for me. The word I wrote was "Dad."

If you want to take a peek into your dreams, you should set an alarm for a time when you're usually fast asleep, especially in the early morning hours, when we tend to have our longest and deepest REM cycles. Forcing yourself to wake up in the middle of a dream is the only possible way to actually get a conscious glimpse of your dreams. Freud and Jung made the same recommendations to their patients because they knew that when we sleep and awaken naturally (without an alarm or some other waking mechanism), we tend to wake up in between REM cycles. That's why we often feel like we had a peaceful night of dreamless slumber, even though we know for a fact that we all go through several REM cycles every night. If you don't wake up in the middle of a dream, you will have absolutely no conscious memory of that dream. So as a rule, we don't remember our dreams. That fact in and of itself disabuses the "dream as message" construct because why would the brain go through the trouble of creating literally thousands and thousands of messages that will never be seen by its recipient? Also, if dreams are messages, why does the sleep/dream process itself make it highly unlikely that we will have any conscious knowledge of the vast majority of our dreams? The only possible explanation is that dreams are not messages at all and that they don't take waking consciousness into consideration at all. In fact, dreaming as a process is millions and millions of years older than consciousness itself. *For all dreams know, consciousness doesn't even exist.* That's the conclusion I reached by observing my own dreams personally and by observing Daisy's doggy dreams from a distance. As a dog, Daisy does not experience waking consciousness as verbal thought, which makes it highly unlikely that her dreams are unconscious messages to her doggy consciousness. Yet, still she dreams. That to me is proof enough that dreaming as a process is not interested or even aware of our conscious mind. Dreams represent a primordial consciousness that we share with all mammals and birds. They are far older than humanity itself, far older than consciousness, and far wiser than we are. If there *is* a spiritual dimension to existence, it's something I've never been able to relate to consciously, but I know for sure that it's something I dream about.

Conclusion
The Message/Medium Mind Flip

> *The role of the metaphor is the elevation of hidden ground into sensibility.*
> —Marshall McLuhan

You're probably familiar with the construct of a figure/ground reversal, such as in the image provided, which portrays a sax player in the foreground (the figure of your perception), while the background portrays a woman's face. The moment you see the woman's face rather than the sax player is a figure/ground reversal (I call them "flips," following Marshall McLuhan). Your perception flipped from figure to ground, allowing you to see something that was previously hidden in plain sight in the ground of your perception because of the perceptual blindness we experience when focusing on the figure of our attention.

The visual artist must always be broadening her perception, perceiving both figure and ground, to reveal relationships between images that only they can see and then representing (re-presenting) that insight to the world. That is the trick of the artist. The trick of the thinker is to construe figure/ground reversals in cognition rather than perception—revealing hidden blind spots in the way we *think* about something rather than in how we *see* it. Marshall McLuhan

"Figure/Ground Reversal"

was the premier thinker of his generation in terms of the cognitive figure/ground flip. His revelation—"*the medium is the message*"—is actually just a simple "flip." If a "message" such as the one you're reading is the content of a "medium," then your cognitive attention is invariably focused on the words of this message—the "figure" of your attention—rather than the medium of your cognition, your ability to think, read, and write in words. "*The medium is the message*" because the medium itself is molding the way you think constantly and forever, while the message or content of your medium only affects your cognition for a passing moment.

McLuhan's insight was just one flip. Limitless others exist, hidden in plain sight. What do you tell a heartbroken friend, for example, whose partner abandoned him? You very well might say, "*There are plenty of fish in the sea.*" This is a flip. Your friend is focusing on the one fish he doesn't have (the figure of his attention), and your advice is for him to flip his cognition to consider the ground of the entire sea and all the fish that he might have within it. The hidden ground of his attention offers limitless fish if he only stopped focusing and pining on the one fish he doesn't have.

Your final thought experiment is to flip a figure/ground way of thinking in your own world. The experiment is a deliberate study in broadening your worldview, a method of intentionally opening your eyes wider, to perceive the hidden grounds in your own existence that may be eluding you. Some flips may be eye opening, others more mundane, but continue flipping until you experience an insight. To help you in your search, remember that everything you see can be interpreted as a metaphor for a deeper reality. Your task is to seek and find that metaphor, elevating the "*hidden ground*" of that insight into your everyday "*sensibility.*" That task isn't just a one-off thought experiment; it's the true meaning and benefit of media mindfulness. If you can look past the figure of your attention in all media environments to discern the mechanisms at work within the ground of the media itself—and if you can construe the effects of those mechanisms on your own thoughts and behavior—then you're truly being mindful of the medium you're engaged in within the moment of engagement, and your behaviors and thoughts will then follow, balancing themselves of their own accord.

Epilogue
Stop Fighting Your Self

The biggest personal challenge for my own media mindfulness was when my university recalled its furloughed faculty and I went back to my pre–Covid-19 work schedule. It's one thing to balance my engagement across eight different media during an extended period of spending all of my time at home, but it's quite another to do the same when I have to go to campus and work there several days a week. I don't think you'll be surprised to hear that my post–Covid-19 mindfulness practice has been going just fine. Here are some important keys to maintaining your practice over the long term.

If you stress out about having time to do everything, you're defeating the purpose of the practice, which in large part is about avoiding the pitfall of obsessing over the construct of time as duration. You can't do everything. Do not stress. Do one thing at a time and do it mindfully, and you'll be fine. The point of the practice is to trust your intuition and to let it naturally guide you away from stressful thoughts and activities. If the practice itself becomes a stressful thought and activity, you're doing it wrong because you're fighting your Self. ***Stop fighting your Self.***

Another important key to finding time to spread out your engagement is to cut back on sedentary, passive, receptive media engagement, which suck up time like a vacuum while typically offering little return in terms of personal development. Watching TV, reading social media, bingeing on bad news, doomscrolling, and similar forms of engagement place you either in the consumer role of passive viewer or the narcissus role of reflective observer. When we work all day with information, we tend to think we're both physically and mentally exhausted by the end of the day, but usually, it's just saturation fatigue because informational work is not physical. Your body doesn't need to rest or recuperate from staring at screens all day, so you may need to rile yourself up a bit and push yourself into an active expressive mode of engagement, such as biking, gardening, walking the dog, or my personal favorite, playing music. Once you get into the habit of practicing more active and expressive modes of engagement even after working all day, you won't need to find the energy to do those things because your mind and body will begin to crave those fun and joyful activities, and the activities themselves will generate more energy than they consume.

Don't worry about having enough time for media balancing because you have all the time in the world to master the practice—the rest of your life, in fact, and that's quite a long time, considering that you're going to live until you're 120. Don't worry about time or the number of media you engage in; just be mindful of what you're doing as you do it. Pursue the activities that allow you to be expressive and creative, as well as anything that gets you outdoors and moving, anything that gets you together with real people in real time, or anything that gets you in your own personal "flow zone." Don't worry about your thoughts, and don't worry about worrying. Most important, stop turning your Self into a loser by defeating your Self with negative thought patterns. ***The only way to win inner peace and balance is to stop fighting your Self and simply allow your Self to be your Self.*** At this point in the book, I've given you all the useful suggestions for accomplishing media mindfulness and balancing that I can think of. Now it's up to you. Remember, the first step and the last step are one and the same: ***Change your behaviors, and your thoughts will follow.***

Chapter Notes

Preface

1. You will notice that I occasionally write the word "self" as a capitalized proper noun. This is a reference to Carl Jung's construct of the "Self," a way of envisioning your identity as a dynamic balance of many different traits and attributes so that you are not defined by the traits themselves but by the way you balance them within your Self.

Introduction

1. "Servo-mechanisms" is a term borrowed from Marshall McLuhan.

Chapter One

1. McGilchrist (2019).
2. Gardner (2011), 13.

Chapter Two

1. Bergson (1911), 291–92.
2. There's an easier way to do this, by the way, and it's called going to sleep.
3. Parasocial relationships are the unidirectional relationships we form with subjects in our media environments, such as the characters in our favorite TV show. They often feel real to us, but they're obviously not real relationships, and they can be harmful if we allow them to take the place of real relationships with real people.
4. Cognitive dissonance is the uneasy feeling we have when we knowingly contradict ourselves, such as when we continue to eat even though we're completely full.
5. One reader, commenting on my last book, said it "made my brain hurt." I'll do my best to lighten up a bit with this book.
6. The same basic phenomenon is also known as "pseudo-fatigue," a construct often attributed to Dale Carnegie, author of the best-selling self-help book *How to Win Friends and Influence People* (1936).
7. We have six (not five) senses if you include "proprioception," the sense of the position and equilibrium of your body in movement through time and space (i.e., your sense of "balance").
8. The work media I regularly overengage in out of necessity are linguistic and mathematical, and the same is true for most of you, I'm guessing.
9. The aphorism "*Well begun is half done*" is generally attributed to Aristotle.
10. Carr (2010).
11. Gardner (1993), 70.

Chapter Three

1. Sartre, *La nausée* (1938).
2. Sir Edward Dyer (16th century).
3. Shorter (2013), 86. The statement by Hippocrates was documented by Galen (130–210 AD). Shorter was quoting Galen who was paraphrasing Hippocrates.
4. See Indick (2021), chap. 5.
5. Daudet, *Notes sur la vie* (1899).
6. Jaynes (1976), 462.
7. William Shakespeare, *Henry IV, Part II* (ca. 1596–1599).

Chapter Four

1. McGilchrist (2009), 279.
2. McLuhan (1964), 136.
3. Indick (2015), 193.

4. Marvell, "To His Coy Mistress" (1681).
5. The distinction between a "human being" and a "human doing" is often attributed to Erik Erikson.
6. John Wheeler (the physicist who coined the term "black hole"), as quoted in the film, *A Brief History of Time*.
7. Timequake: A sudden disruption in the perceptual experience of time. I stole this term from Kurt Vonnegut.
8. Remembrances of Things Past: I stole this phrase from the title of Marcel Proust's famous novel *Remembrance of Things Past*.
9. Friedman (1990), 88: "In the pagan religious view of the universe, the essential perception of time was the cyclical, the eternally recurring reality of nature."
10. *Bhagavad Gita*, as quoted in Huxley (1944), 191.
11. McLuhan (1965), 155.
12. Ibid.
13. Ibid.
14. Epicurus, as quoted by Seneca, "On Groundless Fears."
15. Dr. Joseph Bogen (1969), as quoted in McLuhan & Powers (1989), 75.
16. Nietzsche, *The Gay Science* (1862).
17. Dostoevsky, *Notes from Underground* (1864).
18. If you take issue with my argument that retirement is bad for you and should be avoided until absolutely necessary because you desperately look forward to retiring, my response is that you should carefully read all of my arguments for why retirement is bad for you, and then if you still desperately want to retire, I suggest you search your feelings about your job. Is the issue that you really want to retire, or is the issue that you hate your job? If you hate your job, then you have a much more pressing issue than retirement to resolve.
19. Bjorklund & Earles (2019).
20. FOMO is the fear of missing out.
21. While you're still "young"—by that I mean, if you're less than 100 years old, you're still quite young, considering the fact that you're living to 120.

Chapter Five

1. Wordsworth, "The World Is Too Much with Us" (1802).

2. McLuhan & Powers (1989).
3. Bob Dylan, "Forever Young" (1973).
4. Maryrose Wood, *The Unseen Guest* (2010).
5. McLuhan (1964).
6. The question of whether a dog or a cat can truly "love" like a human is just semantics. How do you define "love"? The question is summarily dismissed. Also, for the purposes of the pet lover, it doesn't matter whether our pets "truly love" us; it matters only that we *feel* truly loved by them.
7. Buber (1923/1970).

Chapter Six

1. Yeshiva: A parochial school for Orthodox Jewish boys.
2. Gardner (1993), 109.
3. McGilchrist (2009), 105: "So the evolution of literary skill ... progresses from right-hemispheric music (words that are sung), to right-hemispheric language (the metaphorical language of poetry), to left-hemispheric language (the referential language of prose)."
Bradshaw & Rogers (1993), 359–360: "Increasing musical sophistication has been shown to draw more and more processing resources from the right to the left hemisphere.... Music may therefore be a 'playing of the emotions'—like the visual and plastic arts, but in a modality closer to that of speech and linguistic communication."
4. Gardner (1993), 115: "Indeed, recent studies converge on the right anterior portions of the brain with such predictability as to suggest that this region may assume for music the same centrality as the left temporal lobe occupies in the linguistic sphere."
5. McGilchrist (2019), 19: "The right hemisphere is far more important than the left for the appreciation of music—which is organic, which flows, which needs to be appreciated as a whole, and which exists entirely in 'betweenness.' The left hemisphere can appreciate rhythm, as long as it is simple, but little else: melody, timbre, and, especially, harmony are all largely right-hemisphere-dependent, as are complex rhythms, with cross-beats and syncopations." (Professional musicians are an

exception to this right-hemisphere dependency for a number of possible reasons that are interesting in and of themselves. See McGilchrist [2009], 75).

6. William Congreve, "The Mourning Bride" (1697).

7. Steiner (1991), 27.

8. *Ibid.*, 196–197.

9. Andersen (2020).

10. In an interview (I can't recall which one), Ronnie Lane, bass player for The Small Faces and The Faces, said that his uncle told him the advice about learning an instrument and always having a friend. This is doubly true. A musical instrument is indeed a friend. I've spent many a joyful hour with my piano and guitars. It's also true that if you're musical, you can always find a musical friend with whom to play.

Chapter Seven

1. Realtors refer to the hard work we put into maintaining and improving our homes as "sweat equity" because the work increases the monetary value of our homes. If you've been paying attention, you will immediately identify the construct of "sweat equity" as a form of commoditization and pay it no heed. Your home has a personal value to you and your family that is far greater than its list price or "zestimate."

2. Technically, this is untrue. You could actually pay me enough to mow your lawn, but that price would be about $1,000 an hour depending on the size and location of your lawn.

3. https://www.safeaccessnow.org/cannabis_safety.

4. Please note that I'm not talking about psychiatric medications for schizophrenia, bipolar disorder, or any other mental condition other than my own construct of anxious depression.

5. Spartos (2000).

6. Boyer & Shannon (2005): 1112–1120.

7. Entheogen: A substance that facilitates a moment of spiritual transcendence from the "profane" world of work and mundane necessity to the "sacred" world of gods and yearnings of the spirit.

8. "A dab'll do ya" as in a little bit, not the dance move "dab" and certainly not the superpotent form of cannabis smoking, "dabbing," which is definitely too much THC for anyone and doubtlessly a poor life choice.

9. Also, you can always get high later if you want.

Chapter Eight

1. Wallace (1993), 51. All quotations from Wallace are from this source.

2. Meyrowitz (1985), 326.

3. Gardner (1993), 181.

4. Varela et al. (2017), 32.

5. *Ibid.*, 110.

6. I borrow the construct of "instant karma" from John Lennon.

7. *Ibid.*, 121.

8. *Ibid.*

9. *Ibid.*, 235.

10. Saunders (1957).

11. If you were counting, that's only seven media environments in which I have a flow zone. Sorry, Math, you loser! I'd love you more if you'd been introduced to me as comely patterns of quantity in space rather than meagre numerals and operators.

12. I know that words and numbers are in and of themselves symbols, but they are symbols that generally represent one thing and as such could be considered "sign symbols," such as a stop sign, which by design, has one and only one meaning. Symbols representing the Self, such as the music symbol or a national flag, are broader and are likely to have multiple levels of personal meaning.

13. Carl Jung, *Modern Man in Search of a Soul* (1933), 103.

14. In Greek mythology, Psyche is the goddess of the soul, and her name in Greek means both "soul" and "butterfly."

15. I also apologize for the clip art, but using digital media was the most expedient means of illustrating my point in book format.

Chapter Nine

1. McLuhan (1964), 46.

2. "Digitality" is the condition of living in a digital culture.

3. Lanier (2018), 13.

4. https://www.sciencedirect.com/science/article/pii/S0747563216302941.

5. Lanier (2018), 83.

6. *Ibid.*, 81.
7. *Ibid.*, 86. See also https://arxiv.org/abs/1408.3550, https://papers.ssrn.com/sol3/papers.cfm?abstract_id=2886783, https://rsos.royalsocietypublishing.org/content/3/1/150292.
8. McLuhan (1964), 41.
9. Jia Tolentino, "The I in the Internet" (2020).
10. McLuhan (1964), 42.
11. Lanier (2018), 72.
12. Tolentino, "The I in the Internet."
13. https://www.ajpmonline.org/article/S07049-3797(17)30016-8/fulltext.
14. Lanier (2018), 6–7.
15. *Ibid.*, 5.
16. *Ibid.*, 19.
17. *Ibid.*, 32.
18. *Ibid.*
19. Sean Parker, first president of Facebook, as quoted by Lanier (2018), 8.
20. Buber (1923).
21. Lanier (2018), 60.
22. *Ibid.*, 51.
23. *Ibid.*, 21.
24. *Ibid.*, 68.
25. *Ibid.*, 88.
26. Why else would Elon Musk buy Twitter?
27. Palihapitiya as quoted by Lanier (2018), 9.
28. Cybernetics: How people and computers communicate with each other.
29. I use the term "contradiction" to simplify Bateson's more accurate term "contradictory injunctions." R.D. Laing's term "paradoxical orders" is also a good one.
30. This interpretation of Bateson's construct owes more to R.D. Laing than it does to me.
31. Lanier (2018), 93: "How can you be authentic when everything you read, do, or say is being fed into a judgment machine?"
32. Lanier (2018), 158.
33. *Ibid.*, 88.
34. *Ibid.*, 2.
35. https://www.forbes.com/sites/petersuciu/2021/06/24/americans-spent-more-than-1300-hours-on-social-media/?sh=3dd823ae2547.

Chapter Ten

1. William Blake, *The Marriage of Heaven and Hell* (1793).
2. Diphenhydramine (aka Benadryl) is an antihistamine that causes drowsiness, which is why it's also sold as an over-the-counter sleep aid. It makes me sleepy and clears my sinuses so I can breathe better at night, affording me a deeper and more restful sleep. Although I don't recommend sleep aids for everyday use, a simple and safe product like diphenhydramine is an effective way of helping me to "reset" my sleep schedule when necessary.
3. Walker (2017), 8.
4. Paradoxical sleep is another name for dreaming. The paradox is that sleep is meant to be restful, but while dreaming, our brain becomes just as if not more active than it is while we're awake.
5. See Dr. Walker's book (2017) for empirical evidence backing all of these claims.
6. Indick (2015).
7. See Part Two of Walker's book (2017) for evidence that we all need at least eight hours of sleep per night.
8. In the interest of space, I cannot summarize the findings of sleep researchers here, but I encourage the curious reader to see Dr. Walker's comprehensive and illuminating summaries in his book.
9. Memories cannot simply be "replayed" because memory doesn't work that way. We store minuscule neurological associations, not entire intact "memories."
10. Walker (2017), 207.
11. Frankl (1975).
12. Walker (2017), 209.
13. This is a reference to Freud's famous assertion that the conscious ego is "not the master of its own house."
14. May (1991).
15. Ramachandran (1998).
16. A "theophany" is a perceptual experience of a divinity or a spiritual presence.
17. My book *The Digital God* (2015) is all about my construct of "spiritual perception."
18. Indick (2015).
19. See Indick (2015) for a literature review of the psychosocial benefits associated with spirituality.
20. James (1902), 378–379.
21. *Ibid.*
22. Faith deficit disorder is a construct I just made up, but it makes about as much sense as many of the other constructs in the DSM.

23. Maslow (1964), 85.
24. Fromm (1951), 18.
25. *Ibid.*, 6–7.
26. This is a reference to Freud's famous statement that "dreams are the royal road to the unconscious."
27. Maslow (1964), 19.
28. Jung (1938), 45–46, 49..
29. Note that Jung *did not* state that it is *psychoanalysis* that gives a meaning to life.
30. Jung (1964), 89.
31. Atemporality is a state of timelessness in which time as a construct does not exist.
32. Walker (2017), 30–40.
33. For an example of dream-time dilation, see the movie *Inception* (2020) in which time stretches out like an accordion for the dreamers in the film (and also for the viewers in the audience, as they sit through two and a half hours of the same premise).
34. "Pascal's wager," posed in Blaise Pascal's (1623–1662) posthumously published *Pensées*, explores the notion of an individual consciously wagering with his life on the question of whether God exists.
35. Walt Whitman (1892), "Song of Myself."
36. Walker (2017), 234.
37. Feuerbach (1957), as quoted by Guthrie (1995), 187.
38. Huxley (1961).
39. Walker (2017), 56.
40. The sleep/wake flip is complicated because everybody has different schedules. Some people prefer to take midday naps, others work nights and sleep during the day, still others prefer small naps spread out throughout the day. I can only provide some basic general instructions here—you will need to customize the flip to fit your schedule, your innate sleep habits, and your way of doing things.
41. Walter de la Mare, "All That's Past" (1921).

Bibliography

American Psychiatric Association. (2013). *Diagnostic and Statistical Manual of Mental Disorders*. 5th ed. Arlington: American Psychiatric Association.

Andersen, H.C. (2020). *The Complete Fairy Tales and Stories*. New York: Book House Publishing.

Bergson, H. (1911). *Creative Evolution*. New York: Henry Holt.

Bjorklund, B., & Earles, J. (2019). *Journey of Adulthood*, 9th ed. Upper Saddle River: Pearson.

Boyer, E.W., & Shannon, M. (2005). "The Serotonin Syndrome." *New England Journal of Medicine* 352, no. 11: 1112–1120, doi:10.1056/NEJMra041867.

Bradshaw, J.L., & Nettleton, N.C. (1981). "The Nature of Hemispheric Specialization in Man." *Behavioral & Brain Sciences* 4:51–91.

Bradshaw, J.L., & Rogers, L.J. (1993). *The Evolution of Lateral Asymmetries, Language, Tool Use, & Intellect*. New York: Academic Press.

Buber, M. (1923/1970). *I and Thou*. Translated by W. Kaufmann. New York: Scribner.

Buckner, R.L., Andrews-Hanna, J.R., & Schacter, D.L. (2008). "The Brain's Default Network: Anatomy, Function, and Relevance to Disease." *Annals of the New York Academy of Sciences* 1124:1–38.

Campbell, J. (1949). *The Hero with a Thousand Faces*. Princeton: Princeton University Press.

Campbell, J. (1990). *The Hero's Journey*. San Francisco: Harper & Row.

Campbell, J., & Moyers, B. (1991). *The Power of Myth*. New York: Anchor.

Carr, N.C. (2010). *The Shallows: What the Internet Is Doing to Our Brains*. New York: Norton.

Chomsky, N. (1957/2005). *Syntactic Structures*. New York: Martino Fine Books.

Clark, A.D. (2005). *Dyslexia*. New York: Lucent Books.

Deacon, T.W. (1997). *The Symbolic Species: The Co-evolution of Language and the Brain*. New York: Norton.

Delgado, P., Price, L.H., Miller, H.L., Salomon, R.M., Aghajanian, G.K., Heninger, G.R., & Charney, D.S. (1994). "Serotonin and the Neurobiology of Depression: Effects of Tryptophan Depletion in Drug-Free Depressed Patients." *Archives of General Psychiatry* 51(11): 865–874.

Donald, M. (1991). *Origins of the Modern Mind: Three Stages in the Evolution of Culture and Cognition*. Cambridge: Harvard University Press.

Dragioti, E., Karathanos, V., Gerdle, B., & Evangelou, E. (2017). "Does Psychotherapy Work? An Umbrella Review of Meta-analyses of Randomized Controlled Trials." *Acta Psychiatrica Scandinavica* 136(3): 236–246.

Ehmke, R., & Child Mind Institute. (2019). "How Using Social Media Affects Teenagers." Retrieved from https://childmind.org/article/how-using-social-media-affects-teenagers/.

Eliade, M. (1949). *Cosmos and History: The Myth of the Eternal Return*. Translated by W.R. Trask. Princeton: Princeton University Press, 1954. Originally published as *Le Mythe de l'eternel retour: Archétypes et repetition*.

Eliade, M. (1957). *The Sacred and the Profane: The Nature of Religion*. Translated by W.R. Trask. New York: Harvest.

Fardouly, J., & Vartanian, L.R. (2016). "Social Media and Body Image Concerns:

Current Research and Future Directions." *Current Opinion in Psychology* 9:1–5.
Frankl, V. (1975). *The Unconscious God.* New York: Simon & Schuster.
Freud, S. (1900). *The Interpretation of Dreams.* In *The Complete Psychological Works: Standard Edition*, Volumes 4 & 5. London: Hogarth.
Freud, S. (1927). *The Future of an Illusion.* New York: Norton.
Freud, S. (1930). *Civilization and Its Discontents.* London: Penguin.
Freud, S. (1939). *Moses and Monotheism.* New York: Vintage.
Friedman, J. (1990). *About Time: Inventing the Fourth Dimension.* New York: Penguin/Random House.
Fromm, E. (1951). *The Forgotten Language: An Introduction to the Understanding of Dreams, Fairy Tales, and Myths.* New York: Grove Press.
Gardner, H. (1993). *Frames of Mind: The Theory of Multiple Intelligences.* New York: Basic Books.
Gardner, H. (2011). *The Unschooled Mind: How Children Think and How Schools Should Teach.* New York: Basic Books.
Geschwind, N,. & Behan, P. (1984). "Laterality, Hormones, and Immunity." In Geschwind & Galaburda, eds. (1987), 211–224.
Geschwind, N., & Galaburda, A.M. (1987). *Cerebral Lateralization: Biological Mechanisms, Associations, and Pathology.* Cambridge: MIT Press.
Grinspoon, L. (1971). *Marijuana Reconsidered.* New York: Quick American Archives.
Horgan, J. (2004). *Rational Mysticism.* New York: Houghton Mifflin.
Huxley, A. (1944). *The Perennial Philosophy.* New York: Harper.
Huxley, A. (1954). *The Doors of Perception.* New York: Harper & Row.
Huxley, A. (1961). "Visionary Experience." A Speech Delivered at the XIV International Congress of Applied Psychology. Copenhagen, Denmark. In J. White, ed. (1972). *The Highest State of Consciousness.* New York: Anchor Books.
Indick, W. (2015). *The Digital God: How Technology Will Reshape Spirituality.* Jefferson, NC: McFarland.
Indick, W. (2021). *Media Environments and Mental Disorder: The Psychology of Information Immersion.* Jefferson, NC: McFarland.
James, W. (1902). *The Varieties of Religious Experience: A Study in Human Nature.* New York: Modern Library.
Jaspers, K. (1949). *The Origin and Goal of History.* London: Routledge & Kegan Paul.
Jaynes, J. (1976). *The Origin of Consciousness in the Breakdown of the Bicameral Mind.* New York: Houghton Mifflin.
Jones, E. (1951). *On the Nightmare.* New York: Liveright.
Jung, C.G. (1936). *Archetypes and the Collective Unconscious.* (In *Collected Works*, Vol. 9).
Jung, C.G. (1938). *Psychology and Religion.* New Haven: Yale University Press.
Jung, C.G. (1939). *The Integration of the Personality.* (In *Collected Works*, Vol. 11).
Jung, C.G. (1953). *Collected Works.* Edited by H. Read, M. Fordham, & G. Adler. Princeton: Princeton University Press.
Jung, C.G. (1961). *Memories, Dreams and Reflections.* New York: Random House.
Jung, C.G. (1964). *Man and His Symbols.* New York: Doubleday.
Jung, C.G. (1971). *The Portable Jung.* Edited by J. Campbell. New York: Viking Penguin.
Kaas, J.H. (2006). "Evolution of the Neocortex." *Current Biology* 16(21): 1–5.
Kierkegaard, S. (1848). *Christian Discourses.* Copenhagen: Gyldenhal.
Kierkegaard, S. (1957). *The Concept of Dread.* Princeton: Princeton University Press.
Killingsworth, M.A., & Gilbert, D.T. (2010). "A Wandering Mind Is an Unhappy Mind." *Science* 330(6006): 932.
Kohut, H. (1971). *The Analysis of the Self: A Systematic Approach to the Psychoanalytic Treatment of Narcissistic Personality Disorders.* Chicago: University of Chicago Press.
Laing, R.D. (1960) *The Divided Self: An Existential Study in Sanity and Madness.* Harmondsworth: Penguin.
Laing, R.D. (1969). "Transcendental Experience." In J. White, ed. (1972). *The Highest State of Consciousness.* New York: Anchor Books.
Lanier, J. (2010). *You Are Not a Gadget: A Manifesto.* New York: Knopf.
Lanier, J. (2018). *Ten Arguments for Deleting Your Social Media Accounts Right Now.* New York: Knopf.
Lasch, C. (1979). *The Culture of Narcissism:*

American Life in an Age of Diminishing Expectations. New York: Norton.

Lewin, K. (1936). *Principles of Topological Psychology.* New York: McGraw-Hill.

Louv, R. (2005). *Last Child in the Woods: Saving Our Children from Nature-Deficit Disorder.* Chapel Hill: Algonquin Books.

Maslow, A.H. (1964). *Religions, Values, and Peak-Experiences.* New York: Penguin.

May, R. (1953). *Man's Search for Himself.* New York: Norton.

May, R. (1969). *Love and Will.* New York: Norton.

May, R. (1975). *The Courage to Create.* New York: Norton.

May, R. (1977). *The Meaning of Anxiety.* New York: Norton.

May, R. (1983). *The Discovery of Being.* New York: Norton.

May, R. (1991). *The Cry for Myth.* New York: Norton.

McCrone, J. (1991). *The Ape That Spoke.* New York: Avon Books.

McGilchrist, I. (2009). *The Master and His Emissary: The Divided Brain and the Making of the Western World.* New Haven: Yale University Press.

McGilchrist, I. (2012). *The Divided Brain and the Search for Meaning.* New Haven: Yale University Press.

McGilchrist, I. (2019). *Ways of Attending: How Our Divided Brain Constructs the World.* New York: Routledge.

McLuhan, M. (1964). *Understanding Media.* New York: McGraw-Hill.

McLuhan, M. (1965). *The Gutenberg Galaxy: The Making of Typographic Man.* Toronto: University of Toronto Press.

McLuhan, M. (1967). *The Medium Is the Massage.* New York: Random House.

McLuhan, M. (1995). *Essential McLuhan.* Edited by E. McLuhan & F. Zingrone. New York: Basic Books.

McLuhan, M. & Fiore, Q. (1968). *War and Peace in the Global Village.* New York: Simon & Schuster.

McLuhan, M., & Powers, B. (1989). *The Global Village: Transformations in World Life and Media in the 21st Century.* New York: Oxford University Press.

Meyrowitz, J. (1985). *No Sense of Place: The Impact of Electronic Media on Social Behavior.* Oxford: Oxford University Press.

Morris, E. (1991). *A Brief History of Time* (Documentary film). Story by S. Hawking. Netflix films (dist.).

O'Keeffe, G., & Clarke-Pearson, K. (2011). "The Impact of Social Media on Children, Adolescents, and Families." *Pediatrics* 127(4): 800–804.

Ong, W.J. (1982). *Orality and Literacy: The Technologizing of the Word.* New York: Routledge.

Piaget, J. (1929). *The Child's Conception of the World.* London: Kegan Paul, Trench, Trubner.

Piaget, J. (1952). *The Origins of Intelligence in Children.* New York: International University Press.

Piaget, J. (1962). *Play, Dreams, and Imitation in Childhood.* New York: Norton.

Pollan, M. (2018). *How to Change Your Mind: What the New Science of Psychedelics Teaches Us about Consciousness, Dying, Addiction, Depression, and Transcendence.* New York: Penguin.

Raichle, M.E., MacLeod, A.M., Snyder, A.Z., Powers, W.J., Gusnard, D.A., & Shulman, G.L. (2001). "A Default Mode of Brain Function." *Proceedings of the National Academy of Sciences of the United States of America* 98(2): 676–682.

Ramachandran, V.S. (2011). *The Tell-Tale Brain: A Neuroscientist's Quest for What Makes Us Human.* New York: Norton.

Ramachandran, V.S., & Blakeslee, S. (1998). *Phantoms in the Brain: Probing the Mysteries of the Human Mind.* New York: HarperCollins.

Rapin, I. (1982). *Children with Brain Dysfunction: Neurology, Cognition, Language and Behaviour.* New York: Raoen Press

Rossetti, S. (2011). *Why Priests Are Happy: A Study of the Psychological and Spiritual Health of Priests.* Notre Dame: Ave Maria Press.

Rust, J., Golombok, S., & Abram, M. (1989). "Creativity and Schizotypal Thinking." *Journal of Genetic Psychology* 150:225–227.

Sacks, O. (1998). *The Man Who Mistook His Wife for a Hat and Other Clinical Tales.* New York: Touchstone.

Sacks, O. (2013). *Hallucinations.* New York: Vintage.

Sagan, C. (1977). *The Dragons of Eden: Speculations on the Evolution of Human Intelligence.* New York: Ballantine.

Sagan, C., & Druyan, A. (1992). *Shadows of*

Forgotten Ancestors: A Search for Who We Are. New York: Random House.

Sass, L.A. (1992). *Madness and Modernism: Insanity in the Light of Modern Art, Literature and Thought.* Cambridge: Harvard University Press.

Saunders, A. (1957). "Quotable Quotes." *Reader's Digest*, January, 32.

Scribner, S., & Cole, M. (1981). *The Psychology of Literacy.* Cambridge: Harvard University Press.

Seaford, R. (2004). *Money and the Early Greek Mind: Homer, Philosophy, Tragedy.* Cambridge: Cambridge University Press.

Shorter, E. (2013). *How Everyone Became Depressed: The Rise and Fall of the Nervous Breakdown.* New York: Oxford University Press.

Skinner, B.F. (1948/2005). *Walden Two.* Indianapolis: Hackett.

Spartos, C. (2000). "Sarafem Nation." *Village Voice*, December 5.

Steiner, G. (1991). *Real Presences.* Chicago: University of Chicago Press.

Tandoc, E.C., Ferrucci, P., & Duffy, M. (2015). "Facebook Use, Envy, and Depression among College Students: Is Facebook Depressing?" *Computer in Human Behavior* 43:139–146.

Tillich, P. (1999). *The Essential Tillich.* Edited by F.F. Church. Chicago: University of Chicago Press.

Twenge, J., & Campbell, K. (2009). *The Narcissism Epidemic: Living in the Age of Entitlement.* New York: Free Press.

van Os, J. (2004). "Does the Urban Environment Cause Psychosis?" *British Journal of Psychiatry* 184(4): 287–288.

Varela, F.J., Thompson, E., & Rosch, E. (2017). *The Embodied Mind: Cognitive Science and Human Experience.* Cambridge: MIT Press.

Walker, M. (2017). *Why We Sleep: Unlocking the Power of Sleep and Dreams.* New York: Simon & Schuster.

Wallace, D.F. (1993). "E Unibus Pluram: Television and U.S. Fiction." *Review of Contemporary Fiction* 13(2): 151–194.

Weeks, D., & James, J. (1995). *Eccentrics: A Study of Sanity and Strangeness.* New York: Villard Books.

West, T.G. (1997). *In the Mind's Eye: Visual Thinkers, Gifted People with Dyslexia and Other Learning Difficulties, Computer Images and the Ironies of Creativity.* New York: Prometheus.

Index

active expressive engagement 32–33
anxious depression 50–62, 69, 77–79, 83–88, 120–123
Aristotle 210–212

Bateson, Gregory 197–199
Bergson, Henri 19, 75, 131
Blake, William 171–172, 203
bodily-kinesthetic media 15, 126–155
Bogen, Joseph 78
Buber, Martin 99, 189–192, 201

Campbell, Joseph 13, 109
Carnegie, Dale 28
Carr, Nicholas 40
cognitive dissonance 23
commitment resistance 34–42
commoditization 69–71
Csikszentmihalyi, Mihaly 169–170

Daudet, Alphonse 56
default mode network 61–62
deliberation 76–77
displacement principle 21–2, 108
Dostoevsky, Fyodor 78
double bind 197–199
dreams 203–227
Dylan, Bob 92

Eliade, Mircea 73, 218–219
enhancement-obsolescence dichotomy 29–31
Epicurus 76

Feurbach, Ludwig 221
flow 169–170
Frankl, Victor 209
Freud, Sigmund 63, 91, 95, 209–212, 214, 217, 224–226
Fromm, Erich 216

Gardner, Howard 11, 14–15, 46, 102, 122

Hippocrates 50
homo nervusus 60–62, 76, 80, 87, 104, 133

Huxley, Alduous 221
hyperconsciousness 58–62

inhibition energy 29, 41
interpersonal media 15, 176–202
intrapersonal media 15, 203–227

James, William 107, 215–218
Jaynes, Julian 56
Jung, Carl 91, 122, 171–175, 216–218, 224–225

Lanier, Jaron 176–200
lateral growth 43–44, 92–95
Lennon, John 76, 110, 147
Lewin, Kurt 16
linguistic media 15–65
logical-mathematical media 15, 66–89
Louv, Richard 89

mandala 171–175
Mantle, Mickey 79
marijuana 135–155
Marvell, Andrew 71–72, 74, 100
Maslow, Abraham 215–216
May, Rollo 209–210
McCulloch, Warren 66
McGilchrist, Iain 13–14, 68–69, 141
McLuhan, Marshall 7, 10, 27, 29–32, 44, 70, 74–75, 90, 156–158, 161–162, 176, 181, 185, 196, 207–209, 229–230
media appetites 20–21
media flipping 25–27, 32–33
media switching 24–27
meta-anxiety 58
Meyrowitz, Joshua 159
multitasking 39–42
music therapy 101–125
musical media 15, 100–126

naturalistic media 15, 89–100
Nietzsche, Friedrich 78, 122, 152

parasocial relationships 157–159
passive expressive engagement 32–33
Pater, Walter 100, 108

perseveration 57–62
Pope, Alexander 142
primary media environment 53–62, 68
principle of least action 32–33
procrastination 36–42
productivity paradox 33–34

Ramachandran, V.S. 212
retirement 83–88
retrieval-reversal dichotomy 31–32
rumination 58–9

Sacks, Oliver 121
Sagan, Carl 140–142
Saint Augustine of Hippo 66
Sartre, Jean-Paul 22–24, 47
saturation fatigue 28–29
saturation nausea 22–29
saturation principle 20–22
Saunders, Allen 76, 167
Shakespeare, William 15, 61
Skinner, B.F. 129
sleep 203–227
social media 27, 176–201
specialization 92–95, 102–105, 130–135
spectator anxiety 168
spiritual perception 212–227

Steiner, George 118
subliminal development 95–96
switching costs 36–42

television addiction 22–26, 156–159
thought experiment 62–65
Tillich, Paul 91
time as duration 72–88, 97–98, 148–149
toxic media environment 2
Trachtenberg, Joshua 214

videogames 161–170
visual-spatial media 15, 156–175
Vygostky, Lev 169–170

Walker, Matthew 203–212, 218–219, 221–223
Wallace, David Foster 156–159
Weber, Max 78–9
Wheeler, John Archibald 88
Wilson, E.O. 219–221
Wordsworth, William 89–90

YoDEM 126–135, 154–155
Yoga 132–135

Zhuang Zhou 126
zone of proximal development 169–170